C0-BXA-847

WITHDRAWN
HARVARD LIBRARY
WITHDRAWN

Lily Montagu's Shekhinah

Judaism in Context

Judaism in Context is a series of monographs and collections focusing on the relations between Jews, Judaism, and Jewish culture and the other peoples, religions, and cultures among whom Jews have lived and flourished.

Lily Montagu's Shekhinah

Luke Devine

gorgias press

2011

Gorgias Press LLC, 954 River Road, Piscataway, NJ, 08854, USA

www.gorgiaspress.com

Copyright © 2011 by Gorgias Press LLC

All rights reserved under International and Pan-American Copyright Conventions. No part of this publication may be reproduced, stored in a retrieval system or transmitted in any form or by any means, electronic, mechanical, photocopying, recording, scanning or otherwise without the prior written permission of Gorgias Press LLC.

2011   ٦

ISBN 978-1-61143-684-6   ISSN 1935-6978

Library of Congress Cataloging-in-Publication Data
Devine, Luke.
  Lily Montagu's shekhinah / by Luke Devine.
      p. cm.
  Includes bibliographical references and index.
  1. Montagu, Lilian Helen, 1873-1963. 2. Reform Judaism--Great Britain. 3. Jews--Great Britain--Biography. I. Title.
  BM755.M57D48 2011
  296.8'341092--dc22

2010049222

Printed in the United States of America

CONTENTS

Yankee 18165

9/13/2012

PREFACE

During my time at the University of Southampton, nearly five years ago now, I had the opportunity to explore the often dusty shelves of the Parkes Library. The collection holds books spanning three-thousand years of Jewish history. Although I was studying the Jewish ritual murder accusation, I had the occasion to read up on nineteenth-century Anglo-Jewry (particularly another Anglo-Jewish writer, Amy Levy). Indeed, the University holds an annual Claude Montefiore lecture, and the library contains many of Lily Montagu's books and essays. Having read some of these works, and scanned others, I turned to the extant historiography. I would like to say that I was surprised to find little mention of Lily Montagu, the *founder* of Liberal Judaism in England, but aware as I am of the androcentrism that has blighted Anglo-Jewish scholarship since its inception, I was hardly shocked. Moreover, I was disheartened to find that where Montagu was mentioned, it was often with secondary consideration. Certainly, the majority of historiography preferred to minimize her role in the foundation of Liberal Judaism in England, and to focus on Claude Montefiore.

Although as we will see, a few recent studies have sought to correct this injustice, it remains an unfortunate truism that Lily Montagu, and her biography, continue to suffer from historiographical neglect. My book seeks to redress the balance – to provide a counter to the men-only history of Liberal Judaism. Thus, my innovative re-reading of Montagu's oft-ignored novel, *Naomi's Exodus,* and the introduction of little known archival material, will generate a more accurate picture of Montagu biography, her theological writing, and her activism.

Indeed, my account will reveal a Lily Montagu that is unfamiliar to students and scholars alike: a Lily Montagu that is not a disciple of Claude Montefiore, rather, a woman with latent fiery temperament and revolutionary spirit, deep held theological convictions, along with the intellectual prowess to develop and articulate these theological reflections. *Lily Montagu's Shekhinah* maps the history of Liberal Judaism at the *fin-de-siècle* and the development of Montagu's proto-feminist and spiritual aspirations, finally culminating in her theological discourse of "gender completion" and elaboration on the feminine aspect of the divine presence, commonly known to Jewish feminists as the *Shekhinah*.

Luke Devine
Worcester, England
September 2010

ACKNOWLEDGMENTS

This book would not have been possible without the helpful advice and encouragement of Professor Melissa Raphael whose knowledge of Jewish feminist theology has once again proven invaluable. I must also thank the London Metropolitan Archives for the use of their facilities, as well as the Parkes Library of the University of Southampton, which holds many of the books and pamphlets vital to this monograph.

This book is dedicated to Georgina May Taylor

INTRODUCTION

Lily Montagu was born on December 22, 1873 (died, 1963), the sixth child of Ellen Montagu (formerly Cohen) and the wealthy Samuel Montagu (First Lord Swaythling). The family owned two homes, one in Swaythling, Hampshire, and the other at Kensington Palace Gardens in London. Lily Montagu, who would eventually be acknowledged as a "rabbi-without-title,"[1] suffered a spiritual crisis at the age of fifteen. She was unable to align her proto-feminist ambitions with the Orthodox "legalism," or "rabbinism," enforced by her strict father. As we will see, her situation was perhaps paradigmatic of the confrontation between traditional Judaism and liberal modernity.[2] Montagu, unwilling to compromise her Jewishness, emerged determined that she would minister to, and spiritually vitalize, the Anglo-Jewish community, and she helped establish Liberal Judaism in England. Montagu, typical of many upper-class philanthropists, and in line with Liberal Judaism's commitment to the prophetic tradition,[3] was committed to social justice, in particular, towards the poverty stricken Jewish communities of London's East End. Montagu, unsurprisingly given the interpretive liberty of Reform and Liberal Judaisms, appropriated the Christian Evangelical designation of women as moral and spiritual redeemers (although

---

[1] Linda Gordon Kuzmack, review of *Lily Montagu and the Advancement of Liberal Judaism: from Vision to Vocation*, by Ellen Umansky, *Journal for the Scientific Study of Religion* 24, no. 3 (1985): 337.

[2] Ellen Umansky, *Lily Montagu and the Advancement of Liberal Judaism: from Vision to Vocation*, Studies in Women and Religion, vol. 12 (New York: Edwin Mellen Press, 1983), 220.

[3] The Jewish feminist project has always been aligned with prophetic Jewishness as represented by modern Jewish ethical thought.

within an Anglo-Jewish context),[4] and notions of the reclamation of the individual. She did not, however, consider conversion; though similar to most Liberal thinkers she recognized the importance of assimilating the values and norms of the host culture to counter the attractions of Christian society. Indeed, although Montagu replicated Protestant criticisms of traditional Judaism as narrow-minded, amoral, and legalistic, her fiction, despite similarities to conversionist novels portraying Jewish women as uneducated, oppressed by Jewish materialism, and under the stern control of legalistic fathers, did not conclude with the heroine embracing Christianity. Montagu were aware of, and internalized, conversionist criticisms of traditional Judaism's response to the "Woman Question," figuring the community as both retrogressive and "Oriental," yet sought to transform Judaism along proto-feminist lines, and to combat secularization, rather than to abandon her faith. Certainly, Montagu's commitment to Liberal Judaism led to estrangement from her Orthodox father, who warned her inheritance would be forfeited if she continued to promote the movement. He was ignored.

Lily Montagu wrote numerous sermons, liturgies, essays, and novels that dissect Jewish biblical, prophetic, and mystical themes. Paradoxically, she might be described as an *Orthodox* Liberal Jew, more so given her application of classically Jewish themes such as *binah*.[5] Indeed, she kept kosher throughout her life.[6] For Montagu,

---

[4] Despite the prohibition on the copying of gentile practices known as *chukkat ha-goy* (Leviticus 18:3-4, 20:23), even rabbinic Judaism has frequently borrowed from Christianity. In fact, Talmud Sanhedrin concludes that a gentile practice can be followed if there is biblical precedent (Michael Hilton, *The Christian Effect on Jewish Life* (London: SCM Press Ltd, 1994), 5).

[5] *Binah* is capitalized in reference to the mystical (Kabbalah) as opposed to the rabbinic tradition. *Binah* is the notion of women's inherent intellectual superiority, which conveniently dovetails with the "cult of true womanhood."

[6] Kosher refers to food fit for consumption according to halakhah (Jewish law: "the way"); *kashrut*: the observance of the dietary laws. Halakhah consists of 613 *mitzvot*. There are 248 positive *mitzvot* (actions to perform) and 365 negative *mitzvot* (prohibitions). Halakhah, halakhot (plu-

the divine presence, monotheism, the universal God of Liberal Judaism, was omnipresent. However, her application of Liberal theology ensured the immediacy of the divine in ways that are perhaps more characteristic of Second-Wave Jewish feminist theology. Indeed, her reading of Isaiah, and the mystical tradition, informed her appropriation of the feminine aspect, the immanent *Shekhinah* ("She Who-Dwells-Among-Us"), not as a separate deity but as the attribute of presence within the Godhead. The Protestant orientation of Liberal Judaism toward the individual encouraged synagogue attendance for women, ensuring their personal and immediate experience of the divine presence was private, solemn, and dignified. Montagu also sought to refigure both the liturgy and the service toward gender inclusionism.

Lily Montagu challenged conventional Jewish perceptions concerning the accepted religious role of women.[7] In her study of Jewish women as radicals, Naomi Shepherd describes the mood at the *fin-de-siècle*:

> The potential for rebellion, the desire for radical change among Jewish women, was all the stronger as they glimpsed for the first time the chance to rid themselves of traditional disabilities … It led them into political activity; it also encouraged them to seek a relationship with men hitherto unknown in Jewish society.[8]

Montagu's adoption of an ethically selective approach to the tradition, common to Reform and Liberal Judaisms, enables the retro-

---

ral), and halakhic (adjective) refer to the corpus of law, both oral and written Torah. The opposite of halakhah is *aggadah*, the rabbinic literature which is regarded as homily, or story, rather than legal.

[7] Although religious leadership was the exception as opposed to the rule for *fin-de-siècle* Anglo-Jewish women, Christian women had been involved in local Church leadership for many years. See Olive Banks, *Faces of Feminism: A Study of Feminism as a Social Movement* (Oxford: Basil Blackwell, 1988).

[8] Naomi Shepherd, *A Price Below Rubies: Jewish Women as Rebels and Radicals* (London: Weidenfeld and Nicolson, 1993), 6-7.

gressive and gender discriminatory layers to be marginalized, while the "modern," egalitarian, and gender inclusive aspects are retained. As we will see, Montagu's innovative approach develops religious and theological discourse reflecting the intellectual capacity of women (*binah*) using mystical and traditional perspectives, and seeks to align Claude Montefiore's Liberal theology with her own proto-feminist aspirations by acknowledging the feminine aspect of the divine presence. In sum, Montagu redefined for her contemporaries the role of the Jewish woman beyond the traditional stereotype of wife, mother, and educator of children. Instead, by merging Christian Evangelicalism with quintessentially Jewish themes through the interpretive liberty of Liberal Judaism, her writing lionizes Jewish women as the agents of social, religious, and theological transformation, and challenges the masculinist theologies, liturgies, and sacred texts of the tradition.

However, because so many scholars working in women's studies lack expertise in the theological dimensions of Jewish women's experience, examination of the theological aspects that underpin Lily Montagu's writing and activism has been completely overlooked by the extant historiography. This oversight has been compounded by the general neglect of her biography. Moreover, Montagu is rarely cited by contemporary Jewish feminists, despite the fact that she was the founder of Liberal Judaism in England.[9] This is problematic as women's religiosity and the history of Liberal Judaism cannot be "subsumed into that of men," as Melissa Raphael argues by referring to the exclusion of women from traditional Judaism in general:

> From the rabbinic period to the present, and despite some recent changes to a degree permitted by men regarding women's opportunities to study and pray, Orthodox male discursive, interpretive and practical dominance privileges masculinity as the

---

[9] The label "Jewish feminist" I apply to any man or woman influenced by First, Second, or Third-Wave Jewish feminism who remains loyal to a cultural, religious, political, or ethnic sense of being Jewish. Additionally, the "tradition" refers to mainstream rabbinic/Orthodox Judaism unless otherwise clarified.

primary likeness of God. It is masculinity that has been and remains generative of religious and historical knowledge, and authority and leadership in both the domestic and public religious spheres.[10]

From here, chapter one evaluates and critiques the extant historiography. Chapter two overviews the failure of Reform Judaism in England alongside the context of First-Wave feminism and the "Woman Question." Chapter three outlines the onset of Liberal Judaism, and in particular, Lily Montagu's biography and central role in the movement. Chapter four analyzes *Naomi's Exodus* and the influence of Christian Evangelicalism on Montagu's novel and the nascent Liberal Jewish movement. Finally, chapter five explores Lily Montagu's employment of the *Shekhinah*, and theological perspectives of gender completion, and her appropriation of the cult of true womanhood through the traditional and mystical concept of *Binah* or the "higher *Shekhinah*."

---

[10] Melissa Raphael, *The Female Face of God in Auschwitz: A Jewish Feminist Theology of the Holocaust* (London: Routledge, 2003), 1, 3.

1 ANGLO-JEWISH HISTORIOGRAPHY AND THE ERASURE OF LILY MONTAGU

It is an unfortunate truism that very little has been written on Lily Montagu. Aside from sporadic references,[1] the earliest efforts did not come from academia at all but were produced by individuals close to the Liberal Jewish cause in England. Both Nellie Levy, a member of Montagu's West Central Jewish Girls' Club,[2] and Eric Conrad, a nephew of Montagu's, published short biographies.[3] Chaim Bermant's *The Cousinhood*, published in 1971, seems to have been the first significant study of Montagu's career,[4] although his conclusions reflect the androcentrism indicative of Anglo-Jewish historiography prior to the 1990s.[5] Thus, Judith Romney Wegner rightly questions in her analysis of women in the tradition that if Montagu was the founder of Liberal Judaism, why did no one choose to write about her sooner?[6] Bermant's history of the Anglo-

---

[1] See Ramsay MacDonald, *Margaret Ethel MacDonald: a Memoir* (London: Hodder & Stoughton, 1913).

[2] Nellie Levy, *The West Central Story and Its Founders the Hon. Lily H. Montagu CBE, JP, DD and the Hon. Marian Montagu: 1893-1968*, club pamphlet (London: Leeway Business Services).

[3] Eric Conrad, *Lily H. Montagu: Prophet of a Living Judaism* (New York: National Federation of Temple Sisterhoods, 1953).

[4] Chaim Bermant, *The Cousinhood: The Anglo-Jewish Gentry* (London: Eyre & Spottiswoode, 1971).

[5] Androcentrism refers to the assumption that maleness is constitutive of humanity (Judith Plaskow, *Standing Again at Sinai: Judaism from a Feminist Perspective* (1990; rpt. New York: HarperCollins Publishers, 1991), 241 n12). Other similar terms include phallocentrism and gynophobia.

[6] Judith Romney Wegner, *Chattel or Person? The Status of Women in the Mishnah* (New York: Oxford University Press, 1988), 187-88.

Jewish elite marginalizes Montagu's role in the formation of Anglo-Liberal Judaism, and describes her, rather insultingly, as "less intelligent than [Claude] Montefiore … She played Sister Clare to his St Francis."[7] This assumption is particularly inaccurate as Montefiore frequently maintained that Montagu had been the founder of the movement. In fact, it is doubtful that he, as a timid intellectual, would have been spurred to the leadership had she not persuaded him.[8] As Montagu herself noted: "[Montefiore had been] prepared to accompany me in my adventure," and "he was *glad* to help."[9] Nonetheless, Stephen Bayme (1982) would draw similarly negative conclusions in his study of the origins of Liberal Judaism, describing Montagu merely as a "devoted communal worker" who maintained a type of leadership role.[10]

Aside from some minor contributions,[11] Ellen Umansky's, *Lily Montagu and the Advancement of Liberal Judaism*, published in 1983, seems to have been the first (and only) book-length study of Montagu's role as religious leader.[12] Umansky's path-breaking study reintroduced Montagu to a new generation of feminist scholars and uniquely revealed the extent of her role in the organizational formation of Liberal Judaism as a movement:

---

[7] Bermant, *The Cousinhood*, 210. See Edward Kessler, *An English Jew: The Life and Writings of Claude Montefiore* (London: Vallentine Mitchell, 1989).

[8] Conrad, *Lily H. Montagu*, 46.

[9] Lily Montagu, *The Faith of a Jewish Woman* (London: George Allen & Unwin, 1943), 24, 28.

[10] Steven Bayme, "Claude Montefiore, Lily Montagu and the Origins of the Jewish Religious Union," *Transactions of the Jewish Historical Society of England* 27 (1982): 61.

[11] See Sidney Bunt, *Jewish Youth Work in Britain: Past, Present and Future* (London: Bedford Square Press, 1975); Lawrence Rigal, *A Brief History of the West Central Liberal Synagogue* (London: West Central Synagogue, 1978).

[12] For abbreviated versions of Umansky's study see Ellen Umansky, "Lily H. Montagu: Religious Leader, Organizer and Prophet," *Conservative Judaism* 34, no. 6 (July/August 1981): 17-27; Ellen Umansky, "The Origins of Liberal Judaism in England: The Contribution of Lily H. Montagu," *Hebrew Union College Annual* 55 (1984): 309-22.

Lily Montagu used her organizational talent to transform Liberal Judaism from a way of thinking to a way of life. In founding the Jewish Religious Union [the forerunner to the JRU for the Advancement of Liberal Judaism], she gave the religious ideas of Claude Montefiore greater public expression and support.[13]

Umansky's research draws several useful conclusions, namely, that Montagu provided her women with access to all spheres of religious life previously denied to them by Orthodoxy, and that she might be regarded as a "feminist in action" rather than a "feminist theorist."[14]

However, although Lily Montagu was, first and foremost, an organizer and social worker, these labels neglect to account for her religious and theological aspirations. There are several aspects of Ellen Umansky's biography that, having been followed up by subsequent research, including my own, are perhaps unsustainable. Umansky argues, for example, that Montagu rarely suggested specific ways in which new roles for women could be created,[15] while the opposite is in fact true. Montagu frequently encouraged women to participate in the synagogue and castigated Orthodoxy for socializing girls towards "domestic observances."[16] Instead, Montagu regularly urged her girls to write their own prayers,[17] and to develop their own rituals. Surprisingly, while Umansky demonstrates the centrality of Montagu's role in the development of Liberal Judaism as a movement she undercuts her assertion by systematically dismissing Montagu's intellectual and theological contribution:

---

[13] Ellen Umansky, *Lily Montagu and the Advancement of Liberal Judaism: from Vision to Vocation*, Studies in Women and Religion, vol. 12 (New York: Edwin Mellen Press, 1983), 208-09.

[14] Umansky, *Lily Montagu*, 224.

[15] Umansky, *Lily Montagu*, 224.

[16] Lily Montagu, "August 12th, 1916," in "Addresses Given on the Club Holiday at Littlehampton, August 1916," London Metropolitan Archives, ACC/3529/3/7, 11.

[17] See *Prayers, Psalms, and Hymns for Jewish Children*, eds. Lily Montagu and Theodora Davis (London: Eyre & Spottiswoode, 1901).

Lily Montagu made little if any attempt to present her thoughts systematically. In most of her writings, she focused on specific topics (e.g., the relation of conduct to belief, the significance of ceremonialism, human and divine justice, the power of personality), while in others she randomly moved from one idea to the next. Her intention was not to offer clear-cut theological statements, but simply to share her faith with others. …

Much of Lily Montagu's religious thought can at best be characterized as naive. …

The most striking feature of Lily Montagu's religious thought is that it never seemed to develop. Though she described Liberal Judaism as evolving from one age to the next, her own ideas remained static. … Once she formulated her beliefs, they neither changed nor expanded. … For this reason, one can view her writings as a unified whole, attaching little if any significance to the date of composition, the situation to which she was responding, or the audience being addressed.[18]

The comment that Montagu did not present "clear-cut" theological statements and had simply intended to "share" her faith is inadequate, even unpersuasive. As we will see, the majority of Montagu's writing explores theological issues. Umanky's conclusion that Montagu neglected to develop her religious thought is equally disconcerting. Actually, it had been due to Montagu's flexibility that the Jewish Religious Union (the organizational base of Liberal Judaism) had become an autonomous movement. Initially, she had not intended the movement to be schismatic, and had advised Liberal Jews to seek reform within the existing structure (the United Synagogue, established in 1870 by Act of Parliament). By 1909, however, the movement, by her instigation, had become an independent organization. Perhaps most surprisingly, Umansky repeats Chaim Bermant's negative evaluation of Montagu as Claude Montefiore's disciple:

---

[18] Umansky, *Lily Montagu*, 181, 189, 191-92.

Lily Montagu frequently relied upon the insights of others, rather than trusting insights of her own. Though congregants and Club members frequently turned to her for guidance, she relied almost completely upon Claude Montefiore and Israel Mattuck. …

She continually referred to herself as Montefiore's disciple. As Chaim Bermant perceptively has noted, it was although he were St. Francis and she St. Clare. …

Lily Montagu's reliance upon Montefiore and Mattuck clearly was as much emotional as it was intellectual. She felt that she *needed* them, that she would be useless without their "full sympathy and faith." Similarly, though she might not have realized it, she remained intellectually and emotionally attached to her father.[19]

These comments ignore the evidence that Montagu had been frustrated by Montefiore's cautious approach.[20]

Ellen Umansky's edited collection of Lily Montagu's *Sermons, Addresses, and Letters* which followed in 1985, and included a sizable proportion of previously unpublished material, although timely, did not revive interest in the founder of Liberal Judaism in England,[21] and consequently little noteworthy was written until the 1990s. Despite her writing for the Jewish feminist movement, Umansky presents Montagu as little more than a dowdy social organizer bereft of individuality whose unquestioning devotion to, and pining after, Montefiore enabled the formation of the Liberal Jewish movement. As Judith Plaskow notes concerning the rediscovery of women's history:

It is one thing to see the importance of rediscovering women's history, however, and another to accomplish this task in a

---

[19] Umansky, *Lily Montagu*, 194-96.

[20] Daniel Langton, *Claude Montefiore: His Life and Thought* (London: Vallentine Mitchell, 2002), 77.

[21] See Lily Montagu, *Lily Montagu: Sermons, Addresses, Letters, and Papers*, ed. Ellen Umansky (New York: Edwin Mellen Press, 1985).

meaningful way. First of all, qua historian, the Jewish feminist faces all the same problems as any feminist historian trying to recover women's experience: Both her sources and the historians who have gone before her recover male activities and male deeds in accounts ordered by male values. What we know of women's past are those things men considered it significant to remember, seen and interpreted through a value system that places men at the centre.[22]

Umansky is a self-identified feminist and theologian, but, problematically, by reconfirming the centrality of Montefiore, and the other male leaders, to the Liberal Jewish movement, she perpetuated the masculinist version of Liberal Judaism's history and allowed Montagu's commitment to the cult of true womanhood,[23] and her recognition of women's "natural" role as moral and spiritual redeemers, to overshadow those aspects of her writing that are salvageable for contemporary Jewish feminism, such as her appropriation of the *Shekhinah*, her production of innovative feminist liturgies, and the gender equalizing aspects of her theological discourse.

Linda Gordon Kuzmack's *Jewish Woman's Movement*, published in 1990, also overviews Lily Montagu's activism, though declines to develop any new conclusions or to approach Montagu's theological writing. Kuzmack argues that as the first female leader of an organized Jewish movement, Montagu had:

undergirded the … campaign for religious and communal, as well as secular, suffrage, by providing a theological framework for the "religious and moral basis for enfranchisement." … Linking women's emancipation with Liberal Judaism, Montagu

---

[22] Plaskow, *Standing Again at Sinai*, 32.
[23] Montagu would not have applied the term "cult of true womanhood." I have used this label as it summarizes the *fin-de-siècle* notion, internalized by contemporaneous feminists, of women's role as spiritual and moral redeemers, resonant of the idea of female superiority.

also became the spirit guide of the Jewish League for Woman Suffrage.[24]

Kuzmack rightly notes that although Montagu was a committed suffragist and desired that women be incorporated into all aspects of religious life and leadership, she sought to expand women's opportunities to fortify their primary role as wives, mothers, and moral guardians. Montagu, according to Kuzmack, believed in the nobility of motherhood and the responsibilities inherent to class privilege.[25]

Aside from the republication of several of Lily Montagu's sermons,[26] and a number of terse biographies,[27] little else was written during the 1990s. Even Israel Finestein's study of Anglo-Jewry, 1840-1914, assumes that "[Claude] Montefiore was the principal founder of the Liberal Synagogue," and neglects to refer to Montagu at all.[28] Although several articles refer to her social work,[29] the first notable study of Montagu's career since the millennium was by Daniel Langton in 2002. While his research focuses on Claude Montefiore, he rightly elevates Montagu's status beyond the "naive," malleable disciple of Ellen Umansky's interpretation. Indeed,

---

[24] Kuzmack, *Woman's Cause*, 136.

[25] Kuzmack, *Woman's Cause*, 137-38.

[26] See *Four Centuries of Jewish Women's Spirituality: A Sourcebook*, eds. Ellen Umansky and Diane Ashton (Boston: Beacon Press, 1992).

[27] Margaret Yacobi, "Lily Montagu – A Pioneer in Religious Leadership: A Personal Appreciation," in *Hear Our Voice: Women in the British Rabbinate*, ed. Sybil Sheridan (Columbia: University of South Carolina Press, 1998), 9-15.

[28] Israel Finestein, *Anglo-Jewry in Changing Times: Studies in Diversity, 1840-1914* (London: Valentine Mitchell, 1999), 200.

[29] Jean Spence, "Lily Montagu: a Short Biography," *Youth and Policy* 60 (1998): 73-83. See Annemarie Turnbull, "Gendering Young People – Work, Leisure and Girls' Clubs: the Work of the National Organization of Girls' Clubs and its Successors 1911-1961," in *Community and Youth Work*, eds. Tony Jeffs and Jean Spence (Leicester: Youth Work Press, 2001), 95-110; Jean Spence, "Working for Jewish Girls: Lily Montagu, Girls' Clubs and Industrial Reform 1890-1914," *Women's History Review* 13, no. 3 (2004): 491-509

he argues for a "much needed corrective to the traditional down-playing of Lily Montagu's role in the Jewish Religious Union."[30] Langton notes that Montagu seemed content to allow Montefiore to represent the intelligentsia of the movement, and instead focused herself upon the religious education of women and the administration. Montefiore, who valued her ability, allowed her to guide the agenda. Moreover, Langton suggests, Montagu's "revolutionary fervor" left her disappointed with Montefiore's cautious, less confrontational approach.[31] This reappraisal, though brief, at least recognizes Montagu's organizational and intellectual independence from Montefiore.

In 2004, Lawrence Rigal and Rosita Rosenberg produced an equally complimentary study on Lily Montagu's role in the movement, although their approach was perhaps expected given that both are affiliated to Liberal Judaism.[32] Certainly, Rigal was a Liberal Jewish Youth Leader and had ministered to six Liberal congregations, while Rosenberg, aside from being a member of the Liberal Jewish Youth Movement, had been a member of the organization's professional staff. Their study was the first book-length history of the Liberal Jewish movement, which is surprising given that the movement has its basis in the 1890s. Rigal, who takes the first half of the book, notes that Montagu frequently stirred Montefiore into action,[33] yet neglects to assign any intellectual or theological attributes to her activism:

> Claude Montefiore was the philosopher and theologian who gave the distinctive teachings which inspired the teaching of the Liberal movement in the early years; Lily Montagu was the

---

[30] Langton, *Claude Montefiore*, 35.

[31] Langton, *Claude Montefiore*, 77.

[32] Lawrence Rigal and Rosita Rosenberg, *Liberal Judaism: The First Hundred Years* (London: Union of Liberal and Progressive Synagogues, 2004).

[33] Rigal and Rosenberg, *Liberal Judaism*, 13.

dedicated and spiritually-minded one, whose piety warmed the hearts of those she met and talked to.[34]

Nevertheless, Rigal elucidates Montagu's central role in the movement's organization, administration, and formation, particularly in her gathering of supporters and persuading Montefiore to take up the presidency. Rigal also acknowledges that Montagu's *Prayers for Jewish Working Girls* was the first Liberal Jewish prayer book.[35] Likewise, Rosenberg praises Montagu as an inspiration to women and notes the extent of her gender equalizing initiatives, including her determination that women should preach,[36] though, similar to her co-author there is scant evaluation of Montagu's theological or fictional writing.

Since 2004, little has been written on Lily Montagu.[37] Geoffrey Alderman's entry in the *Oxford Dictionary of National Biography*, however, draws several derogatory conclusions:

> Now in her mid-twenties, this excessively plain, nominally Orthodox Jewess was drawn to the personality and the pronouncements of the handsome Claude Goldsmid Montefiore. … It is clear that Montagu had formed an emotional attachment to Montefiore (then a widower); it is equally clear that this affection was not reciprocated.[38]

---

[34] Rigal and Rosenberg, *Liberal Judaism*, 14.

[35] See Lily Montagu, *Prayers for Jewish Working Girls* (London: Wertheimer, Lea & Co., 1895).

[36] Rigal and Rosenberg, *Liberal Judaism*, 57, 243.

[37] See Clare Midgley, "Ethnicity, 'Race' and Empire," in *Women's History: Britain, 1850-1945. An Introduction*, ed. June Purvis (London: Routledge, 2004), 247-75.

[38] Geoffrey Alderman, "Montagu, Lilian Helen," in *Oxford Dictionary of National Biography, 38: Meyrick – Morande*, eds. H. Matthew and Brian Harrison (Oxford: Oxford University Press, 2004), 753.

In his 1998 study of Anglo-Jewry, Alderman even describes the spiritual crisis of Montagu's youth as a "mental" episode.[39]

In sum, the scholarship that has analyzed Lily Montagu's role in the foundation and development of Liberal Judaism has neglected to examine the theological underpinnings of her writing. Instead, successive studies have preferred to focus on her social work, her organizational attributes, her role as an educator of children, and her subordinate status to Claude Montefiore. By overlooking Montagu's theological writing an important part of the picture is missed, and describing her as intellectually insecure (although it may be true and a symptom of women's experience in patriarchal milieus) merely perpetuates the androcentrism that frequently undermines Anglo-Jewish historiography. It is equally noticeable that scholarship has generally avoided analysis of her fiction. This is surprising given the importance of the novel to women's public representation at the *fin-de-siècle*.[40] Judith Plaskow argues that "Historiography as one aspect of the feminist reconstruction of Jewish memory challenges the traditional androcentric view of Jewish history and opens up our understanding of the Jewish past";[41] indeed, the very intention of this book.

Accordingly, my new reading of Lily Montagu's writing, sermons, and activism makes an original contribution to the feminist reconstruction of Jewish memory, more specifically, the history of Liberal Judaism, and the history of Jewish feminism in *fin-de-siècle* England, by firstly, examining the relationship between Christian Evangelicalism and the proto-feminist aspirations of the fledgling Liberal Jewish movement primarily through Montagu's oft-ignored novel, *Naomi's Exodus*;[42] and secondly, by revealing for the first time Montagu's innovative theological discourse couched in the perspective of "gender completion," and recognizing the masculine

---

[39] Geoffrey Alderman, *Modern British Jewry*, new ed. (Oxford: Clarendon Press, 1998), 202.

[40] See Michael Galchinsky, *The Origin of the Modern Jewish Woman Writer: Romance and Reform in Victorian England* (Detroit: Wayne State University Press, 1996).

[41] Plaskow, *Standing Again at Sinai*, 36.

[42] Lily Montagu, *Naomi's Exodus* (London: T. Fisher Unwin, 1901).

and feminine aspects of the divine presence through the *Shekhinah*. Moreover, this book contextualizes Montagu's theological reflections alongside more recent Second and Third-Wave Jewish feminist analyses of *Shekhinah*.[43]

This study and its woman-centered, gendered analysis,[44] presents a feminist challenge to the androcentric history of Liberal Judaism that has become representative, as Joan Wallach Scott notes: "Feminism has provided focus, commitment, and critical stimulus for those of us who have undertaken to write history from its perspective, while history has provided an important and sobering corrective to the essentialist tendencies of feminist politics."[45] Moreover, Melissa Raphael: "The halakhic inadmissibility of women as most forms of witness, or as scholar or judge, as well as the exemption (or exclusion-in-effect) of women from most time-bound religious observances is closely connected to [their experience]."[46] This does not suggest, however, that gender reflects or

---

[43] By First-Wave feminism I refer to the period 1792-1918; between the publication of Mary Wollstonecraft's *Vindication of the Rights of Woman*, ed. Carol Poston (1792; rpt. New York: W. W. Norton, 1975), and the suffrage campaign that resulted in women (only those aged over thirty) being granted the franchise in 1918 in England. Second-Wave Jewish feminism refers (1971-1984) to activism in the United States beginning with Rachel Adler's classic article: "The Jew Who Wasn't There: Halacha and the Jewish Woman," *Response: A Contemporary Jewish Review* (1971; rpt. Summer 1973): 77-82, and culminating in the mid-1980s. Third-Wave Jewish feminism (1990s onwards), if we can even call it that, refers to the most recent generation of Jewish feminists in the United States, unless otherwise clarified. However, the periods are as much conceptual as they are historical. Indeed, Jewish feminists continue to write from First and Second-Wave perspectives.

[44] Recent feminist research has tended to be gender-inclusive rather than women-centered.

[45] Joan Wallach Scott, *Feminism & History* (Oxford: Oxford University Press, 1996), 5.

[46] Melissa Raphael, *The Female Face of God in Auschwitz: A Jewish Feminist Theology of the Holocaust* (London: Routledge, 2003), 4-5. Although women are disqualified from being witnesses, there are exceptions. Women's testimony, for example, concerning whether they were raped when taken captive is deemed believable if it is to their own disadvantage.

implements "natural" and "fixed" physical characteristics to women and men.[47]

Recently, the Victorian era has become the subject of particular interest for critics who see the onset of both modern anti-Semitism and modern Jewish identity articulated in nineteenth-century writing. Moreover, applying gender as a category to analyze Anglo-Jewish history reveals the effect of modernity on Jewish domestic ideology, the feminization of religion, and the difference between Jewish men and women's experience of religious reform. The influence of feminist theory on Jewish studies continues to makes these aspects of modern Jewish experience more visible. Indeed, the uniqueness of Anglo-Jewish literary history is that it is the sole modern Jewish literary history in which women are pre-eminent as writers and intellectuals.[48] Alternatively, Anglo-Jewish men, compared to their continental contemporaries, produced little polemical writing. They preferred to stand for office or to use their wealth and influence rather than to write books. Likewise as regards to religious reform, Anglo-Jewish men were less inclined than the German Reformers to write on the matter, possibly because they had nothing to say.[49] In sum, this book offers "an alternative to the men-only story that has been transmitted as the history of ... Anglo-[Jewry]";[50] a religio-historical reconstruction of Lily Montagu's role in the rise of Liberal Judaism. Indeed, this book follows recent literary critics to develop a new reading of modern Jewish literary history which focuses "its discussions of Jewish modernity – immigration, acculturation, emancipation, reform, socialism, Zionism, and feminism – not on the literature of Russian, German, American, or Israeli Jews, but on the literature of the Jews of England."[51] Earlier generations of literary critics paid little attention to nineteenth-century women writers, and when they did notice them

---

[47] Joan Wallach Scott, *Gender and the Politics of History* (New York: Columbia University Press, 1988), 2.

[48] Michael Galchinsky, "The New Anglo-Jewish Literary Criticism," *Prooftexts* 15, no. 3 (September 1995): 281.

[49] Galchinsky, *The Origin*, 19, 24.

[50] Galchinsky, *The Origin*, 22.

[51] Galchinsky, "The New Anglo-Jewish," 272.

there was a propensity to dismiss them as unimportant. Since the 1980s, however, critics have attempted to bridge the disciplines of Jewish studies and English literary criticism. Thus, feminist criticism has turned from analysis of how male writers represented women to what women writers had to say about themselves. Similarly, critics of minority literatures have sought to recover forgotten sources. Hence, the minority ceases to be a figure of someone else's anxieties or a foil against the hegemonic culture, but an interpreter of her own subculture's story.[52] Additionally, the "cultural studies" approach here applied necessitates that representations of Jews and Jewish thought must be placed within their proper historical contexts.[53]

Jewish feminism, and Jewish feminist theology, particularly during the First-Wave of activism, has generally been a literary phenomenon.[54] This book is augmented by a plethora of primary material that has been collected by the London Metropolitan Archives (ACC/3529) on Lily Montagu, most of which has rarely been viewed. Ellen Umansky had used a number of these essays and sermons in her 1985 edition, yet much has been overlooked, including numerous Liberal sermons, letters, and addresses to the West Central Jewish Girls' Club and its supporters. Furthermore, Montagu's published material, although sometimes difficult to locate, is employed extensively throughout this book, and includes Montagu's keynote article, "Spiritual Possibilities of Judaism To-Day" (1899),[55] and her novel *Naomi's Exodus* which, aside from being auto-biographical, and acting as an unacknowledged "manifesto," outlines the proto-feminist aspirations of the Liberal Jewish movement. Moreover, the following texts are integral to this study: Montagu's *Prayers for Jewish Working Girls* (1895), which is the first

---

[52] Galchinsky, "The New Anglo-Jewish," 272-73, 276,

[53] Galchinsky, "The New Anglo-Jewish," 280.

[54] See David Cesarani, *The Jewish Chronicle and Anglo-Jewry, 1841-1991* (Cambridge: Cambridge University Press, 1994). The Second-Wave, however, was more academic in focus.

[55] Lily Montagu, "Spiritual Possibilities of Judaism To-Day," *Jewish Quarterly Review* 11 (1899): 216-31.

Liberal Jewish liturgy; *Thoughts on Judaism* (1904),[56] which outlines Montagu's Liberal theology; and her: "The Girl in the Background" (1904), which overviews her early proto-feminist thought.[57] The theological aspects of Montagu's writing are perhaps omnipresent, as are her frequent references to the prophets. Accordingly, the autobiographical monographs, including *My Club and I: the Story of the West Central Jewish Club* (1941),[58] and *The Faith of a Jewish Woman* (1943), are essential. Many of these texts will be unfamiliar to readers as they have only recently been rediscovered by literary critics and are rarely, if at all, available for purchase.

---

[56] Lily Montagu, *Thoughts on Judaism* (London: R. Brimley Johnson, 1904).

[57] Lily Montagu, "The Girl in the Background," in *Studies of Boy Life in Our Cities*, ed. E. Urwick (1904; rpt. New York: Garland Publishing Inc., 1980), 233-54.

[58] Lily Montagu, *My Club and I: the Story of the West Central Jewish Club* (London: Herbert Joseph, 1941).

2   BEGINNINGS: THE FAILURE OF REFORM JUDAISM IN ENGLAND

By the nineteenth-century, following three millennia of women being idealized by traditional Judaism as wife and mother, the industrial revolution brought about important social and sexual changes. Given men's customary propensity to undertake Talmudic study, Jewish women in Eastern Europe were often the major, or even sole, breadwinner of the family. Prior to the nineteenth-century it was possible for women in England to undertake paid work at home. However, industrialization shifted employment outside of the home, introducing Jewish women to the secular opportunities of Victorian society. In the traditional Orthodox community, women were viewed as the hidden "Other" as they were not expected to regularly attend synagogue, and not obligated to perform time-bound religious tasks (*mitzvot*) that interfered with domestic duties.[1] Although women were permitted to attend synagogue, they were required to remain behind a screen or *mechitzah* curtain, or were sequestered to the gallery. They could not be counted in the prayer quorum (*minyan*),[2] nor could they recite the blessings over the Torah,[3] read from the scroll (*Aliyah*),[4] or study

---

[1] *Mitzvah* – commandment or "good deed."

[2] Classical halakhah has no interest in women's prayer behavior with other women, so long as they do not interfere with the *minyan*. The *minyan*, traditionally, requires a quorum of ten males.

[3] The five books of Moses, or can refer to the scroll containing them, and indeed, generally, all Jewish teaching.

[4] Or *aliyah* la-Torah, *aliyot* (plural). The person who undertakes *aliyah* ("ascent") normally reads the blessings while a rabbi or cantor chants Torah.

21

the sacred texts.[5] In short, women were excluded, not only from the leadership of the community, but from the aspects of Judaism that define traditional male identity.

By the mid-nineteenth-century, however, these gender inequalities, augmented by the counter-attractions of secular society, and the rise of Reform and Liberal communities in, for example, England and Germany, were contributing to women's alienation from the tradition. Accordingly, breaking away, reversing this alienation, disregarding the legal minutiae of halakhah, and ensuring Jewish survival in modernity became integral to reformative Judaisms, and to some, Jewish women's experience. Moreover, Jewish men and women had grown tired of the traditional services, as Nicholas de Lange notes:

> It is true that even the regular services left a great deal to be desired from a modern western aesthetic point of view. Their flavor can still be judged from traditionalist services today. There was a minimum of formal ceremonial. The service did not begin promptly at an advertised time, but tended to gather momentum gradually, the worshippers arriving in trickles, taking their places with some commotion, greeting their friends, engaging in often animated conversation and even heated arguments (sometimes occasioned by the sale of honors to the highest bidder during the service). The synagogue could easily appear to resemble a stock exchange rather than a house of prayer. That this was an old problem is clear from exhortations to decorum and attention, particularly during the reading of the Torah, in the traditional codes of conduct. In the early nineteenth century, in the face of increasingly outspoken dissatisfaction, steps finally began to be taken in many western European synagogues to remedy the situation.[6]

---

[5] Linda Gordon Kuzmack, *Woman's Cause: The Jewish Woman's Movement in England and the United States, 1881-1933* (Columbus: Ohio State University Press, 1990), 4-5.

[6] Nicholas de Lange, *Judaism* (Oxford: Oxford University Press, 1987), 44.

Individual Jews probably visited England before the Roman occupation, yet the first settlement did not occur until after the Norman invasion.[7] During the early years relations with gentiles were generally amicable. Although Jews maintained their own cultural and religious institutions, and their social ties remained largely with other Jews, they were involved in commerce, local, and national politics through the monasteries, arguments or amiable debates with clerics, the Crown, and medicine. While the community was confined to distinct areas (streets or quarters) it was not ghettoized. As recent arrivals to England, the Jews were not part of the feudal hierarchy and were directly responsible to the king, who was overseer of their legal and financial rights through royal charter. The monarch, while able to protect the community, could withhold the right to settle or trade, and could even intervene in issues such as marriage, the building of cemeteries, and education. The status of the Jews in England was thus unstable, more so when usury became the dominant trade. The community was barred from other employment. Artisans were required to belong to a guild, but these were exclusively Christian, and agricultural trade required the owning of land and the hiring of Christian labor; both prohibited to Jews. Hence, money-lending, barred to Christians by Canon Law, was one of the few options available to Jewish entrepreneurs, and Jews obtained an unintentional monopoly. Those responsible for collecting unpaid debts aroused particular resentment, especially given the wealth thereby acquired. Tales of Aaron of Lincoln's financial dealings, for example, spread throughout Europe and his personal wealth was such that on his death in 1186 a special branch

---

[7] See Cecil Roth, *Essays and Portraits in Anglo-Jewish History* (Philadelphia: Jewish Publication Society of America, 1962); James Picciotto, *Sketches of Anglo-Jewish History* (London: Soncino Press, 1956); *The Encyclopaedia Judaica*, ed. Cecil Roth (Jerusalem: Keter, 1972); V. Lipman, *The Jews of Medieval England* (London: Jewish Historical Society of England, 1967); Louis Ginsberg, *The Legends of the Jews*, 7 vols. (Philadelphia: Jewish Publication Society, 1909-1938); Heinrich Graetz, *History of the Jews*, 6 vols. (1895; rpt. Philadelphia: JPSA, 1956); Salo Baron, *A Social and Religious History of the Jews*, 18 vols., 2nd ed. (New York: Columbia UP, 1952-1983); Abraham Geiger, *Judaism and Its History*, trans. Charles Newburgh (New York: Bloch, 1911).

of the Exchequer (*Scaccarium Aaronis*) had to be formed to deal with his estate, which became the property of the Crown.

During the twelfth and thirteenth-centuries, anti-Jewish sentiment increased due to two causal factors: the ritual murder accusation and the Crusades.[8] The charge of ritual murder, or blood libel,[9] has appeared throughout the history of Europe, Africa, and the Americas. However, the first accusation probably originated in Norwich during 1144, recurring in York, Bristol, Bury St Edmunds, Gloucester, and Lincoln. Despite the unfounded, ridiculous nature of the charge, the allegation was widely believed among the Christian community given its dissemination by the Church to an already superstitious population (the accusation, in fact, persists to the present day). The Crusades further ignited anti-Jewish sentiment, and during preparations for the Third Crusade in 1190, the Jews of York were massacred at Clifford's Tower.[10] In the Magna Carta of 1215, out of sixty-two clauses, two focus on Jews and money-lending.[11]

By the mid-thirteenth-century, the position of the Jews was becoming untenable, particularly given Church hostility toward money-lending. The Church had acquired astronomical debts, ironically the result of money borrowed from Jewish moneylenders to finance the building of cathedrals, churches, and monasteries. Royal pressure was also mounting as successive monarchs chose to tax the community to finance the Crusades. In 1253, the Mandate

---

[8] See Jacob Marcus, *The Jew in the Medieval World* (New York: Atheneum, 1974). For an outline of mediaeval anti-Semitism see Gavin Langmuir, *Toward a Definition of AntiSemitism* (London: University of California Press, 1996).

[9] There is a difference between the terms, although many historians use them interchangeably. "Ritual murder" refers to the re-enactment of the crucifixion with a Christian child taking the place of Jesus, while "blood libel" came later and refers to the Jewish use of Christian blood for supernatural purposes, or, for example, to make unleavened bread for Passover.

[10] See Richard Dobson, *The Jews of Medieval York and the Massacre of March 1190* (York: Anthony's Hall Publications, 1974).

[11] These clauses were designed to protect minors and widows from Jewish debtors.

to the Justices issued restrictions on the Jews to limit Jewish-Christian relations. Indeed, Jews were to wear a badge of identification, and were prohibited from eating with Christians, barred from buying meat at Lent, and prohibited from entering towns without the king's permission.[12] By Edward I's reign, the Jewish community had become widely impoverished as a result of the Crown's taxation and the Church's desperation to end usury. In 1275, Jews were forbidden to lend money on interest and encouraged to take up mercantile and agricultural trades. However, by 1290 Edward realized that the Statutes of Jewry had been a failure, and decided to expel the Jews wholesale with the backing of Church, Parliament, and the Christian population. The official reasoning behind the expulsion was that Jewish converts to Christianity were returning to Judaism, and that usury was being practiced in secret.

The seventeenth-century rise of the Puritans ushered in a new attitude towards the Jews in England. Indeed, the Puritans believed that the conversion of the Jews could bring about the coming of the Messiah. Oliver Cromwell thus readmitted the Jews in 1656 and a small group of Sephardim from Amsterdam led by the theologian Manasseh ben Israel arrived in London.[13] It was perhaps stipulated that the Jews should not proselytize, although this condition has never been substantiated. The first synagogue was established in 1657 in Creechurch Lane. Subsequently, the number of immigrants steadily increased as the Sephardim were joined by their Ashkenazi co-religionists.[14] As the Sephardim had escaped the Catholic Inqui-

---

[12] See J. Rigg, *Select Pleas, Starrs and Other Records from the Exchequer of the Jews, 1220-1284* (London: Jewish Historical Society of England, 1902). The badge (two tables of yellow felt six inches by three) referred to Jews over the age of seven years.

[13] See Lucien Wolf, *Manasseh ben Israel's Mission to Oliver Cromwell. Being a Reprint of the Pamphlets Published by Manasseh ben Israel to Promote the Re-admission of the Jews to England, 1649-1656* (London: 1901).

[14] See Albert Hyamson, *The Sephardim of England* (London: Methuen, 1951); David Katz, *Philo-Semitism and the Readmission of the Jews to England, 1603-1655* (Oxford: Oxford University Press, 1982); Martin Gilbert, *Exile and Return* (London: Weidenfeld and Nicolson, 1978). For a history of the Anglo-Sephardim see Moses Gaster, *History of the Ancient Synagogue of the Spanish and Portuguese Jews* (London: 1901).

sition in Spain and Portugal, the Ashkenazim were fleeing persecution in Eastern Europe. When the Tsar, Alexander II was assassi-
nated in 1881, the Russian government launched an anti-Semitic
campaign. The Jews responded by emigrating *en masse*. Between
1881 and 1914 over three million Jews made their way to the West.
Most went to the United States, although 100,000, at least, chose to
settle in England. The first Ashkenazi community was established
in 1690, and their first synagogue, the Great Synagogue, was constructed in 1722. The Sephardim and the Ashkenazim, however,
differed, particularly as the Napoleonic and Revolutionary wars had
brought a temporary halt to immigration, resulting in a balance between foreign-born and native Jews. Each had a particular dialect:
the Sephardim: Ladino, and the Ashkenazim: Yiddish.[15] The Sephardim were more affluent having been involved in the trading
opportunities of the Spanish and Portuguese colonies. By contrast,
the economically disadvantaged Ashkenazim were devoted to study
of the sacred texts as opposed to commercial venture. Their financial ambition rarely stretched beyond selling watches, buttons,
buckles, pencils, and old clothes, and the burden of their poverty
normally fell on the synagogues (although later, welfare services
were made available). Synagogue practice and appearance were
also different. London's Sephardic Jews went to their own synagogue, Bevis Marks. Yet, by the late-Victorian period the two
groups had become more unified, particularly after the formation
of the London Committee of Deputies of the British Jews which
included representatives from both communities. Ashkenazi immigration had come to outstrip the Sephardim and across Europe and
the Americas the Ashkenazi population exploded. By 1815, of the
20,000 Jews in England,[16] the Sephardim numbered less than
2000.[17]

---

[15] The Sephardim, aside from speaking English, Spanish, and Portuguese use Ladino, an intermingling of Hebrew and Spanish. Yiddish
(*jüdische*) is a combination of Hebrew, Slavic, and German languages.
[16] See Cecil Roth, *A History of the Jews in England* (Oxford: Clarendon
Press, 1964); Todd Endelman, *The Jews of Georgian England: Tradition and
Change in a Liberal Society* (Philadelphia: Jewish Publication Society of England, 1979); V. Lipman, *Three Centuries of Anglo-Jewish History* (London:

As early as 1714, the free-thinking liberal John Toland called for the naturalization of the Jews on the basis that all citizens should be declared equal. By 1753, despite vehement opposition, an Act of Parliament, "the Jew Bill," sought to allow foreign Jews naturalization providing they had resided in Britain for three years, though this was limited to the wealthy and property owners. The bill was repealed in the following year due to widespread opposition.[18] Despite possessing economic and social liberty, Jews were prohibited from political office due to the necessity of swearing the oath: "upon the true faith of a Christian." A bill demanding emancipation was defeated in the House of Commons in 1830, but the issue refused to disappear and further bills were presented, and defeated, in the House of Lords.[19] In 1831, Thomas Babbington Macaulay announced his support for the removal of disabilities, and the struggle to win municipal rights was brought to a successful conclusion with the Jewish Disabilities Removal Act. However, the political disabilities remained. Lionel de Rothschild, elected

---

Jewish Historical Society of England, 1961); H. Richardson, *The English Jewry Under Angevin Kings* (London: Jewish Historical Society of England, 1960); Israel Abrahams, *Jewish Life in the Middle Ages* (New York: Atheneum, 1973); Joseph Jacobs, *The Jews of Angevin England* (Farnborough: Gregg International Publishers, 1969); V. Lipman, *Social History of the Jews in England, 1850-1950* (London: Watts, 1954); V. Lipman, *A History of the Jews in Britain Since 1858* (Leicester: Leicester University Press, 1990).

[17] By 1830, the Sephardic community of London was past its prime due to intermarriage, migration, and the marriage of its women to the Ashkenazi communities, by which it was substantially outnumbered (Geoffrey Alderman, *Modern British Jewry*, new ed. (Oxford: Clarendon Press, 1998), 34). In 1860, Sephardic hegemony was broken as of the entire Jewish population, eighty-six percent were Ashkenazim (Daniel Elazar, "Sephardim and Ashkenazim: the Classic and Romantic Traditions in Jewish Civilization," *Judaism* 33, no. 2 (April): 147).

[18] Jewish politicians were encouraged to seek political emancipation by the Catholic Emancipation Act of 1829.

[19] See Israel Abrahams and S. Levy, *Macaulay on Jewish Disabilities* (Edinburgh: Jewish Historical Society of England, 1909); M. Salbstein, *The Emancipation of the Jews in Britain – The Question of the Admission of the Jews to Parliament, 1828-1860* (London: The Littman Library of Jewish Civilization, 1902).

four times by the City of London, was unable to take his seat because of his refusal to take the oath. David Salomons (the first Jewish sheriff of London), likewise, caused a commotion when he refused to take the oath. By 1858 matters reached crescendo during
the Conservative administration of the Earl of Derby and Benjamin
Disraeli. The Liberal majority of the Commons threatened to permit Rothschild to take his seat, despite the Lords forbidding his
entry. Nevertheless, Disraeli, who would later become Prime Minister, who was himself a Jewish convert to Christianity, pressurized
Derby into a compromise through which each house could deter-
mine the form of the oath to be applied. Rothschild was finally able
to take his seat.[20] Subsequently, the Jewish presence in the legislature grew, to the consternation of the communal leadership, with
embarrassing speed. By 1865 six Jews sat in the Lower House,
augmented by two others during the 1865-1868 Parliament. Compared to the total proportion of Jews in the United Kingdom,[21]
they were overrepresented and it was assumed, by both critics and
supporters of the emancipation, that Jewish MPs would become
spokesmen for their coreligionists. However, the opposite was in
fact true as Jewish members were generally committed to serving
their constituents as citizens, not as Jews.[22] Alongside the struggle
for political emancipation, First-Wave feminism was born.

Traditional Judaism's attitude toward sex-role differences affected all aspects of women's lives, particularly as no formal public

---

[20] See Abraham Guilam, *The Emancipation of the Jews in England: 1830-
1860* (New York: Garland, 1982). Sir George Jessel was the first Jewish
judge to be appointed to the High court Bench, while Nathaniel de Rothschild was the first Jewish member of the House of Lords. Full emancipation was not achieved until 1890 when the Jews were permitted to occupy
the positions of Lord Chancellor and Lord Lieutenant for Ireland.

[21] By 1850 there were approximately 50,000 Jews residing in England.

[22] Alderman, *Modern British Jewry*, 56, 63-64. See Geoffrey Alderman,
The Jewish Community in British Politics (Oxford: Oxford University Press,
1983); Todd Endelman, *The Jews of Britain, 1656 to 2000* (Berkeley: University of California Press, 2002); Daniel Gutwein, *The Divided Elite: Economics,
Politics and Anglo-Jewry, 1882-1917* (Leiden: Brill Academic Publishers,
1992).

acts of worship are accorded to women. Traditionally, women are glorified as wife and mother and only expected to perform private acts of charity and to maintain the Jewish home. Rabbinic prohibitions ensure women cannot take positions of leadership over men. In those exceptions during the Talmudic and mediaeval periods when women did teach religious law or write prayers it was normally done behind a screen. Despite these restrictions, however, women have always worked. Indeed, historically, given that men devoted their lives to study, women have often supplemented the family income as only the public *religious* sphere is defined in Judaism as public. Paid work constitutes the private realm to which women have more or less equal access. Their employment does not violate halakhah, and could, prior to industrialization, be undertaken at home. The social change that necessitated that women work outside of the home proved crucial to the emergence of Jewish women's movements,[23] and their involvement in secular feminism.[24]

First-Wave feminism normally refers to a period from the early to mid nineteenth-century, through to the early twentieth-century.[25] The movement is renowned for its militant campaigns for women's suffrage that resulted in women over the age of thirty being given the vote.[26] The First-Wave possibly originated with the publication of Mary Wollstonecraft's *Vindication of the Rights of Woman* in 1792.[27] This tract, bound up in separate spheres ideology,

---

[23] Kuzmack, *Woman's Cause*, 4-5.

[24] See *Jewish Women: a Comprehensive Historical Encyclopedia*, ed. Paula Hyman (Jerusalem: Shalvi Pub., 2006).

[25] See Olive Banks, *Becoming a Feminist: The Social Origins of "First Wave" Feminism* (Brighton: Wheatsheaf Books, 1986); *Women's History: Britain, 1850-1945. An Introduction*, ed. June Purvis (London: Routledge, 2004); Mary Lyndon Stanley, Feminism, Marriage and the Law in Victorian England, 1850-95 (Princeton: Princeton University Press, 1993).

[26] See Brian Harrison, *Separate Spheres: The Opposition to Women's Suffrage in Britain* (London: Croom Helm, 1978) for an outline of the opposition to the movement. For the fullest account written by a participant see E. Pankhurst, *The Suffragette Movement* (London: Virago, 1977).

[27] Mary Wollstonecraft, *Vindication of the Rights of Woman*, ed. Carol Poston (1792; rpt. New York: W. W. Norton, 1975). See Jacob Bouten,

represents one of the first clear statements endorsing women's political and civil equality. This was followed by reform in the following century. In 1839, mothers of "unblemished character" were given access to their children in the event of divorce, and in 1848 women were admitted to London University (the University Tests Act of 1871 abolished compulsory attendance of Church services and membership in the Church of England, resulting in the admission of Catholics, and Jews, to Durham, Cambridge, and Oxford Universities). Subsequently, in 1854 Cheltenham Ladies College was founded, and in 1857 the Matrimonial Causes Act gave women limited access to divorce. In 1870, the Married Women's Property Act enabled women to retain £200 of their own earnings per annum, and the Education Act guaranteed girls an elementary education. However, demands for women to be given the franchise by both men and women began long before the twentieth-century. In 1832, William Fox published an article discussing female suffrage, and in 1867, the philosopher John Stuart Mill demanded that women be given the franchise. The right to vote, financial independence, and education became the central issues of First-Wave activism.[28] It was integral that women be able to vote on issues that affected them, that women be given access to formal educational opportunities, and that women be able to pursue professional careers beyond, though also within, the domesticity and philanthropy assigned to them by separate spheres ideology.[29]

The history of First-Wave feminism in England is bound up with the ideology of Protestant, often Evangelical,[30] sectarian, dis-

---

Mary Wollstonecraft and the Beginnings of Female Emancipation in France and England (Philadelphia: Porcupine Press, 1975).

[28] See Jane Lewis, *Women and Social Action in Victorian England* (Aldershot: Edward Elgar, 1991).

[29] See *Suffer Be Still: Women in the Victorian Age*, ed. Martha Vicinus (Bloomington: Indiana University Press, 1973); Ronald Walton, *Women in Social Work* (London: Routledge & Kegan Paul, 1975); Frank Prochaska, *Women and Philanthropy in Nineteenth-Century England* (Oxford: Clarendon Press, 1980); Frank Prochaska, "Women in English Philanthropy, 1790-1830," *International Journal of Social History* 19 (1974): 426-45.

[30] See Kathleen Heasman, *Evangelicals in Action: An appraisal of Their Social Work* (London: G. Bles, 1962); Alan Gilbert, *Religion and Society in*

senting individualism, expressed within an idea of the family, marriage, and sexuality that acknowledges women's moral purity and influence, not only on the family, but also on the social order. The radicalism of Protestant sects such as the early Quakers allowed women considerable religious freedom, to the extent that they even produced proto-feminist leaders. The political ideas of the Enlightenment (natural rights and political democracy), and the French and American Revolutions, were a vital influence upon the feminist movement. However, the First-Wave was largely a middle-class phenomenon. These women, by contrast to their working-class contemporaries, had the education and political connections necessary for activism,[31] not to mention the leisure time to translate concepts of rebellion into direct political action.[32] The Protestant emphasis on domestic virtue blossomed into the cult of domesticity: women endowed the home with symbolic, transcendental qualities. The cult of true womanhood developed out of, but in tune with, the ideology of separate spheres. Contemporary Evangelicalism idealized women, who, possessing "special" feminine nature, by their virtue of moral purity, patience, gentleness, and kindness, could be both protector and the protected, and usher the moral regeneration of society at large through the exercise of their feminine skills and virtues.[33] Olive Banks argues:

> The cult of domesticity became transformed into the ideal of female superiority, and the doctrine of separate spheres into the attempted invasion of the masculine world not simply by

Industrial England: Church and Chapel in Social Change 1740-1914 (London: Longman, 1976).

[31] See Philippa Levine, *Feminist Lives in Victorian England: Private Roles and Public Commitment* (Oxford: Basil Blackwell, 1990).

[32] See Kathryn Gleadle, *The Early Feminists: Radical Unitarians and the Emergence of the Women's Rights Movement, 1831-51* (Basingstoke: Macmillan, 1995).

[33] Olive Banks, *Faces of Feminism: A Study of Feminism as a Social Movement* (Oxford: Basil Blackwell, 1988), 4-5, 85-86, 89-90. See also, Martha Vicinus, *A Widening Sphere: Changing Roles of Victorian Women* (Bloomington: Indiana University Press, 1973).

women, but, potentially even more revolutionary in its impact, by womanly values. Moreover, the process by which this change occurred was bound up … with the transformation of woman from Eve the eternal temptress to Eve the innocent victim. According to this new ideology, it was now the male who was naturally evil; the female was essentially good, and through her goodness and purity was able to redeem mankind from sin.[34]

The cult of true womanhood, the "feminization of religion," and the notion of "female superiority" gained widespread acceptan-:e by the *fin-de-siècle*,[35] and also penetrated the Anglo-Jewish community.

In mid Victorian England, there was no official Jewish feminist movement and no recognizable institution with religio-feminist aspirations for women (until the Liberal Judaism of the *fin-de-siècle*). This is not to say that Jewish women, similar to their gentile contemporaries, were not influenced by, or involved in, First-Wave feminism. Michael Galchinsky notes that the political emancipation of the Jews, and their liberation from England's oppressive political laws, suggested to Jewish women the possibility of an internal emancipation from Jewish gender exclusionism.[36] Jewish women also participated in national feminist movements. Constance Rothschild Battersea, for example, was active in the International Council of Women, and in 1901 was elected president of the National Union of Women Workers. Louisa, Lady Goldsmid, joined the Women's Protective and Provident League and persuaded the Jewish Board of Guardians to assist in its attempts to organize women workers excluded by the tailors' unions. Both May Abraham and Emily Routledge would later join the organization. By interacting with the community and their non-Jewish peers, Jewish women participated in the new social services, socialist feminism, and equal rights activism. They were active in almost all of the ma-

---

[34] Banks, *Faces of Feminism*, 90.

[35] Banks, *Faces of Feminism*, 91.

[36] Michael Galchinsky, *The Origin of the Modern Jewish Woman Writer: Romance and Reform in Victorian England* (Detroit: Wayne State University Press, 1996), 30.

jor national feminist ventures, including trade union, suffrage,[37] and welfare feminism. Consequently, Jewish groups emerged to mirror these organizations,[38] such as the Conference of Jewish Women, which convened in 1902; the Jewish League for Woman Suffrage, founded in 1912; the Jewish Ladies' Visiting Association, the Society of Jewish Maternity Nurses, and the World Council of Jewish Women, established in 1923. The Jewish maternal welfare organizations were middle-class institutions set up to assist the Yiddish-speaking, destitute immigrants. Accordingly, Jewish women realized, as much as their Christian contemporaries had, that careers did exist beyond the stereotype of wife and mother. They began to envisage a Bat Mitzvah (Daughter of the Commandment), a seat in the synagogue alongside the men, and access to the sacred texts.[39]

At the *fin-de-siècle*, the cultural symbol of the New Woman represented social and political transformation in contrast to the ancient institutions of aristocracy, class, race, and separate spheres.[40] The extent of the phenomenon was such that concerns were voiced regarding the demise of English virility. The New Woman

---

[37] See Aileen Kraditor, *The Ideas of Woman Suffrage Movement 1890-1920* (New York: Columbia University Press, 1965).

[38] Kuzmack, *Woman's Cause*, 1.

[39] Galchinsky, *The Origin*, 30.

[40] See Ann Ardis, *New Women, New Novels: Feminism and Early Modernism* (London: Rutgers UP, 1990). The term "New Woman" was for the first time coined in 1894 in an article by Sarah Grand (*Sally Ledger, The New Woman: Fiction and Feminism at the Fin de Siècle* (Manchester: Manchester University Press, 1997), 2; Lucy Bland, *Banishing the Beast: English Feminism and Sexual Morality 1885-1914* (London: Penguin Books, 1995), 144). However, the term had been in circulation for many years. An account of a dinner on 31 May 1889 that appeared in *The Women's Penny Paper* records that: "Mrs. Meynell, speaking on behalf of Poetry, remarked that poetry from the New Woman would have a very distinct note in the future" (quoted by Christine Pullen, "Amy Levy; Her Life, Her Poetry and the Era of the New Woman" (Ph.D. diss., Kingston University, 2000), 7). In short, "New Woman" refers to women's appearance in the public arena at the *fin-de-siècle* at the forefront of political causes, living and working independent of family and husbands, attending universities, travelling alone, and joining intellectual clubs, in stark contrast to the traditional institutions of marriage, domesticity, and motherhood.

could take the form of a feminist activist, reformer, careerist, an unruly wife, or a lesbian.[41] She was also a writer, an intellectual, an independent spirit, and could be seen riding a bike. The various images of the New Woman were delivered through contemporary literature and journalism, and represented the culmination of the Victorian women's movement. This included political causes such as socialism (Isabella Ford), social purity (Sarah Grand),[42] anti-vivisection (Mona Caird),[43] the peace movement (Evelyn Sharp), anti-imperialism (Olive Schreiner),[44] and pacifism.[45] Jewish women, largely of German and Sephardic descent, also protested against the trade union movement that denied them equal wages. Indeed, by the late nineteenth-century, many of the recent Jewish immigrants had turned to the trade union and socialist movements. Poor Jewish women often organized rent strikes or neighborhood protests, and some belonged to the Zionist movement. Thus, acculturated *Jewish* New Women were visible, not only in the gallery of the Reform Synagogue, which only constituted a minute proportion of the total number of Jewish women in England, but also in the libraries, universities, and social clubs.

By the 1880s, assimilated women who were no longer content with marriage, domesticity, and motherhood, were pursuing careers in the public sphere, participating in literary salons, acting as entre-

---

[41] Female relationships were rarely condemned in the period, although the fact that such women were unmarried, or un-chaperoned, was viewed as unconventional. See Yopie Prins, *Victorian Sappho* (Princeton: Princeton University Press, 1999).

[42] See Judith Walkowitz, *Prostitution and Victorian Society: Women, Class and the State* (Cambridge: Cambridge University Press, 1980).

[43] See Carol Lansbury, *The Old Brown Dog: Women, Workers, and Vivisection in Edwardian England* (Wisconsin: The University of Wisconsin Press, 1985); Mona Caird, *The Daughters of Danaus* (New York: The Feminist Press, 1989).

[44] Ann Heilmann, *New Woman Fiction: Women Writing First-Wave Feminism* (Basingstoke: Macmillan, 2000), 1-2, 4-5.

[45] See Heloise Brown, *"The Truest Form of Pacifism": Pacifist Feminism in Britain, 1980-1902* (Manchester: Manchester University Press, 2003).

preneurs, and smoking cigarettes.[46] Aside from joining Jewish organizations, these women were active in secular movements and saw themselves as much a part of the "sisterhood" as any other feminists in the period.[47] However, Jewish members of secular feminist organizations were sometimes viewed with suspicion or prejudice, as the early leaders of the feminist movement were overwhelmingly Christian.[48] As is the case with feminism and Judaism, the relationship between Jewish and Christian feminists was, and is, often unstable. By joining secular feminist movements, Jewish women created friction between their respect for the tradition, their hope for acculturation, and their wariness of anti-Semitism.[49] Many women felt they had to choose between their feminist and their Jewish identities because their Jewishness was not always accepted by secular and Christian feminists, and some felt that the sexism of the tradition was incompatible with feminism. It was during the early years of the nineteenth-century that Anglo-Jewish women's writing became a distinguishable subculture.

The *Haskalah* movement, a Jewish variation on the Enlightenment, began in Berlin, Germany, in the late eighteenth-century and subsequently spread throughout Europe.[50] Moses Mendelssohn was aware of the decline in traditional Jewish education, and of diminishing respect for the rabbinic authorities. He proposed improvements to secular education and sought to "rationalize" Judaism. The *Haskalah*, however, would go further: "*Wie es sich Christelt, so Juedelt es sich*" ("as the Christian, so the Jew"). The movement argued that religion should invoke spiritual fulfillment and move away from legality and obedience, that authority should shift from the Talmud to the Bible, and that prayer should reveal the immedi-

---

[46] Susan David Bernstein, introduction to *The Romance of a Shop*, by Amy Levy, ed. Susan David Bernstein (1888; rpt. Ontario: Broadview Press, 2006), 18, 40.

[47] See *The New Woman in Fiction and in Fact: Fin-de-Siècle Feminisms*, eds. Angelique Richardson and Chris Willis (Houndmills: Palgrave, 2001).

[48] Kuzmack, *Woman's Cause*, 3-4.

[49] Kuzmack, *Woman's Cause*, 5.

[50] The term "*Haskalah*" literally means "cultivation of the intellect," and represented an attempt to translate the German, *Aufklarung*, or "Enlightenment," into Hebrew.

acy of the divine. The *maskillim* (devotees of the *Haskalah* movement) derided the alleged primitivism, opposition to change, and
superstitionism of the rabbis, advocated the importing of secular
values, and demanded the replacement of traditional Jewish education with more Westernized styles of schooling. As early as the
eighteenth-century, Rabbi Jonathan Eybeschuetz of Metz stated:

> Look at the Christians among whom we live. We learn from
> them styles of clothing and haughtiness, but we do not learn
> from them silence during prayer. We are like them in eating
> their cheeses and their wine, but we are not like them in regard
> to justice, righteousness and honesty. We are like them in shav-
> ing our beards or styling them like theirs, but we are not like
> them in their refraining from swearing or cursing in God's
> name. We are like them in frequenting underground game
> rooms, but we are not like them in turning from vengeance
> and refraining from bearing hatred in our hearts. We are like
> them in fornicating with their daughters, but we are not like
> them in conducting business affairs with faithfulness and fair-
> ness.[51]

The Anglo-Jewish *Haskalah*, however, was unique in that it gener-
ated a number of unprecedented opportunities for women. Breaking centuries old taboos on demonstrating learning or highlighting
their education in public,[52] Jewish women from middle and upper-
class backgrounds began to publish novels, poems, essays, short-
stories, manuals, recipe books, and historical tracts.[53]

---

[51] Quoted by Michael Hilton, *The Christian Effect on Jewish Life* (London: SCM Press Ltd, 1994), 9. Many Jewish practices have been adopted
from Christian culture since the mediaeval period. These were not innovations of the rabbis but had been taken on by the Jewish population and
assimilated to the tradition. However, the law of *chukkat ha-goy* was frequently cited following the Enlightenment by Orthodox rabbis against the
Reformers (Hilton, *The Christian Effect*, 10).

[52] Galchinsky, *The Origin*, 36.

[53] An overview of Anglo-Jewish women's writing is beyond the
scope and remit of this book. See, for example, Maria Polack, *Fiction With-*

For Anglo-Jewish women, writing was one of the few means of public self-expression. Although Jewish women had occasionally written in the past, in England their novels represented the inception of a distinctive subculture.[54] These writers, aside from arguing for women's access to formal education, showcased the scholarly abilities of women for their Jewish and Christian audiences,[55] and demonstrated awareness of the omnipresent threat of anti-Semitism.[56] Michael Galchinsky has concluded that Anglo-Jewish women used the novel not only to lobby for liberation in Jewish society, but also for Jewish emancipation in the Christian world.[57]

During the early nineteenth-century, Anglo-Jewish women writers employed the historical novel, stressing the victimization,

---

out Romance; or the Locket Watch, 2 vols. (London: Effingham Wilson, 1830); Grace Aguilar, *Collected Works*, 8 vols. (London: R. Groomridge, 1861); Grace Aguilar, *Grace Aguilar: Selected Writings*, ed. Michael Galchinsky (Peterborough: Broadview Press, 2003); Celia Moss and Marion Moss, *Tales of Jewish History*, 3 vols. (London: Miller and Field, 1843); Charlotte Montefiore, *Caleb Asher* (Philadelphia: Jewish Publication Society, 1845); Emily Harris, *Estelle*, 2 vols. (London: George Bell, 1878); Emily Harris, *Benedictus*, 2 vols. (London: George Bell, 1887). For an introduction to Anglo-Jewish men's literature see Cecil Roth, *The Evolution of Anglo-Jewish Literature* (London: Edward Goldston, 1937); Edward Calisch, *The Jew in English Literature, as Author and Subject* (New York: Kennikat Press, Inc., 1969); Michael Galchinsky, "The New Anglo-Jewish Literary Criticism," *Prooftexts* 15, no. 3 (September 1995): 272-82.

[54] Galchinsky, *The Origin*, 19. In the United States, for example, Minna Cohen Kleeburg had written poems, called for a Bat Mitzvah ceremony, and demanded access to formal education. Similarly, Rebecca Graetz devoted herself to Jewish philanthropy, while Emma Lazarus wrote extensively to defend Jewish rights across the world and to promote Zionism. See Diane Lichtenstein, *Writing Their Nations: The Tradition of Nineteenth-Century American Jewish Women Writers* (Bloomington: Indiana University Press, 1992). Rather than a subculture, these women writers attest to the diversity of feminist issues in nineteenth-century America.

[55] See Angela Leighton, *Victorian Women Poets: Writing Against the Heart* (Charlottesville: University Press of Virginia, 1992).

[56] See *Philosemitism, Antisemitism and "the Jews": Perspectives from the Middle Ages to the Twentieth Century*, eds. Tony Kushner and Nadia Valman (Aldershot: Ashgate Publishing Limited, 2004).

[57] Galchinsky, *The Origin*, 36.

persecution, and suffering of the Jewish community, as well as its similarities to the host culture, to arouse Christian sympathy and deflect criticism. They aligned Anglo-Jewry to the prejudices of the host culture to demonstrate solidarity, making their novels specifically anti-Catholic. In short, the early writers sought to present the community as a benevolent influence on English life, leading Bryan Cheyette to label this pre-emancipation subculture an "apologetic" tradition. By stark contrast, he labels the later writing of the 1880s onwards a "revolt" against the earlier tradition.[58] Certainly, these writers, the radically assimilated daughters of the assimilation, were more concerned with portraying Anglo-Jewry realistically as opposed to idealistically.[59] It was in this period that the mass immigration of Eastern European Jews came to be regarded as a problem in England, not only for the Christian community, but more so for assimilated Anglo-Jews.

The new arrivals, escaping persecution in the Russian Empire, had previously lived in the ultra-Orthodox *shtetls* (little towns) away from the trappings of modernity. These introverted communities, even throughout the violent Pogroms (anti-Semitic rioting) of the early nineteenth-century, had remained, at least superficially, socially, religiously, and culturally unchanged, although in reality the *shtetl* had been in decline for some time. Hence, the practices of the *shtetl* and their religio-social composition, arrived in England with the immigrants, as did an "us-them" mentality – the result of years of persecution. Of the men, nearly all were committed to Talmudic study and the religious life of the community, as had been the cus-

---

[58] See Bryan Cheyette, "From Apology to Revolt: Benjamin Farjeon, Amy Levy, and the Post-Emancipation Anglo-Jewish Novel, 1880-1900," *Transactions of the Jewish Historical Society of England* 29 (1982-86): 253-65.

[59] For example, Amy Levy, *Reuben Sachs: A Sketch* (London: Macmillan, 1888); Mrs. Alfred Sidgwick [pseud. Mrs. Andrew Dean], *Isaac Eller's Money* (London: Unwin, 1889); Julia Frankau [pseud. Frank Danby], *Dr. Phillips; A Maida Vale Idyll* (London: Vizitelly, 1887). I have borrowed the term "radical assimilation" from Todd Endelman's study of acculturated Jewry. See his *Radical Assimilation in English Jewish History: 1656-1945* (Bloomington: Indiana University Press, 1990); "The Frankaus of London: A Study of Radical Assimilation, 1837-1967," *Jewish History* 8, no. 1-2 (1994): 117-54.

tom for hundreds of years. Economic necessity ensured that many of the women sought employment in order to support their husband's traditional role as scholar.[60] Indeed, while in the established Anglo-Jewish community the role of women mirrored society at large, designating men the duty of sole breadwinner and assigning women the task of managing the kosher home,[61] the immigrants turned the normal division of labor on its head. The husband was committed to the *yeshivah* (religious fraternity) and study of the sacred texts, while his wife was duty bound to supplement the family income (accordingly, the spiritual male committed to religious scholarship contrasted the material sphere of the female).[62] Immigrant wives normally took up employment in sweatshops, and buttonholing, but also worked independently as grocers, market traders, credit drapers, cap-makers, and dressmakers. Some even turned their parlors into retail outlets or opened factories.[63] However, the curious "foreign" appearance of the immigrants, and their Yiddish dialect, along with their stubborn refusal to assimilate, became a source of anger, even anti-Semitism, for the acculturated community also.[64] For existing Ashkenazi Anglo-Jews, the immigrants were an unwelcome reminder of their Eastern European origins, and of the latent prejudices of the host culture.[65] The ultra-Orthodoxy of the arrivals, or "aliens," was in stark contrast to the

---

[60] See Ricky Burman, "'She Looketh Well to the Ways of Her Household': the Changing Role of Jewish Women in Religious Life, c. 1880-1930," in *Religion in the Lives of English Women, 1760-1930*, ed. G. Malmgreen (London: Croom Helm, 1986), 234-60; Frances Guy, *Women of Worth: Jewish Women in Britain* (Manchester: Manchester Jewish Museum, 1992); L. Marks, *Working Wives and Working Mothers: A Comparative Study of Irish and East European Jewish Married Women's Work and Motherhood in East London 1870-1914* (London: PNL Press, 1990).

[61] Alderman, *Modern British Jewry*, 197-98.

[62] Clare Midgley, "Ethnicity, 'Race' and Empire," in *Women's History: Britain*, 249.

[63] Alderman, *Modern British Jewry*, 199.

[64] See Esther Panitz, *The Alien in Their Midst: Images of Jews in English Literature* (London: Associated University Presses, 1981).

[65] See Bernard Gainer, *The Alien Invasion: The Origins of the Aliens Act of 1905* (New York: Crane, Russak & Co., 1972) for an overview of the Anglo-Jewish response to the immigrants.

anglicized Reform Synagogue, and even Anglo-Orthodoxy, which had itself assimilated Protestant religious norms.

In 1836, several members of the Bevis Marks Synagogue in London demanded alterations similar to those adopted by the German Reform synagogues. Their requests resulted in greater decorum at the services, and, for example, the chanting and the traditional singsong came to be replaced with plain oratory. However, in 1839 further demands were made concerning the length of prayers, the convenience of Shabbat services, the abolition of the second holy day, the possibility of sermons being delivered in English, and regarding a choir. These requests were rebuffed, and subsequently, the Reformers asked if they could open a synagogue closer to their homes in the West End. The Bevis Marks leadership refused and was ignored, and on April 15 1840 the West London Synagogue of British Jews was formed. The newly organized leadership took immediate steps to bring ritual in line with the German model. They supported the political emancipation, and hoped that British Jewry would accommodate Protestant congregational norms and abandon its claim to a separate national destiny.[66] The links to the German movement were initially strong, as sermons were translated into English and a bibliocentric (focus on biblical rather than rabbinic authority) approach, along with the abolition of the second day of festivals (which is a rabbinic as opposed to a biblical institution), was adopted. Thus, although the Ten Commandments were absent from synagogue liturgies in the Orthodox community, the West London Synagogue reintroduced them in 1841. Anglo-Reform Judaism, from the outset, was guided by the morals and ethics of the Hebrew prophets, more so than the legal portions of the Pentateuch (the five books of Moses), yet still preserved the reading of the Torah from a manuscript, emphasizing the primacy of the first reading or more implicitly, the primacy of Judaism over Christianity.[67] However, the newly issued prayer book, by contrast to German Reformism, did not include any radical alterations. The texts calling for the restoration of the Temple and the coming of the Messiah, for example, were retained.

---

[66] Alderman, *Modern British Jewry*, 57.
[67] Hilton, *The Christian Effect*, 106, 108.

The German Reformers of the 1840s, including Abraham Geiger, the essential founder of the movement, analyzed traditional Judaism as an "Oriental," primitive religion. Geiger concluded that the tradition was stagnant as the rabbis obeyed whatever was passed down.[68] The term "Oriental," in the Victorian secular context, refers to the treatment of women in the East, as Linda Hunt Beckman notes: "Victorian feminists attempted to reform Western patriarchal attitudes by developing a discourse that targeted the East for particularly atrocious treatment of women while making comparisons between British and "Oriental" men so as to shame the former into being more enlightened."[69] For the Reformers, Orthodoxy was outdated, particularistic, and based on the legalistic "bogus" authority of the rabbis. According to the Reformers, Orthodoxy dichotomized the life of its members between an onerous, unaesthetic, complex, alienating religion, and an aesthetic, modern, host nation offering the benefits of secular education. For Riv-Ellen Prell, this left Orthodox individuals out of synch as their Judaism continually separated them from the Occident.[70] In Germany, the Reformers specifically targeted the "Woman Question" as one of their key issues.[71] Again Prell: "The proposals of classical Reform paralleled German feminist demands for 'freedom from oppression' and 'their own exercise of critical judgment.' Feminism and Reform both embraced the Enlightenment commitment to progress, democracy and universalism."[72] The focal issues were: women's exclusion from the *minyan*, the exemption of women from

---

[68] See Abraham Geiger, *Judaism and Its History*, translated by Charles Newburgh (New York: Bloch, 1911).

[69] Linda Hunt Beckman, *Amy Levy: Her Life and Letters* (Athens: Ohio University Press, 2000), 304 n27.

[70] Riv-Ellen Prell, "The Dilemma of Women's Equality in the History of Reform Judaism," *Judaism* 30, no. 4 (Fall 1981): 418-26, 419. The Occident: Westernized world.

[71] See David Philipson, *The Reform Movement in Judaism: A Sourcebook of its European Origins* (New York: World Union for Progressive Judaism, 1963) for an overview of the Reform movement in Europe.

[72] Prell, "The Dilemma," 423.

all time-bound positive *mitzvot* incumbent on men,[73] the segregation of the sexes in the synagogue,[74] and the prohibition on women taking up formal education.[75] At the Reform Conference of 1845, held in Frankfurt, Germany, Rabbi David Einhorn, along with Samuel Adler, and A. Adler, discussed several proposals they hoped would promote gender inclusionism. Their report was presented at the 1846 Breslau conference. Einhorn argued that women could be obligated to perform the *mitzvot* reserved for men, that women could form a *minyan*, that women should be given legal independence in divorce, that the age of religious majority should be thirteen for both sexes,[76] and that the morning prayer, during which the men thank God for not having "made me a woman," should be

---

[73] In Jewish tradition there are three *mitzvot* exclusively assigned to women: *nerot* (the lighting of candles), *challah* (separating a portion of dough), and *niddah* (ritual immersion at the end of the menstrual period).

[74] The divider is intended to preserve modesty on the basis that an individual's mind should be on prayer, and not on an attractive woman sat close by. In Orthodoxy, the concept of modesty, *tzniut*, forbids sexual relations outside of marriage and requires that both men and women substantially cover their bodies. In the ultra-Orthodox Haredi community, women are further required not to wear bright colors, to cover their hair, and men may not, generally, hear women sing (*Kol isha*).

[75] The rights of women in traditional Judaism, at least prior to the nineteenth-century, were greater than they were for non-Jewish women. Halakhically, women have the right to buy, sell or own property, to draw up contracts, and to be consulted regarding marriage (numerous halakhot protect women from domestic violence and rape). Women are conferred particular respect and assumed to have been endowed with superior *binah* (intelligence, intuition, and understanding) than men. Even theologically, while the traditional texts have frequently been criticized, and even discarded by the adherents of feminist reform as too inhospitable to women, traditionalists have argued that the equality of men and women begins with God. By contrast to Christianity, Judaism maintains that God, despite the masculine language of the sacred texts, is neither male nor female. Accordingly, the divine presence possesses both masculine and feminine traits. Apologists for the tradition have concluded that masculine terminology is applied merely for convenience, as God has no physical form and therefore no genitalia.

[76] Although boys are given the Bar Mitzvah ceremony, no such rite existed, at least then, for girls.

abolished. Although radical, these proposals were neither discussed nor confirmed, and only a proportion of German synagogues adopted them.[77] The German Reformers, even given their critique of the tradition, were in actuality, less revolutionary than their rhetoric implied. For example, the resolution declaring that the use of Hebrew was not essential to public worship was followed by an instant decision to retain it for fear of offending older generations of worshippers.

First and foremost the German reformers hoped that Judaism would "catch up" with the rest of Europe. It had not escaped their notice that across the Continent women were coming to dominate the social services, and in Germany a fledgling feminist movement was developing.[78] However, rather than developing a unique Judaism from the salvageable remnants of the tradition, the Reformers, and their synagogue services, came to resemble Protestantism. The music, designed to spiritually liven the services, was of Western origin, prayers were said as a group, and proceedings were calm and ordered. While these changes initially differentiated Reform and Orthodox services, they were neither theologically nor halakhically radical.

By the 1880s, Upper Berkeley Street (West London Reform Synagogue) had become a fashionable sanctuary for acculturated middle-class Jews unable, and unwilling, to accommodate the halakhic minutiae of Orthodoxy to their highly anglicized lifestyles. Synagogue attendance, similar to church on Sunday, was often more essential to family respectability than to spiritual fulfillment. The Anglo-Reform congregation placed specific emphasis on decorum (which encouraged worshippers to behave as spectators rather than as active participants), permitted English prayers, a mixed sex choir, and replaced particularistic prayers, such as the call for a return to Israel, with universalistic ones. The services were shorter, English sermons were provided on Sabbath (in London, delivering sermons in the vernacular began in the early nineteenth-century), being called up to read was abolished, and Orthodox notions of the Messiah were replaced by hope for a Messianic age initiated, not by

---

[77] Prell, "The Dilemma," 421-23.
[78] Prell, "The Dilemma," 423.

an individual, but by the Jewish people. Moreover, preaching became part of the new style adopted by ministers. Indeed, the chief
rabbi, Nathan Adler, helped establish the Jews' College in 1855.
This modern rabbinical seminary considered the training of
preachers integral to their mission. However, the service remained
little different from Orthodoxy. The modifications were a product
of middle-class Jewry's intention to appear anglicized, and of their
awareness of Evangelical charges of ritualism at the expense of
inner-spirituality. The influence of the German movement was, in
fact, minimal and only become noticeable in the 1930s. Orthodox
complaints, on the grounds of *chukkat ha-goy*, were cited against the
organ (introduced in 1859 at the Reform Synagogue), the adoption
of gentile names, and the rabbi or cantor (*hazzan*) wearing a gown
and tie. By the late nineteenth-century, cantors increasingly came to
have a musical education reflecting the influence of both the
Church and the opera house. Nevertheless, the Reformers were
able to find in rabbinic and biblical sources precedents for these
innovations.[79] Though, as David Feldman argues, Christian Evangelicalism was the primary influence:

> Notwithstanding this recognition that the influence of evan-
> gelicalism did not stand alone, the parallels between religious
> reform and the evangelical critique of Judaism are impressive.
> … By the 1830s, the majority of the Anglo-Jewish upper and
> middle class looked upon the revival of political reform in
> Britain as a movement likely to create a polity more rich with
> opportunity for Jews rather than one fraught with danger. But
> if these aspects of evangelicalism did "not take," it is possible
> to highlight striking parallels elsewhere; above all in the em-
> phases on "unmysterious" forms of worship and vital religion
> of the heart.[80]

---

[79] Hilton, *The Christian Effect*, 10.
[80] David Feldman, *Englishmen and Jews: Social Relations and Political Culture, 1840-1914* (New Haven: Yale University Press, 1994), 62-63.

The Reform practice of a professional leader or rabbi taking public prayer, for example, is taken from the Church. Stephen Sharot argues that reforms made by the Orthodox synagogues actually brought the denominations closer together. The *Jewish Chronicle* commented that there was little difference between members as the leadership of both denominations acted in unison for the Board of Guardians, the Board of Deputies, and the Jewish Religious Education Board.[81] Members presided at each other's synagogues during award ceremonies, and there was little to differentiate ministers. Not only were their beliefs similar, they performed the same roles.[82]

The Orthodox service also moved toward the Church model. Newly built synagogues became larger, more elaborate, and architecturally mirrored the churches. Certainly, the New Synagogue built in London in 1837 was far too big for the area's requirements, and no part of the tradition states that such a building was necessary. The Chief Rabbi, likewise, adopted dress associated with Christian clergy, including a dark clerical gown with white neck band.[83] From 1850, Orthodox synagogues introduced choirs, English sermons, a reverential atmosphere, elaborate pulpits, and began using quintessentially Protestant titles such as warden, guardians, reverend, and vestry. Even the terms "Reform" and "Orthodox"

---

[81] See Charles Emanuel, *A Century and a Half of Jewish History Extracted from the Minute Books of the London Committee of Deputies of the British Jews* (1910; rpt. Charleston: BiblioBazaar, 2009); V. Lipman, *A Century of Social Service 1859-1959 – The History of the Jewish Board of Guardians* (London: Routledge and Kegan Paul, 1959); Aubrey Newman, *The Board of Deputies of British Jews, 1760-1985* (London: Vallentine Mitchell, 1987).

[82] Stephen Sharot, "Reform and Liberal Judaism in London: 1840-1940," *Jewish Social Studies* 41, no. 3/4 (Summer/Fall 1979): 217. See Bernard Homa, *Orthodoxy in Anglo-Jewry, 1880-1940* (London: Jewish Historical Society of Great Britain, 1969); Aubrey Newman, *The United Synagogue, 1870-1970* (London: Routledge and Kegan Paul, 1977); Geoffrey Alderman, *The Federation of Synagogues, 1887-1987* (London: Federation of Synagogues, 1987); W. Gunter Plaut, *The Rise of Reform Judaism* (New York: World Union for Progressive Judaism, 1963).

[83] See Hyman Simons, *Forty Years a Chief Rabbi: The Life and Times of Solomon Hirschell* (London: Robson Books, 1980).

are borrowed from the Church.[84] The Anglo-Reform leadership, representative of the upper-class elite, remained affiliated to Orthodoxy, and members from both denominations maintained social ties.[85] The Reform prayer book included only minor changes, and the wearing of prayer shawls and phylacteries continued.[86] In fact, 1880s Reform Judaism failed to generate any sizable defection from the Orthodox community. Aside from Upper Berkeley Street no other synagogues were founded in London in the period.[87] Reform Judaism impacted little upon the community and reflected the interests of an elite determined that the movement assimilate the host culture, including its bibliocentrism, anti-ritualism, and anti-Talmudism. David Feldman concludes:

> In all but their decision to dispense with some customary holidays, the doctrinal innovations of Reform Judaism in Britain were notably moderate. … In Britain, reformers wedded themselves to the word of the Bible. This limited their innovations but it also led them to abolish the second day of festivals for which there was no scriptural authority; something beyond the agenda of European reform.
> This particular programme of change reflected the force in Britain of a bibliocentric critique of Judaism. … In Britain it was the evangelical bibliocentric attack on Judaism that was loudest and most persistent before 1860.[88]

Anglo-Reformism was a response to criticism from the non-Jewish world. The Reformers published elaborate bibliocentric critiques of the tradition aware of charges of "rabbinism" and rejection of the "spirit."[89] Accommodating contemporaneous Evangelical ideas, the

---

[84] Hilton, *The Christian Effect*, 142-45.

[85] Sharot, "Reform and Liberal," 213-14, 217-18.

[86] Phylacteries: two boxes containing scripture worn on the arm and head respectively.

[87] See Peter Renton, *The Lost Synagogues of London* (London: Tymsder Publishing, 2000).

[88] Feldman, *Englishmen and Jews*, 63-64.

[89] Feldman, *Englishmen and Jews*, 65.

Reformers concluded that ritualism had no basis in scripture, and that the rabbis, through halakhah, had corrupted biblical law. Accordingly, sermons delivered by Reform Rabbi David Marks during the 1840s condemned Orthodoxy for being incapable of meeting the spiritual requirements of women.

Due to its low membership, the West London Reform Synagogue did not hold any daily services. According to a contemporary religious poll, nine out of ten seats were unoccupied during a Sabbath service in 1891, and a visitor in 1895 could only count eighteen male worshippers.[90] By contrast, the ladies gallery was full. Indeed, in 1885 a minister concluded that without the women there would be little requirement for services. By 1896, the Synagogue invited its female members to discuss reforms, although did not give them the right to vote.[91] Their regular presence was indicative of middle-class women during the period. These women had sufficient leisure time to attend, and many sought to emulate women's increased role in Church affairs. The creation of Christian sisterhoods and the revival of the deaconesses provided new opportunities for unmarried women to be of service. Nearly twice as many women of all Christian denominations attended churches compared to men.[92] Likewise, Jewish women assumed new religious roles. The Anglo-Jewish elite,[93] which prided itself on being "British" and receptive to new ideas, reconsidered women's role in the light of Victorian trends.[94] As Stephen Sharot argues: "The high, sometimes predominant, proportion of female worshippers at the Reform synagogue is an index of the high degree of acculturation

---

[90] In 1886 the Bevis Marks leadership considered selling the Synagogue as attendances were so low.

[91] Sharot, "Reform and Liberal Judaism," 215.

[92] Brian Heeney, *The Women's Movement in the Church of England, 1850-1930* (Oxford: Clarendon Press, 1988), 5.

[93] See Todd Endelman, "Communal Solidarity Among the Jewish Elite of Victorian London," *Victorian Studies* 28, no. 3 (Spring 1985): 491-526.

[94] Ellen Umansky, *Lily Montagu and the Advancement of Liberal Judaism: From Vision to Vocation*, Studies in Women and Religion, vol. 12 (New York: Edwin Mellen Press, 1983), 36.

of the Reform congregants to Christian patterns of behavior."[95] As men were absorbed in Torah study, providing one's daughters with a secular education became a visible symbol of Jewish adaptability. Well-to-do families encouraged their daughters to acquire knowledge of foreign languages and literature. However, once these women recognized their capacity for knowledge, the justifications for their exclusion from religious study and their unequal participation in the community no longer seemed valid. Although the majority of these women chose to remain within the fold, many expressed dissatisfaction with their religious role.[96] By the late 1880s, Jewish women were demanding greater access to public life.[97] Their increased role in volunteer philanthropy and teaching had, according to Linda Gordon Kuzmack:

> triggered a search for equality in religious life … They [women] could not have chosen a better time, for Jewish men were leaving the synagogue in droves, bored by long, incomprehensible services in Hebrew, dry sermons, and the need to work on the Sabbath. The loss of congregants, combined with the impact of Darwinism, the rise of secularism, and modern Biblical criticism, generated a debate over modernizing worship that filled Jewish newspapers and journals.[98]

As the men were turning away from the synagogue, Anglo-Jewish women were attending services and performing the charitable work. Since fewer men were visible, the activities of women became central to synagogue life.[99]

According to Olive Banks, late Victorian feminism altered the perceived traits of women's character without actually rejecting separate spheres: "The feminists changed, sometimes in highly sig-

---

[95] Sharot, "Reform and Liberal Judaism," 215.

[96] Umansky, *Lily Montagu*, 27-28.

[97] See Patricia Hollis, *Women in Public 1850-1900* (London: Allen and Unwin, 1979).

[98] Kuzmack, *Woman's Cause*, 47.

[99] Kuzmack, *Woman's Cause*, 47.

nificant ways, the view of women's character and destiny without ever totally rejecting the basis of the doctrine, which implied not only a special feminine nature but also a grounding of that nature in women's domestic and ultimately, her maternal role."[100] The cult of true womanhood developed alongside separate spheres: men were the stronger and harder sex, less emotional, and physically able to cope with the ruthless world of the market-place. However, as women required the protective walls of the home, they possessed maternal qualities. Their greater moral purity made them the ethical inspiration for their husbands and the moral guardians of children.[101] As the "subordinate" being, women were delicately equipped by God and nature for their role in the home and family. Hence, the Church was the guardian of a basic conservatism rooted in the Pentateuch and enshrined in the Pauline epistles.[102] Although this stereotype persisted, and was internalized by feminist activists, women's spiritual role, by the 1880s, spilled over into public life. The woman's movement in the Church rejected the doctrine of female subordination and automatic submission to husbands, fathers, and brothers. Indeed, as women sought to overcome these restrictions, they became involved in philanthropy on an unprecedented scale. They also took up pre-professional positions in the Church.[103]

The cult of true womanhood was based on the Evangelical theology of Christian femininity outlined by William Wilberforce in the eighteenth-century. Women's qualities of devotion and self-sacrifice were applicable to motherhood and homemaking. This ensured the division of labor and the divine ordering of nature. The emphasis on women's superior religiosity, however, contradictorily, sat alongside the traditions of her disobedience and original sin, which explained her subjection to male authority. Evangelicals located this theology in Genesis, and in St Paul's analysis in 1 Corinthians 11, and 1 Timothy 2. Nonetheless, the idea that women were more sinful than men, yet more pure, had to be resolved through

---

[100] Banks, *Faces of Feminism*, 86.
[101] Banks, *Faces of Feminism*, 86.
[102] Heeney, *The Women's Movement*, 6, 9.
[103] Heeney, *The Women's Movement*, 6, 19.

distinction between the innocent, chaste, passionless middle-class Christian woman, and the depraved "fallen woman" of the street. Although Evangelical theology provided a conservative and limiting definition of femininity, it presented justification for women's role in social reform as a natural extension of their maternal and spiritual duties. This case suited the Evangelicals as it confirmed, rather than confronted, contemporary expectations regarding women's role.[104] David Bebbington concludes that Evangelicalism did more than the feminist movement to expand women's sphere:

> At a time when respectability (often reinforced by Evangelical arguments) closely circumscribed the role of women, church work was one of their few outlets. Although Sunday School teachers were overwhelmingly male in the early nineteenth century, they were chiefly female by its end. Philanthropy was a major channel for women's energies. Missionary support work, the YMCA, Christian Endeavour and the Student Volunteer Movement all springing from Evangelical soil, contributed to what one writer called the "Epiphany of Women." Women could even occupy official positions – as deaconesses in the Church of England from 1862, as preachers among the Quakers, the Primitive Methodists and the Bible Christians and as officers in the Salvation Army. It has been persuasively argued that Evangelical religion, despite its emphasis on the domestic role of women, was more important than feminism in enlarging their sphere during the nineteenth century.[105]

Similarly, Olive Banks notes that Evangelicalism was key to the development of a feminist consciousness, conservative in that it conformed to traditional constructions of femininity, but radical in that it expanded women's role into the public sphere.[106] In the Jew-

---

[104] Sean Gill, *Women and the Church of England: From the Eighteenth Century to the Present* (London: SPCK, 1994), 77-79.

[105] David Bebbington, *Evangelicalism in Modern Britain: A History from the 1730s to the 1980s* (London: Unwin Hyman, 1989), 129.

[106] Banks, *Faces of Feminism*, 13-27.

ish community too, women's commitment to organized philanthropy, which began in the 1840s, grew to accommodate the mass immigration. This included the formation of maternal welfare organizations and the Jewish Association for the Protection of Girls and Women. By 1902, the level of women's voluntary work was such that the Union of Jewish Women was created to act as an umbrella organization. Although this was formed to be an "all-embracing sisterhood," it was dominated by women of the Anglo-Jewish elite, and concentrated on providing educational training for middle-class women.[107]

The failure of Reform Judaism in nineteenth-century England, particularly regarding the "Woman Question," can be attributed to many factors: Daniel Langton argues that the Reform movement's paralysis was due to its meager response to biblical criticism. The Anglo-Reformers demonstrated no notable interest in biblical criticism until after 1860, when the movement had already taken shape. Whereas the German Reformers provided a modern, scientifically informed alternative to Orthodoxy, Anglo-Reformism was not ready to approach evolutionary theory. According to Langton, Rabbi David Marks' Karaite-like reliance on the Bible proved disastrous for English Reform.[108] Indeed, theological reforms, such as of the prayers, were often slow to happen. Disputed passages were often retained, or written in Hebrew to avoid criticism (many congregants could not read Hebrew), and offensive prayers were usually rephrased. Riv-Ellen Prell argues that while the liberalism of the Enlightenment provided proto-feminist opportunities, it became problematic for the status of women in Judaism. By selecting the emancipation model to address the issue of gender, that is, by seeking legal equality, classical Reform diminished the unique legal

---

[107] Midgley, "Ethnicity, 'Race' and Empire," 250-51.
[108] Daniel Langton, *Claude Montefiore: His Life and Thought* (London: Vallentine Mitchell, 2002), 72. Karaism is a Jewish minority that believes in strict interpretation of the scriptures without rabbinic interpretation.

status assigned to women. Thus, as they became equal they also became invisible as women.[109] Nicholas de Lange argues:

> Changes have come about, where they have, in a piecemeal and somewhat haphazard way, and almost always in the face of conservative opposition, even in Reform synagogues. (The Reform synagogue in London was described by the novelist Israel Zangwill, at the end of the nineteenth century, as "a body which has stood still for fifty years admiring its past self.")[110]

In fact, Anglo-Reformism failed on multiple levels: as the brainchild of the upper-class elite, it held no appeal to the immigrants, its Sabbath attendances for the late 1880s were the lowest for all synagogues, and most members attended only once a year, normally on Yom Kippur. The majority of Reformers were dissatisfied with the movement's limitations, and by the late 1880s they lobbied for the service to be shortened (traditional services, generally, had no set times), for the prophets to be read in English, and for the prayer for the restoration of the sacrificial rite to be removed.[111] However, even by 1896 a proposal by the ministers of the Reform Synagogue that the amount of English in services be increased was rejected. Furthermore, attempts to shorten the service to two and a half hours were hampered by the dignified application of readings and prayers, and the musical embellishment, which actually lengthened proceedings. Additionally, the employment of officiates and musicians, along with the supervision of the choir, made the synagogue seem "professionalized."[112] In sum, perhaps too little differentiated Reform and Orthodox services, and some of the Reformers, including Claude Montefiore, growing impatient with the con-

---

[109] Prell, "The Dilemma," 418. For an overview of Reform Judaism in England see *Reform Judaism*, ed. Dow Marmur (London: Reform Synagogues of Great Britain, 1973).

[110] Lange, *Judaism*, 43.

[111] Hilton, *The Christian Effect*, 146-47.

[112] Lange, *Judaism*, 48, 51.

servative, even hit-and-miss, pace of Anglo-Reformism, looked for something more radical.

3   LILY MONTAGU AND THE ONSET OF LIBERAL JUDAISM IN ENGLAND

Lily was one of ten children born into the upper-class Montagu (originally Samuel) household. The family emigrated to England from Northern Germany in the mid eighteenth-century and became synonymous with the Anglo-Jewish elite. Despite her wealthy background, however, Lily Montagu was unable to accommodate her father's Orthodoxy.[1] She stated:

> I was brought up in a home impregnated with the Jewish atmosphere. In spite of the fact that my father had many public duties to perform in connection with his life as a member of Parliament and subsequently as a Peer, all the members of his household knew him primarily as a great Jew. His Jewishness was the central fact of his life.[2]

Instead, she would later seek to develop a more subjective version of Judaism. However, her inability as a child to observe and embrace the rigorous Orthodoxy of the family home caused her, at

---

[1] Chaim Bermant, *The Cousinhood: The Anglo-Jewish Gentry* (London: Eyre and Spottiswoode, 1971), 208-09. See Lily Montagu, *Samuel Montagu, First Baron Swaythling: A Character Sketch* (London: Truslove and Hansom Limited) for a biography of her father. As an energetic merchant banker and philanthropist, Samuel Montagu was active in Anglo-Jewish communal, economic, and religious politics, though never allowed his commercial interests to interfere with the application of his religion.

[2] Lily Montagu, *The Faith of a Jewish Woman* (London: George Allen & Unwin, 1943), 1.

the age of fifteen, to undergo a spiritual crisis. Many years later she described her childhood:

> I was not conscious of any personal spiritual experience stimulated by the Sabbaths and festivals, but I could become very enthusiastic over the symbols, and if asked, should have unhesitatingly said that their preservation was required by God.
> …
> I can trace my first questioning of the utility of observances if pursued as ends in themselves to experiences connected with Passover … I remember rushing up to my eldest brother … and expostulating. "I feel ashamed," I said, "at the behavior of many of the people. How dare they think they are praying? If that is religion, I hate it."[3]

As a child, Montagu regularly attended synagogue without engaging in prayer, and her awareness of Hebrew, unsurprisingly, was minimal. As such, she felt unable to pray in a language she did not understand, and was concerned that her relegation to the gallery limited her participation. She found limited solace, however, in the encouragement of her mother.[4] Although she maintained a traditional household, she did not dismiss new ideas and permitted criticism of the tradition, as Montagu recalled:

> As we grew to adolescence, and asked our father rather radical questions, we could count on our mother's sympathy and support if our questions, in her view, were not altogether unreasonable. … My mother would add, in the depths of her unformulated thoughts, gently and wistfully to herself, that the life of the past was not likely in any of its aspects to be good enough for her children. It must be better.[5]

---

[3] Montagu, *The Faith of a Jewish Woman*, 8-9.

[4] Lily Montagu, *My Club and I: The Story of the West Central Jewish Club* (London: Herbert Joseph Limited, 1941), 19.

[5] Montagu, *The Faith of a Jewish Woman*, 5-6.

Her mother's support allowed Montagu to question Orthodoxy from a young age. By contrast, although she frequently downplayed any rift, her relationship with her father was paradigmatic of the confrontation between modernity and Orthodoxy. As early as the eighteenth-century, many women discovered they could not accommodate themselves to the religion of their parents. Some, like Montagu, sought a spiritual course they hoped would be personally meaningful and acceptable, while others abandoned Judaism. Montagu's plight, as she understood it, resulted from a desire to unearth a means of remaining modern, while continuing to be fully Jewish. Hence, she needed to redefine what it meant to be "Jewish" in order to identify Judaism with what she deemed to be "true" religion.[6]

Lily Montagu's spiritual crisis (medically, the crisis may have been the result of a nervous condition), and her conclusion that Orthodoxy was undermining her self-expression, forced an intense conviction that she was destined to minister to the community, and had she been a man the rabbinate might have beckoned.[7] Montagu would later state: "I was immensely interested in my part as leader of the services, and spent a great deal of time preparing my little talks. We aimed at awakening a spirit of worship; in getting the children to join in the services and feel that it was their own."[8] Even her childhood illnesses, which seem to have been frequent, could not diminish her unshakable, providential belief in herself:

> I was once more taken to the benevolent old doctor, who assured me that I was wonderfully better, but must not be surprised or discouraged if I got bad again before long, as I had been too ill to be expected to get well so quickly. My spirit of

---

[6] Ellen Umansky, *Lily Montagu and the Advancement of Liberal Judaism: from Vision to Vocation*, Studies in Women and Religion, vol. 12 (New York: Edwin Mellen Press, 1983), 210-11, 220.

[7] Geoffrey Alderman, *Modern British Jewry*, new ed. (Oxford: Clarendon Press, 1998), 202-03.

[8] Montagu, *The Faith of a Jewish Woman*, 17.

resistance was at once roused, and I promised myself that I *should* surprise everybody and not get ill in the same way again.[9]

Montagu's education was unique for the period. She received regular schooling until the age of fifteen, and was then allowed to choose her own course of study. Thus, under the instruction of a variety of tutors, Montagu spent the next four years reading up on social philosophy. Her research was augmented by lessons from the Rev. Simeon Singer, who introduced her to the Hebrew prophets.[10] Montagu's attraction to Jewish ethics never wavered, yet despite possessing the spirit of rebellion, she adhered to Orthodoxy, if only to please her rigid father. Indeed, throughout her life she remained kosher, she recited the memorial prayers for her parents, and was even buried at the (Orthodox) Edmonton Federation Cemetery.[11]

Lily Montagu rejected the possibility of conversion; for her, only Judaism could provide spiritual enlightenment.[12] However, she was concerned that traditional ritual had become mere ceremony devoid of inner-spirituality, and moreover, she was troubled that Orthodoxy had failed to assign a formal religious role to women.[13] For Montagu, traditional reluctance to accommodate modernity was leading to the secularization of the community. Certainly, secularization had been evident in England since the mid eighteenth-century, and extenuated in the mid nineteenth-century by Darwinism, scientific discoveries, and biblical criticism. The conflict between faith and science forced many individuals to question their beliefs. In the acculturated Jewish community, as we have seen, attendance of the Reform Synagogue was low, religious observance was declining, and there was little interest in Jewish learning. Mon-

---

[9] Montagu, *The Faith of a Jewish Woman*, 13.

[10] Montagu, *The Faith of a Jewish Woman*, 11.

[11] Montagu, *My Club and I*, 43. For an outline of Montagu's personal views on, and praise of, the basic Jewish observances see her *Thoughts on Judaism* (London: R. Brimley Johnson, 1904), 90-115.

[12] Lily Montagu, "Sept. 20. 1919," sermon, London Metropolitan Archives, ACC/3529/3/7, 5.

[13] See Lily Montagu, "Liberal Judaism in Relation to Women," *Jewish Religious Union Bulletin* (June 1914), 5.

tagu hoped that Liberal Judaism would reach out to both assimilated and immigrant Jews alienated from the tradition. She was particularly inspired by Claude Montefiore,[14] and with him, sought to develop a Liberal alternative to Orthodoxy.[15] From the age of twenty-one until her death, she would publish novels,[16] essays, religious monographs, and present numerous addresses, sermons, and lectures. Additionally, along with her sister Marian, Montagu helped tutor working-class girls living in London's East End, and together they formed the West Central Jewish Girls' Club. Montagu's involvement in social work was part of the "more personally involved pattern of charitable activity" of the mid nineteenth-century that involved "the expenditure of time and effort as well as … money."[17] Philanthropy was regarded as a leisured woman's most viable outlet for self-expression, and active benevolence was a compelling moral, spiritual, and practical option for women. All Christian denominations stressed the necessity of charitable conduct.[18] Certainly, many assimilated single Jewish women and recently arrived immigrants were attracted to the charity of Christian benefactors due to an initial scarcity of Jewish institutions. Accordingly, Montagu, aside from welcoming the arrivals to her Club, is-

---

[14] Montagu never denied her admiration for Montefiore, see *Thoughts on Judaism*, 1, 6. For a biography of Montefiore see Lucy Cohen, *Some Recollections of C. G. Montefiore* (London: Faber & Faber, 1940). For an outline of their professional relationship see Steven Bayme, "Claude Montefiore, Lily Montagu and the Origins of the Jewish Religious Union," *Transactions of the Jewish Historical Society of England* 27 (1982): 61-71.

[15] Montagu, *The Faith of a Jewish Woman*, 5.

[16] For her two novels see Lily Montagu, *Naomi's Exodus* (London: T. Fisher and Unwin, 1901); Lily Montagu, *Broken Stalks* (London: R. Brimley Johnson, 1902). The latter does not approach Jewish themes. For her short-stories see Lily Montagu, *What Can A Mother Do? And Other Stories* (London: George Routledge & Sons, 1926).

[17] Geoffrey Best, *Mid-Victorian Britain, 1851-1875* (New York: Schocken Books, 1972), 134.

[18] Frank Prochaska, *Women and Philanthropy in Nineteenth-Century England* (Oxford: Clarendon Press, 1980), 5-6, 8-9.

sued a response to the press defending the immigrants and praising England's "passion for liberty."[19]

Anglo-Liberal Judaism, as a philosophy, was theorized by Claude Montefiore during the 1880s and 1890s. He had championed numerous Reform initiatives, but the movement's conservative-minded leadership refused to sanction his ideas, such as for the psalms to be sung in English. A sizable number of Reform congregants became disillusioned, and began to consider radical alternatives, such as those put forward by Montefiore. His own brand of Liberal Judaism has its roots in classical German Reformism, and is based on the writings of Abraham Geiger and Samuel Holdheim. Accordingly, monotheism, the spiritual and moral teaching of the prophets, and the tradition down the ages, were features deemed salvageable in a new Judaism. Indeed, Montefiore, by adhering to the interpretive liberty of classical Reformism, or the "pick and choose" approach to the tradition, did not reject the rabbinic tradition *in toto*. He respected the philosophers and exegetes of the middle-ages, although he rejected intermediaries – the rabbis – between the individual and the divine presence. Furthermore, Montefiore never intended to do away with or replace the major festivals. However, Liberal Judaism, similar to Anglo-Reformism, internalized the Christian Evangelical critique of Judaism, and adopted its anti-ritualism, anti-rabbinism, and bibliocentrism.[20] Montefiore developed a theology that was neither nationalistic nor ritualistic. He rejected Orthodox claims that the Bible was the Word of God, and that the Talmud had correctly interpreted that Word. In his speech at the West London Reform Synagogue on February 1 1896, Montefiore outlined the new religion.[21] In the *new* Judaism, to

---

[19] Lily Montagu, "What Some of Our Critics Are Saying," sermon, December 13 1924, London Metropolitan Archives, ACC/3529/3/7, 7.

[20] At his college, Balliol, Montefiore came under the influence of Benjamin Jowett, and his moral and liberal ideas. He had also been a pupil of the German academic, Solomon Schechter, the only rabbinic scholar present in England at the close of the nineteenth-century. See Norman Bentwich, *Solomon Schechter: A Biography* (Philadelphia: Jewish Publication Society of America, 1940).

[21] *Jewish Chronicle*, February 14, 1896, 19-20. See Claude Montefiore, *Judaism, Unitarianism, and Theism*, Papers for Jewish People, 4 (London:

be a good Jew is to be a good citizen and to lead a truthful and righteous life. The application of ritual was to be personally applicable – dependent on the individual and their own subjective liberty. Indeed, Liberal Judaism would encourage freedom of conscience and moral conduct. Jewish particularity was to be minimized and accommodated to the civic life of the host nation. Theologically, Liberal Jews would not be a collective, or *community*, before God, as in the tradition, but individuals able to commune *personally* with the divine presence. Furthermore, nascent Liberal Judaism determined that the Torah no longer possessed the authoritative status relevant to Orthodoxy as many of its prescriptions were irrational and outdated. It was concluded, for example, that kosher law has no religious justification. Additionally, Montefiore committed Liberal Judaism to the equalization of the sexes, with Anglo-Reformism's failure concerning the "Woman Question" in mind. However, these radical theories were mere talk; there was still no organized movement or political agenda.

Unsurprisingly, the traditionalists accused Claude Montefiore of aligning Judaism with Protestantism. However, he condemned intermarriage,[22] rejected the substitution of Sunday worship for Saturday prayers, advised against the use of the New Testament in Jewish ritual, and insisted on the retention of circumcision. In fact, Liberal Judaism, as Montefiore maintained, only came about as a response to acculturation. He concluded that the problem of assimilation, and its solution, must relate to the cultural force to which Anglo-Jewry seemed to be integrating itself. Accordingly, Montefiore believed that Jews needed to understand and engage with Christianity, so applied himself to both Christian and Jewish texts.[23] As Michael Meyer notes:

Jewish Religious Union, 1908); Claude Montefiore, *Liberal Judaism: An Essay* (London: Macmillan 1903).

[22] A. Hanson, "Claude Montefiore, a Modern Philo," *The Modern Churchman* 20, no. 3 (Spring 1977): 110.

[23] Maurice Bowler, "C. G. Montefiore and His Quest," *Judaism* 30, no. 4 (Fall 1981): 453-54, 456, 458.

The Protestant environment gave a crucial impetus to Reform. It provided a model for theological, not merely formal reformation, for the rejection of an old hierarchy, and for liturgy in the vernacular. Protestantism placed the sermon at the centre of the service; it focused on words spoken and sung, not physical ritual acts; and as a religion which had itself revolted and developed further, it raised the hope that, in its liberal formulations, it would go far toward meeting Judaism on common religious ground.[24]

Montefiore assumed that Anglo-Jews were so "Christianized" that "five-sixths of their conception of life is Christian," and praised Christianity for its ethical concerns, which he viewed as closer to Liberal Judaism than the rabbinic tradition.[25] The Reformers, and subsequently Liberal Judaism, were intent on minimizing Jewish defection to the Church, and assumed that to counter Christian initiatives Judaism would have to develop corresponding ideas. Since the early eighteenth-century, acculturated Anglo-Jews had moved with ease in gentile society, and many famous names from the Georgian communal nobility had been lost, motivated by their inability to gain social acceptance while remaining Jewish. The Reformers assumed that a style of prayer closer to the Church might actually encourage the conversion to Judaism of non-Jewish partners. Accordingly, the Reform congregation of Berlin, Germany, became known as an "alliance against apostasy."[26] However, both Montefiore and Lily Montagu were aware that Reform Judaism had not gone far enough, as she would later state: "The cry was no longer for changed externalities such as were secured by the Reform Synagogue already established for seventy years, but for a restatement of Jewish doctrine in the light of scientific truth."[27]

---

[24] Michael Meyer, *Responses to Modernity: A History of the Reform Movement in Judaism* (New York: OUP, 1988), 143

[25] Quoted by Michael Hilton, *The Christian Effect on Jewish Life* (London: SCM Press Ltd, 1994), 155, 204.

[26] Hilton, *The Christian Effect*, 147-48, 195.

[27] Montagu, *The Faith of a Jewish Woman*, 28.

Lily Montagu "always felt deeply moved by any effort at social amelioration,"[28] and began social work in the East End in the early 1890s. She provided a children's service based on an English liturgy and in 1893, following the establishment of the West Central Jewish Girls' Club, she produced a prayer book for the children.[29] The Club was intended to provide social, intellectual, and spiritual opportunities for young women, whose re-engagement with Judaism, regardless of their Orthodox or Reform affiliation, was integral to Montagu, as she noted:

> I had a number of girl friends who were loyal Jews, but to whom the new revelation had not been brought. Judaism was not a valued possession if its observance seemed to clash with the achievement of personal happiness. I saw some of my friends give up their allegiance very early and drift into intermarriage. They did not see they were giving up everything. The treasures of Judaism lay hidden form them.[30]

As Montagu aligned her own beliefs to Liberal Judaism, she became convinced that to bear testimony to the reality of God action was required rather than mere words or blind conformity to ritual. Nellie Levy described Montagu's mission thus:

> A young girl dreamed and behold a vision appeared and she saw her sisters, and they lacked much that had been bestowed on her, some needed guidance and friendship, some to be lighted out of squalor and shown the light; some seemed mere children forced to become breadwinners; some ran to and fro to snatch at pleasures that were transitory and left bitterness and disillusionment; some cried "Give us opportunities denied us, we to need light, space, knowledge"; others sat and waited

---

[28] Montagu, *The Faith of a Jewish Woman*, 11.

[29] See Montagu, *My Club and I; Nellie Levy, The West Central Story and Its Founders the Hon. Lily H. Montagu CBE, JP, DD and the Hon. Marian Montagu: 1893-1968*, club pamphlet (London: Leeway Business Services).

[30] Montagu, *The Faith of a Jewish Woman*, 27.

to enter the world of literature and art, and again, others feared to tread, for the path seemed strewn with giants, who could be overcome only by strength which they lacked, and still others groped towards those frailer than themselves and longed to hold out a helping hand but knew not how. ...

"To this vision I [Montagu] consecrate myself, and its fruition I will labor unceasingly. I will break down barriers, establish friendships and give opportunities. I will share, bind up those who are broken, and I will set before them light and good through a Faith in Judaism, so that they have strength wherewith to live."[31]

Accordingly, in 1899 Montagu published "Spiritual Possibilities of Judaism To-Day" with the intention of providing the Liberal Jewish cause with some much needed direction. In fact, the article, revealing Montagu's latent fiery temperament, was groundbreaking, even savage in its criticisms. In the essay, Montagu sets about castigating the Orthodox community for its commitment to "ceremonialism," which, she concluded, had replaced "true" religion:

> Until Jews are honest enough to recognize that the majority of them are either devoted to ceremonialism at the expense of religion, or indifferent both to ceremonialism and to religion; until they have energy to examine their religious needs and courage to formulate them, they are courting comfort at the expense of truth.[32]

According to Montagu, the Judaism of the East End had become a glorified cult based on obedience, while in the affluent West End religious calling had been replaced with "callousness."[33] For Mon-

---

[31] Levy, *The West Central Story*, 1.

[32] Lily Montagu, "Spiritual Possibilities of Judaism To-Day," *Jewish Quarterly Review* 11 (1899): 216.

[33] Montagu, "Spiritual Possibilities," 216, 218. By "East End" Montagu was referring to the recent immigrants, and by "West End" she was alluding to acculturated Anglo-Jewry.

tagu, it was vital that Judaism accommodate modernity if the community was to survive.[34]

Many in the Orthodox community had rejected political emancipation as irrelevant and dangerous to the community given their fear that political integration would lead to social assimilation. A prevalent view emerged across all Jewish denominations that acculturated Jewry was morally, culturally, and physically degenerate. Indeed, British-Jewry was in a state of tension created by the determination of the anglicized elite to retain control over communal organization, and conflated by the stubborn determination of the immigrants to exert equal authority. Democracy was confronted by oligarchy, laxity by Orthodoxy, social radicalism by political conservatism, synagogal centralism by the independence of the *chevrot* (fraternities from central and Eastern Europe), the numerical dominance of London by the provincial Jewries, and the communal self-help societies by the philanthropy of the Board of Guardians.[35]

The anxiety between the assimilated and immigrant communities rapidly became overwrought, particularly since native-Jews feared the anti-Semitism the recent *Ostjudische* arrivals were arousing. Through the 1880s and 1890s, nativist racism steadily increased as the "Jewish Question" became interlinked with the "Alien Question" in British politics.[36] However, if the immigrant community was criticized for importing unwelcome foreign practices, assimilated Jewry was regarded in equally derogatory terms by Jews and gentiles alike. Many novels presented upper-middle-class Jewry as culturally, morally, and religiously retrograde. According to Todd Endelman, these caricatures, while crude and unrelenting, were not completely inaccurate:

> In all fairness, there was a kernel of truth in what she [Julia Frankau] said. Maida Vale Jewry was *nouveau riche* in the literal sense of the term. Most middle-class Jews at this time were not

---

[34] Montagu, *Thoughts on Judaism*, 1.

[35] Alderman, *Modern British Jewry*, 209.

[36] David Feldman, *Englishmen and Jews: Social Relations and Political Culture, 1840-1914* (New Haven: Yale University Press, 1994), 278, 310.

well-educated or inclined to take an interest in art, literature, or science. Nor was Frankau alone in attributing to English Jewry an excessive devotion to card-playing. Among others, the Rev. Simeon Singer of the Bayswater Synagogue, who could hardly be described as a self-hating Jew, thought the community was "far too much addicted to card-playing as the one unfailing resource to kill the demon of ennui [boredom]."[37]

The writing of both Jews and non-Jews in the late nineteenth-century was critical of Anglo-Jewish decadence and ruthless materialism.[38] As we will see in the following chapter, Lily Montagu's novel, *Naomi's Exodus*, is no different. Embarrassed, the heroine, Naomi Saul, confides to her Christian friend: "I thought you would be shocked at my people." We are informed of her friends:

> For the first time Naomi was *ashamed* of her companions. She had not before noticed that the men's dress was showy, that the girls' hats were objectionable, that they had all been talking much too loudly and attracting a great deal of vulgar attention. … That young lady was enjoying herself immensely. She was dressed in a tailor-made costume, with gold buttons. She wore white shoes and stockings, and a large hat with feathers deco-

---

[37] Todd Endelman, "The Frankaus of London: A Study of Radical Assimilation, 1837-1967," *Jewish History* 8, no. 1-2 (1994): 130-31. See Julia Frankau [pseud. Frank Danby], *Dr. Phillips; A Maida Vale Idyll* (London: Vizitelly, 1887). Having severed all ties with Judaism, Frankau's novels demonstrate particular distaste for her former coreligionists. *Dr. Phillips; A Maida Vale Idyll* castigates middle-class Jewish materialism. Indeed, even the women in her Jewish novel are frivolous. By employing the themes of social Darwinism, *Dr. Phillips* analyzes the assimilated Maida Vale community as physically repulsive and morally degenerate, and there is nothing positive to be said of Anglo-Jewry. The anti-hero, the corrupt Dr. Phillips, confronted with financial ruin, murders his wife to obtain her will, and the novel closes by revealing his depraved medical aim "to unsex women and maim men" (341).

[38] Nadia Valman, *The Jewess in Nineteenth-Century British Culture* (Cambridge: Cambridge University Press, 2007), 178.

rated her hair, which was loosely dressed about her ears. She did not like Jacob Mann. Moreover, she was keeping company with one of the other fellows, and did not need his attentions. But when she saw that Jacob had had a row with Naomi, she commenced to talk vigorously with the disconsolate youth. Mary always maintained that she gave jealous people "something to be jealous for."[39]

Naomi's ostentatious, worldly companions contrast her spirituality, sense of mission, and resolve to be of service. On a visit to the palace:

> The party went through the palace as quickly as they could, for pictures bored them. Then they sat in a tea-garden and had ices, and Naomi refused to be treated. ...
> Throughout the drive home Naomi was dumb. When the others sang she looked cross, and in spite of all their efforts to rouse her, she would not speak, not even to give way to the temper which was surging in her heart and almost choked her. She walked home with Jacob in silence.
> At her aunt's door he said in a hard, angry voice which the girl remembered long after,-
> "You've made a fool of me, young lady. You'd better look out. I'll come to-morrow night."[40]

Montagu concluded: "Pleasure calls, and all other considerations are thrown aside in favor of a moment's exciting experience," and "God's laws are defied."[41] The secularization of the community was of specific concern to her, more so given that a number of London synagogues were virtually empty at the *fin-de-siècle*. Certainly, the forces of emancipation, religious indifference, and skep-

---

[39] Montagu, *Naomi's Exodus*, 19.
[40] Montagu, *Naomi's Exodus*, 20-21.
[41] Lily Montagu, "Man's Ambition and God's Law," sermon, January 18, 1919, London Metropolitan Archives, ACC/3529/3/7, 3.

ticism had taken their toll on Anglo-Jewry.[42] Many secularized and assimilated Jews identified themselves primarily as English; viewing Judaism merely as a social aspect that delineated them from the non-Jewish world. The majority of native-born Jews opposed Zionism, and the Anglo-Jewish elite no longer saw themselves as part of an exclusive community. Social contact with gentiles was frequent and some Jews felt no association with the Jewish people at all. Indeed, while Judaism was a source of religious identity, often one imposed by their detractors, the strongest ties for most Jews were not with their coreligionists, but with British citizens. Even the United Synagogue created an aura that was Anglican in appearance. Ministers were clean shaven and wore canonicals rather than the traditional shawl, and they were not expected to possess a rabbinical diploma. Perhaps unsurprisingly, the immigrant rabbis viewed them with contempt. For young Jews, elementary, secondary, and university education introduced them to scientific theories, biblical criticism, and the study of comparative religions, which in turn led them to ask questions regarding the validity of traditional Judaism. By the close of the Victorian period (overall an age of doubt as well as revival), Jewish religious practice was in decline and indifference to Jewish learning was widespread. To many, therefore, the establishment of the Jewish Religious Union was inconsequential, as was the news that its founder, Lily Montagu, was a woman.[43]

Already, Reform congregations in Germany had taken up the mantle of the fledgling Liberal Jewish movement. Thus, in November 1901, having enlisted the support of Claude Montefiore, Lily Montagu issued letters to one-hundred potential sympathizers asking for assistance in the promotion of a progressive religious organization. The letter included a number of questions Montagu

---

[42] Secularization was a problem that afflicted all religious communities in England; a detailed discussion of which is beyond the remit of this book. See Owen Chadwick, *The Secularization of the European Mind in the Nineteenth Century* (Cambridge: Cambridge University Press, 1975); *The Role of Religion in Modern Jewish History*, ed. Jacob Katz (Cambridge: Association for Jewish Studies, 1975).

[43] Umansky, *Lily Montagu*, 13-19, 21-22, 24, 26.

believed a Liberal Jewish organization in England would have to address, even confront:

> I. What are the vital principles of the old Judaism that must be preserved in the new?
> II. If these "vital principles" do not include belief in the miraculous Divine Revelation heretofore accepted, what is the Authority on which we are to rely in judging of right and wrong?
> III. What forms and ceremonies should be retained on account of their historical or ethical or sanitary value? (Special reference to the seventh day Sabbath and to festivals commemorating alleged miraculous events.)
> IV. What is to be the special function of the Jew under the new Judaism?[44]

In February 1902, they established supplementary religious services (to the United Synagogue), announced the holding of lectures, and the issue of publications to promote Liberal Judaism. Although Montefiore, despite his reluctance, was elected President, Montagu brought together its governing committee. In fact, according to Montagu, as a scholar, he "wasn't inclined to lead movements as a partisan, even in the cause of religion."[45] She admitted, rather modestly, "I am not going to talk to you as a scholar because I am unlearned."[46] Her own writing, as we will see, was deliberately simplistic given that the target audience was often the uneducated, the young, and the socially disadvantaged, including the destitute girls of her West Central Club. The aims of the newly formed Jewish Religious Union were stated in a circular, and included the follow-

---

[44] Lily Montagu, "Private Letter" (March 24, 1899), in Lily Montagu, *Lily Montagu: Sermons, Addresses, Letters, and Papers*, ed. Ellen Umansky (New York: Edwin Mellen Press, 1985), 289.

[45] Montagu, *The Faith of a Jewish Woman*, 28.

[46] Lily Montagu, *In Memory of Lily H. Montagu: Some Extracts from Her Letters and Addresses*, ed. Eric Conrad (Amsterdam: Polak and Van Gennep, 1967), 18.

ing aim:[47] "To provide the means for deepening the religious spirit among those members of the Jewish community who are not in sympathy with the present Synagogue Service, or who are unable to attend them."[48] The movement, thus far, did not have a synagogue of its own and was not intended to be schismatic, although Montagu would later write:

> Ever since we started the Jewish Religious Union, I have felt that if we could only get people to listen to our message, the possibilities of founding congregations were endless. We needed itinerary preachers and organizers, men and money, for in every part of the country, besides those who were devoted to the Orthodox presentment, there were many who chafed at the old teaching and found the observances meaningless.[49]

The first meeting of the JRU took place at the home of Henrietta Franklin, while the first service was held in the Wharncliffe Rooms of the Hotel Grand Central.[50] The service was conducted in English, hymns were universal, the prayer book did not include the return to Israel or the rebuilding of the Temple, and there were few Hebrew prayers. The God of Abraham, Isaac, and Jacob was replaced with the universal divine presence, and there was no reading from the Scroll.

At the annual meeting of the West London Reform Synagogue in 1903, the seat holders decided that the Synagogue could be placed at the disposal of the JRU, if they adhered to certain stipulations. Indeed, the proposal stated that the sexes would have be separated, that English prayers would have to be approved, that the Sabbath afternoon service would have to be included, and that the Hebrew portion of the service would have to include the

---

[47] Stephen Sharot, "Reform and Liberal Judaism in London: 1840-1940," *Jewish Social Studies* 41, no. 3/4 (Summer/Fall 1979): 49.

[48] "Jewish Religious Union Circular," *Jewish Chronicle*, June 6, 1902, 11.

[49] Montagu, *The Faith of a Jewish Woman*, 44.

[50] Umansky, *Lily Montagu*, 172.

Kadddish and the *Shema*. The JRU overwhelmingly rejected the offer, with specific objection to the segregation. However, perhaps unsurprisingly, the JRU found the early years of its inception a struggle. By 1903 the Liberal movement had barely 300 members. Both Lily Montagu and Claude Montefiore were perplexed, as she stated (partly in retrospect):

> Although our congregation has made fairly good headway in the West Central district, it has not attracted a multitude of club members. They have, as I have said before, no interest whatever in services of any kind. If attendance involves the slightest effort, the vast majority refuse to make it. The reasons for this complete indifference are numerous. The most important is that the parents are utterly uninterested. In the Polish and Russian villages from which most of these parents came, it was not the custom for girls to attend services at all.[51]

Another branch of the JRU was founded in the East End, largely at Montagu's instigation, although it was only able to attract 200 members, the majority of which were women, with even less regularly attending. Part of the problem was that the JRU services were irregular and held in different halls.

Finally, in 1909 a Liberal Synagogue was established in Hill Street, Marylebone. The movement now had a fixed address and could employ its first minister, Israel Mattuck, an American Reform rabbi, who became spiritual leader of the Synagogue in 1912. By now, Liberal Judaism had developed into a totally independent organization. Indeed, the non-Liberal members of the leadership, cautious that the movement not become schismatic, had resigned. The main service, held on a Saturday, did not call people up to read the Law, and only minor aspects of the traditional service were retained. By 1915, all 496 seats had been let, and two other branches were formed. Nonetheless, the numbers involved were relatively low. Stephen Sharot concludes that prior to the First-World-War,

---

[51] Montagu, *My Club and I*, 46.

Liberal Judaism achieved only partial success.[52] Likewise, Geoffrey
Alderman considers the JRU a failure, which explains why the leadership changed its name in 1909 to the Jewish Religious Union for
the Advancement of Liberal Judaism. Although Lily Montagu had
intended Liberal Judaism to be a uniting communal force, she had
in fact created a schismatic movement that separated the Orthodox
from the non-Orthodox,[53] although this was hardly surprising con-
sidering Montagu's inflammatory tone towards the other Jewish
denominations. Again, her "Spiritual Possibilities":

> The "East End Jew," whose religion is vigorous in spite of its
> deformities, has no confidence in the shadowy faith of the
> "West End Jew," and refuses to be taught by "West End" me-
> thods. Examining this distrust, I find that it arises from the
> recognition of the dissimilarity in the two religions. The "East
> End Jew" is determined to follow the worship of his fathers,
> and spurns the flaccid religion of his "West End" brothers. To
> the pious "East End Jew" religion is obedience glorified into a
> cult; for him, God exists as a just Law-giver, ready to forgive
> and help those who obey the Law, delivered by him to his
> people through his servant Moses, and having misfortune and
> failure in reserve for the rebellious and indifferent. He is con-
> tinually conscious of the "God without," whom he seeks to
> approach at prescribed times and seasons. Every act of obedi-
> ence tends to increase the sum of his righteousness; no evil can
> touch him while pursuing the divine mandate. He does not
> consciously strive to realize the "God within," and to develop
> it by communion with the divine Ideal of Truth and Love ex-
> isting without, for the idea of an immanent divine presence
> does not seem to affect his creed. When he repeats the prayers
> ordered by his fathers, he is less stirred by the effort of the
> soul to hold communion with the Infinite than by a sense of
> righteousness resulting from unquestioning obedience. The

[52] Sharot, "Reform and Liberal," 221. See Lawrence Rigal, *A Brief History of the West Central Liberal Synagogue* (London: West Central Synagogue, 1978).
[53] Alderman, *Modern British Jewry*, 204, 208.

glow which obedience produces, suffuses his daily life, and encourages him to persevere in his rigid observances, and to face
all earthly difficulties with courage and hope. Can we wonder
that the "East End Jew" regards with half-scornful fear the
man who, while still calling himself "Jew," ventures to neglect
the ordinances prescribed of old, and makes no apparent sacrifice in the cause of his faith? For him, prosperity seems to au-
thorize self-indulgence and laxity of conduct.[54]

Montagu later stated: "Cruel things were said about us by the pseu-
do-Orthodox, whose official conscience made them fear our religion lest it should overwhelm their own flimsy edifice."[55]

Despite initial difficulties, in 1918 Lily Montagu preached her
first official sermon, and in 1944 she became lay minister. The Liberal Synagogue, by this time, had obtained larger premises on St
John's Wood Road, London, and membership exceeded that of the
Reform Synagogue.[56] Montagu had been preaching sermons, preparing proselytes, helping at funerals and weddings, and leading
prayers for many years. She was aware that the traditional liturgy
bored the girls of her West Central Club, and believed it imperative
that the synagogue, and prayer, stimulate women. Accordingly,
through communion, Montagu encouraged her girls to experience
the immediacy of the divine presence in both the synagogue and in
the privacy of their own homes to alleviate the tedium of the traditional services.[57] She stated:

Those people, however, who had leisure to attend services
were unwilling to do so because they were sure of being bored.
Their knowledge of Hebrew was scanty, and they needed to
pray in the language in which they were accustomed to think.
Certainly, Hebrew had great beauty as well as historical interest, and it was a bond between different communities that they

---

[54] Montagu, "Spiritual Possibilities," 217-18.
[55] Montagu, *The Faith of a Jewish Woman*, 34.
[56] Alderman, *Modern British Jewry*, 208.
[57] Montagu, *My Club and I*, 45-47.

should have the same liturgy. But the religious bond could only be of real use if it expressed a living faith. There was no use in peoples meeting in various lands and going through identical services, in order to endure identical sense of boredom. Life was *essential*, and the bond of religion must be the bond of life.[58]

For Montagu, as we will see, it was integral to the revitalization of her faith that ritual be gender relevant. Her analysis of the Passover, for example, analogizes the "liberty" of the oppressed, and the escape from enslavement, with the emancipation of the Jewish woman. As she writes in *Thoughts on Judaism*:

An earnest woman who is devoting her whole life to the cause of industrial freedom, tells how her mother worked in the mines in the days before the passing of factory laws, and bore to the day of her death the mark of the overseer's whip on her shoulder. The pain of that blow has inspired a noble life of unselfishness and devotion to the cause of the oppressed. We Jews are the heirs of pain; across those two thousand years which separate us from the slaves of Egypt the sounds of lamentation echo in our ears and inspire us to feel sympathy for all who suffer the misery of persecution, or even the minor pain of loneliness.[59]

Lily Montagu's acceptance as a religious leader was a result of the high degree of acculturation in the Jewish community, as Ellen Umansky concludes:

In light of Anglo-Jewry's desire to appear British, it is not surprising that Lily Montagu eventually gained acceptance as a religious leader. None of the roles which she assumed exceeded those previously assumed by Christian women. Had the Anglo-

---

[58] Montagu, *The Faith of a Jewish Woman*, 29.
[59] Montagu, *Thoughts on Judaism*, 91, 93-94.

Jewish community been more traditional, (i.e., less secularized and acculturated), Lily Montagu's conducting children's services and, perhaps even more so, her establishment of the Jewish Religious Union, would have been met with great alarm.[60]

Montagu, by encouraging her girls to write their own prayers, and by allowing women to actively participate in the synagogue, ensured that Liberal Judaism was an alternative to the counterattractions of secular society. She died in 1963, though her legacy has not had the impact on Second and Third-Wave Jewish feminisms that we might have expected.

---

[60] Umansky, *Lily Montagu*, 39.

4 _NAOMI'S EXODUS_: NASCENT LIBERAL JUDAISM AND THE INFLUENCE OF CHRISTIAN EVANGELICALISM

In 1901 Lily Montagu published _Naomi's Exodus_. The novel outlines many of the religious and theological aspects of Claude Mon tefiore's Liberal Judaism, as summarized by him from the pulpit of the West London Reform Synagogue on February 1 1896. Montagu would consequently establish these theories as an organized _movement_ in England. Indeed, _Naomi's Exodus_ highlights the alienation of female spirituality in the Orthodox Anglo-Jewish community, calling for women's access not only to elementary education (literacy being vital to the reading of the Bible), but to the sacred texts and their authoritative interpretation, gender inclusive liturgies, ritual, and theology. Surprisingly however, Anglo-Jewish literary critics, historians of Liberal Judaism, and Jewish feminist scholars, have persistently neglected _Naomi's Exodus_, and as we have seen, even minimized Montagu's decisive role in the formation of Liberal Judaism in England. In fact, scholars have generally preferred to focus on Montefiore, thus marginalizing Montagu's proto-feminist contribution. Similar to earlier Anglo-Jewish novels, the heroine of _Naomi's Exodus_ is rather sweepingly portrayed as a victim of the Jewish community's retrogressive unwillingness to acknowledge the "Woman Question," its "Orientalism" (the unsavory treatment of women in the East by comparison to Anglo-Jewry's maltreatment of women, particularly with reference to the marriage market), its cultural philistinism, and its vacuous marital economy.[1] The thematic of the novel is underpinned by Christian Evangelicalism and reveals the extent to which Liberal Judaism in England assimilated the religious and congregational norms of the Protestant host culture.[2]

The influence of Christian Evangelicalism on Reform and Liberal Judaisms, and the importation of Protestant congregational norms, has been well documented, particularly regarding the appropriation of bibliocentrism, anti-rabbinism, anti-Talmudism, and anti-ritualism.[3] The impact of contemporaneous Evangelicalism on secular or First-Wave feminism, likewise, has also been analyzed.[4] The relationship between Christian Evangelicalism and the proto-feminist aspirations of the fledgling Liberal Jewish movement, however, is less explored. True, recent contributions have acknowledged the influence of the Evangelical critique of traditional Judaism as law-bound and encumbered by ritual in the Anglo-Jewish novels of the period.[5] Naomi Hetherington, however,

---

[1] See Todd Endelman, *Radical Assimilation in English Jewish History: 1656-1945.* (Bloomington: Indiana University Press, 1990); Nadia Valman, *The Jewess in Nineteenth-Century British Culture* (Cambridge: Cambridge University Press, 2007).

[2] Evangelicalism should not be equated with any single Christian denomination given its wide-ranging influence across churches and institutions (David Bebbington, *Evangelicalism in Modern Britain: A History from the 1730s to the 1980s* (London: Unwin House, 2002), 1). See Boyd Hilton, *The Age of Atonement: The Influence of Evangelicalism on Social and Economic Thought, 1785-1865* (Oxford: Clarendon Press, 1988); George Russell, *A Short History of the Evangelical Movement* (London: A. R. Mowbray and Son, 1915); Nadia Valman, "Hearts Full of Love for Israel: Converting the Jews in Victorian England," *Jewish Quarterly* 182 (Summer 2001): 15-20.

[3] See David Feldman, *Englishmen and Jews: Social Relations and Political Culture, 1840-1914* (New Haven: Yale University Press, 1994); Michael Hilton, *The Christian Effect on Jewish Life* (London: SCM Press Ltd, 1994); *Religion in Victorian Britain*, vol. 3, ed. Gerald Parsons (Manchester: Manchester University Press, 1988).

[4] See Olive Banks, *Faces of Feminism: A Study of Feminism as a Social Movement* (Oxford: Basil Blackwell, 1988).

[5] See Nadia Valman, "'Barbarous and Mediaeval': Jewish Marriage in Fin de Siècle English Fiction," in *The Image of the Jew in European Liberal*

rightly notes: "Evangelical missionary activity ... propagated Orientalist images of Jews and the Jewish faith in contrast to an elevated Christian womanhood. The ways in which Jewish women writers of the fin de siècle ... appropriated this imagery are seldom critically analyzed."[6] Moreover, *Naomi's Exodus* is particularly significant, not just because it appropriates Evangelical inspired Orientalist images of the Jewish community, but also because it is written by the founder of the Liberal Jewish movement in England and reflective of Liberal Jewish ideology and the movement's proto-feminist perspective at the *fin-de-siècle*. In this chapter's long overdue new reading of *Naomi's Exodus*, which is augmented by previously neglected archival material, we will see how the novel's gendered approach to Claude Montefiore's theology of Liberal Judaism delineates the proto-feminist and gender inclusionary principles that would become the hallmark of Montagu's activism, and by doing so incorporates Evangelical assumptions about women's moral, spiritual, and redemptive "nature," not only to her moral parable, *Naomi's Exodus*, but to the Liberal Jewish movement.

Even given the liberal climate of Victorian England, the conversionist societies, sanctioned by the Crown, were determined to proselytize the Jewish population *en masse*. According to David Bebbington, Evangelicalism is based on four themes: "*conversionism*, the belief that lives need to be changed; *activism*, the expression of the gospel in effort; *biblicism*, a particular regard for the Bible; and what might be called *crucicentrism*, a stress on the sacrifice of Christ on the cross. Together they form a quadrilateral of priorities that is the basis of Evangelicalism."[7] The London Society for the Promotion of Christianity among the Jews, established in 1809, specifically targeted women. It was hoped that spiritual Jewish women, or "Jewish Protestants" as they were labeled, would form the van-

---

Culture, 1789-1914, eds. Bryan Cheyette and Nadia Valman (London: Vallentine Mitchell, 2004), 111-29.

  [6] Naomi Hetherington, "New Woman: 'New Boots': Amy Levy as Child Journalist," *Cambridge Studies in Nineteenth Century Literature and Culture* 47 (2005): 259.

  [7] Bebbington, *Evangelicalism*, 2-3.

guard of Anglo-Jewry's conversion.[8] The Evangelical movement venerated the Hebrew Bible and conferred special status on Jews, in particular women, regarding them as agents of transformation. It was believed that their conversion would precipitate the Second Coming. Jesus' sacrificial and redemptive character thus made him a religious icon who Jewish women could supposedly "emulate." The Jews, representative of the fallen nature of humanity, were allegedly held in spiritual stagnation by the "bogus" authority of the rabbis and their Oral Law, just as Church authority was not deemed necessary by the Evangelicals. The conversionists, dominated by pre-millenarians, believed both in imminent Messianism and the literal reading of "Old" Testament prophecy. From 1829, the London Society began actively seeking converts in the capital.[9] Accordingly, as we have seen, the Liberal Jewish leadership, particularly Claude Montefiore, concerned that acculturation would lead to the social extinction of the Jewish community, concluded that the problem of assimilation, and its solution, must relate to the cultural force to which Anglo-Jewry seemed to be integrating itself.[10]

That *Naomi's Exodus* has been neglected by Anglo-Jewish and feminist literary criticism is a regrettable fact. Ellen Umansky's biography and document collection devotes only a few pages to the novel, dismissing it as weak on plot and characterization.[11] Indeed, most biographies of Montagu's career fail to mention the novel at all.[12] The absence of her fiction from historical studies of religion is

---

[8] Michael Galchinsky, "Engendering Liberal Jews: Jewish Women in Victorian England," in *Jewish Women in Historical Perspective*, 2nd ed., ed. Judith Baskin (Detroit: Wayne State University Press, 1998), 211.

[9] Feldman, *Englishmen and Jews*, 54.

[10] Bowler, Maurice. "C. G. Montefiore and His Quest," *Judaism* 30, no. 4 (Fall 1981): 454-56, 458.

[11] Ellen Umansky, *Lily Montagu and the Advancement of Liberal Judaism: from Vision to Vocation*, Studies in Women and Religion, vol. 12 (New York: Edwin Mellen Press, 1983), 129.

[12] The following studies of Montagu's role in Liberal Judaism have neglected to mention *Naomi's Exodus* at all: Ellen Umansky, "Lily H. Montagu: Religious Leader, Organizer and Prophet," *Conservative Judaism* 34, no. 6 (July/August 1981): 17-27; Ellen Umansky, "The Origins of Liberal

all the more surprising given that literary critics have recently focused on forgotten Anglo-Jewish writers such as Grace Aguilar, Judith Montefiore, Benjamin Farjeon, Israel Zangwill, and Amy Levy.[13] Jewish literary criticism, in recent years, has repeatedly examined modernity, immigration, acculturation, Reform Judaism, socialism, emancipation, and feminism.[14] These topics are central to *Naomi's Exodus*, and given the importance of the novel to Jewish women for public representation,[15] and that the book received good reviews leading to a second edition, it is bewildering that *Naomi's Exodus* has been overlooked by Anglo-Jewish feminist and literary studies.

Naomi's Exodus portrays the spiritual coming-of-age of an assimilated Jewish girl growing up in a "ghetto" community in Lon-

---

Judaism in England: The Contribution of Lily H. Montagu," *Hebrew Union College Annual* 55 (1984): 309-12; Eric Conrad, *Lily H. Montagu: Prophet of a Living Judaism* (New York: National Federation of Temple Sisterhoods, 1953); Linda Gordon Kuzmack, *Woman's Cause: The Jewish Woman's Movement in England and the United States, 1881-1933* (Columbus: Ohio State University Press, 1990); Margaret Yacobi, "Lily Montagu – A Pioneer in Religious Leadership: A Personal Appreciation," in *Hear Our Voice: Women in the British Rabbinate*, ed. Sybil Sheridan (Columbia: University of South Carolina Press, 1998), 9-15; Chaim Bermant, *The Cousinhood: The Anglo-Jewish Gentry* (London: Eyre & Spottiswoode, 1971); Geoffrey Alderman, "Montagu, Lilian Helen," in *Oxford Dictionary of National Biography. Vol. 38: Meyrick – Morande*, eds. H. Matthew and Brian Harrison (Oxford: Oxford University Press, 2004), 753-54.

[13] See Bryan Cheyette, "From Apology to Revolt: Benjamin Farjeon, Amy Levy and the Post-Emancipation Anglo-Jewish Novel, 1880-1990," *Transactions of the Jewish Historical Society of England* 24 (1982-86): 253-65.

[14] Michael Galchinsky, "The New Anglo-Jewish Literary Criticism," *Prooftexts: A Journal of Jewish Literary History* 15, no. 3 (September 1995): 272-82.

[15] For an overview of nineteenth-century Anglo-Jewish writing along with bibliographies see Valman, *The Jewess*; Michael Galchinsky, *The Origin of the Modern Jewish Woman Writer: Romance and Reform in Victorian England* (Detroit: Wayne State University Press, 1996); Linda Zatlin, *The Nineteenth-Century Anglo-Jewish Novel* (Boston: Twayne Publishers, 1981); Cecil Roth, *The Evolution of Anglo-Jewish Literature* (London: Edward Goldston, 1937); Edward Calisch, *The Jew in English Literature, as Author and Subject* (New York: Kennikat Press, Inc., 1969).

don.[16] Naomi Saul's figuring as moral and spiritual redeemer is undoubtedly bound up with the Evangelical cult of true womanhood or the doctrine of female superiority. In *fin-de-siècle* novels, the self-sacrifice and suffering of the Jewess came to represent atonement for the excessive desires of the Jewish man of commerce. For these novelists, Jewish distinctiveness was manifested in their primitive attitude toward women.[17] Accordingly, Naomi's plight is potentially regenerative. Stifled by the Orthodox legalism of her aunt's home, she leaves intending to discover her own spiritual path to Judaism. Naomi is determined to retain her Jewishness and learns to reject the blind obedience she associates with Orthodoxy. Through Mrs. Finch, a Christian acquaintance, she learns that Judaism can be a spiritual religion of the heart through which personal and immediate experience of the divine presence is acceptable, and even encouraged, as opposed to the radical separation of the individual and the divine in the tradition.[18] Naomi also learns that ritual can be imbued with personal and spiritual meaning, with Mrs. Finch perhaps serving in the novel as the personification of contemporary Evangelicalism. Naomi's relationship with Mrs. Finch thus sets up a contrast between the charity and warmth of Christianity (the spirit), and the cold nature of her aunt's legalistic home (the letter of the law). Naomi develops numerous associations with Christian women of all social backgrounds and enjoys a brief romance with a Liberal Jewish social worker (who is probably intended to be Claude Montefiore). In short, the book is a proto-feminist manifesto for Liberal Judaism at the *fin de siècle*, though surprisingly,

---

[16] Montagu uses the term ghetto (*Naomi's Exodus* (London: T. Fisher Unwin, 1901), 189), but the area is probably working or lower-middle-class given the book's descriptions. Although "ghetto" is an Italian word that literally means "Jewish quarter" or "street," the term has other connotations that are not relevant to the English setting. The London West End "ghetto" Montagu refers to was not walled, segregated, or legally forced upon the community.

[17] Valman, *The Jewess*, 171, 173. See, for example, Amy Levy, *Reuben Sachs: A Sketch* (London: Macmillan, 1888).

[18] See Setel, T. Drorah. "Roundtable Discussion: Feminist Reflections on Separation and Unity in Jewish Theology," *Journal of Feminist Studies in Religion* 2 (1986): 113-18.

Naomi, rather than joining a Reform congregation, returns home. Her spiritual awakening complete, she approaches Orthodox ritual with renewed vigor and inner-piety, and is able to confidently experience the immediacy of the divine. The fact that Naomi returns to the Orthodox community demonstrates that, at least in 1901, Montagu did not intend Liberal Judaism to become a schismatic movement independent of the United Synagogue.

Lily Montagu, conscious of the requirement for biblical authority against the frequent charges of rabbinism leveled by the Evangelicals at the Jewish denominations, uses Naomi of the book of Ruth as the inspiration for her heroine.[19] The biblical account depicts the two women's struggle for survival in a patriarchal setting during the time of the Judges. The leader, Naomi, shapes the narrative. The story begins with a Judean family travelling to Moab and the narrator subordinates Naomi to Emilech. She is "his wife" and their children are "his sons" (1:1-2). Emilech's death, however, results in transformation. He becomes "the husband of Naomi" and she is "left with her two sons" (1:3). Consequently, Naomi's sons marry Moabite women but bear no progeny. Thus, she is reduced to the position of *almanah* (widow), and her character forfeits subjective agency. Naomi, nonetheless, discovers that God has restored food to Judah and journeys home. She implores her daughters-in-law to return to the "mother house," espousing the "faithfulness" and "loyalty" of God upon them (1:8-9). Naomi's invoking of divine *hesed* (loving kindness) comes from Orpah and Ruth's devotion to the family, and Ruth's willingness, despite her Moabite ancestry, to accept the God of Israel as her own. She swears a solemn oath to Naomi, her people, God, and to divine fate. Naomi presents these non-Jews as examples of God's universal intentions and hopes her *hesed* will be rewarded with divine *hesed*. Displaced and homeless, Naomi offers her daughter's-in-law all she has, kisses them, and weeps with them. Naomi also warns them that no

---

[19] Attempts to accurately date the book of Ruth have been unsuccessful. It was probably written shortly after the Babylonian exile when the Jewish community was becoming more exclusive. The rabbis generally attribute authorship to Samuel, although many scholars do not accept this tradition.

male protection exists and of her inability to bear offspring. It is her hope that God will reward her daughters-in-law with *menuha*: haven.[20] Given her plight, however, Naomi concludes that God has turned against her. The deity she hopes will show *hesed* to her daughters-in-law instead invokes hostility. Naomi therefore instructs Ruth to uncover the feet of the sleeping Boaz and to remind him when he awakes that he has the right to redeem. Hence, Ruth marries Boaz and bears Naomi a grandchild (Obed, David's grandfather). Hence, Boaz's prayer is related to Naomi's as his kindness is braided into the chain of human *hesed* through which divine *hesed* is realized. Naomi gradually understands that God: "has not failed in *hesed* toward the living or toward the dead" (2:20), leading to Ruth's, as well as her own, redemption. The final great act of *hesed* is therefore Ruth's. Ignoring patriarchal genealogies and the laws of ownership, she gives her son to Naomi as a foster-child.[21]

It is easy to understand why Lily Montagu accommodated the biblical narrative to *Naomi's Exodus*. The book of Ruth, its liberality and universality, is perhaps only comparable in the Tanakh to Jonah. Ruth implies that good, loving people always reciprocate.[22] For Montagu, human kindness and charity are the essence, and prerequisite, of "true" religion,[23] much as active philanthropy and humanitarianism were central to Victorian Evangelicalism. A feminist analysis suggests that although Naomi experiences God as an enemy, she gradually gains his blessing through adversity.[24] In

---

[20] Rachel Adler, *Engendering Judaism: An Inclusive Theology and Ethics* (1998; rpt. Boston: Beacon Press, 2005), 149-51.

[21] Adler, *Engendering Judaism*, 153, 155. See Danna Nolan Fewell and David Gunn, "'A Son is Born to Naomi': Literary Allusions and Interpretation in the Book of Ruth," *Journal for the Study of the Old Testament* 40 (1988): 99-108; Ilona Rashkow, *Upon the Dark Places: Anti-Semitism and Sexism in English Renaissance Biblical Translation*, Bible and Literature Series, 28 (Sheffield: Sheffield Academic Press, 1990).

[22] Adler, *Engendering Judaism*, 151.

[23] Montagu, *Naomi's Exodus*, 61.

[24] Phyllis Trible, "Naomi," in *Women in Scripture: A Dictionary of Named and Unnamed Women in the Hebrew Bible, the Apocry-*

Naomi's Exodus also, the heroine leaves home embittered and alienated by the tradition, yet gradually experiences divine immanence. In the book of Ruth, Naomi is subordinated to Emilech, though gains autonomy, while Montagu's heroine, similarly, gradually attains independence from her oppressive suitor, Jacob Mann, and her authoritarian aunt. The biblical account also deals with assimilation. The family, like contemporaneous Anglo-Jewry, lives under the perpetual threat of absorption into the host culture, the people of Moab.

Naomi's Exodus is identifiable by several Evangelical themes, including its bibliocentrism, its critique of halakhah and the letter of the law at the expense of inner-piety, its portrayal of the alienation of female spirituality, Naomi's Saul's spiritual struggle and subsequent regeneration, her active philanthropy, and her direct communion with the divine presence. *Naomi's Exodus* is also both anti-doctrinal and anti-liturgical. It is no surprise that Jewish religious reformers were often labeled the conversionists "parrots."[25] The novel also warns of the detrimental effect on the race caused by denying women their "natural" political freedoms.

Lily Montagu was aware that many young women were bored and alienated by traditional ritual and services. At her West Central Jewish Girls' Club she began to hold Shabbat services on Saturday afternoons to encourage those who worked during the week to attend. These were short, in English, and vitalized with singing. Montagu attempted to deliver sermons that she hoped had "meaning for modern ... Jewesses in the actual circumstances of their lives."[26] Her reinterpretation of Shabbat for the Club shifts the focus from the ceremony to the congregant and their subjective reality, or to the individual rather than the liturgy, while alternatively, traditional Judaism is a communal or family religion and does not place emphasis on the reclamation of the individual. Montagu believed, however, that the major festivals of the tradition, and their

---

phal/Deuterocanonical Books and the New Testament, eds. Carol Meyers et al. (Cambridge: Eerdmans, 2000), 130-31.

[25] Feldman, *Englishmen and Jews*, 57.

[26] Lily Montagu, *My Club and I: The Story of the West Central Jewish Club* (London: Herbert Joseph Limited, 1941), 46.

observances, were worth retaining, as the prophetic tradition demonstrates the vitality of Judaism. She was more concerned at the
spiritual lethargy, disunity, and materialism of the community in
general.[27] Moreover, she had one eye on Evangelical criticisms of
the tradition, and the consequences of ignoring this criticism. Indeed, *Naomi's Exodus*, describing the inflexible Mrs. Saul, states:
"[she] fully appreciated the righteousness of her rigidly Orthodox
life and relished the comfortable certainty that it had brought her
prosperity."[28] "Ritualism" at the expense of inner-spirituality was a
fiercely debated subject for the Evangelicals, who were bitterly recovering from the Catholic emancipation. David Bebbington notes:

> Acts like the elevation of the bread and wine for adoration
> seemed, in the full sense of the word, "idolatrous." A service at
> St Alban's, Holborn, according to Shaftsbury, was outwardly
> "the worship of Jupiter or Juno." Here was an outstanding tar-
> get for a crusade. Ritual prosecutions in the ecclesiastical
> courts began in 1853 with an unsuccessful attempt to remove a
> high altar, its cross, candlesticks, colored cloths and credence
> table from St Paul's, Knightsbridge. Protests against vestments
> at St George's-in-the-East in 1859-60 degenerated into brawls.
> From 1865 there was an Evangelical organization, the Church
> Association, designed to conduct legal cases against ritualists,
> and from 1874, under the Public Worship Regulation Act,
> there was a clear mode of procedure.[29]

Although Montagu recognized the value of ritual, she ensured the
novel would be acceptable to her Christian readers, aware that the
Evangelicals did not consider Judaism a vital religion, but faith
without engagement.[30] However, she maintained in her essays sole-
ly written for Jewish audiences:

---

[27] Lily Montagu, "Spiritual Possibilities of Judaism To-day," *Jewish Quarterly Review* 11 (1899): 216-18, 231.

[28] Montagu, *Naomi's Exodus*, x.

[29] Bebbington, *Evangelicalism*, 146-47.

[30] Feldman, *Englishmen and Jews*, 56.

Only the elect among us can worship at the "Fount of Inspiration" without some assistance in the form of a ritualistic system, and that the perpetuation of Judaism therefore requires the maintenance of certain ceremonial observances. For the essence of a religion cannot be transmitted in all its simplicity to a child, whose mind cannot conceive an abstraction, and a certain discipline of observance is essential to character-training. We can only combat our tendency to self-indulgence and to spiritual sloth by having fasts and holidays reserved for communion with God.[31]

And in her later addresses, referring to Isaiah 29:13: "Surely our ancient Law Givers had inspired foresight into the rush of modern life when they instituted days for fasting and meditation."[32]

Lily Montagu frequently cited Isaiah as her favorite book of the Bible.[33] The prophet argues that, devoid of spirituality, the performance of commandments is meaningless.[34] Montagu concluded that although prayer must continue to be an integral part of Liberal Judaism, the habit of absconding from synagogue is a result of the boredom invoked by traditional services.[35] In "Spiritual Possibilities of Judaism To-Day," Montagu takes stock of Anglo-Jewry's spiritual dissatisfaction, with ceremonialism being the causal factor:

---

[31] Montagu, "Spiritual Possibilities," 225.

[32] Lily Montagu, "The Responsibility of Leisure," paper read, October 1912, London Metropolitan Archives, ACC/3529/3/17, 3.

[33] Lily Montagu, *The Faith of a Jewish Woman* (London: George Allen & Unwin, 1943), 41.

[34] The rabbis repeatedly iterated that ritual performance can only elicit meaning if accompanied by spiritual intention (*kavanah*), and awareness that it is God who has commanded the ritual. During traditional observance, God must remain central to the individual worshipper's thought process for spiritual validity.

[35] Montagu, *My Club and I*, 45.

It is not enough for us to give a frightened glance of recognition at our materialism and spiritual lethargy, and then seek to draw the veil in all speed, hoping impotently that grim facts will grow less grim if left alone. We have ultimately to confess that facts cannot be thus set aside by mere desire. Moreover, these facts prove on examination to be stimulating rather than terrifying, fraught with hope rather than negation. If I appear dogmatic in my efforts to prove my contention that Judaism has been allowed by the timid and the indifferent to lose much of its inspiring force, I can only plead in excuse the sincerity of my convictions.[36]

Only those ceremonies deemed to serve as aids to "holiness" were to be retained in Liberal Judaism:[37] "The festivals were consecrated as symbols illustrating ethical ideals which should make for the sanctification of life."[38] Montagu thus developed a subjective liturgy, regarded as the first Liberal Jewish prayer book, accommodating the personal circumstances of her girls, and reflective of the Evangelical concern that worship be "free" as opposed to liturgical (Evangelical congregations often permitted open prayer sessions). *Prayers for Jewish Working Girls* contains life-cycle prayers and blessings, focuses on spirituality, trust, and loyalty, and offers prayers for those unable to attend Shabbat.[39] Montagu hoped that the booklet would inspire young women to write their own prayers and insisted

---

[36] Montagu, "Spiritual Possibilities," 216-17.

[37] *Kedushah* (holiness), regarded in traditional Judaism as the transcendent unknowable divine presence in radical separation to the individual. *Kedushah* insists upon the sanctity of the family home and heterosexual marriage. Most Jewish feminists reject the concept of holiness as separatist, obsolete, and gynophobic (Melissa Raphael, "Standing at a Demythologized Sinai? Reading Jewish Feminist Theology Through the Critical Lens of Radical Orthodoxy," in *Interpreting the Postmodern: Responses to 'Radical Orthodoxy,'* eds. Rosemary Radford Ruether and Marion Grau (New York: T & T Clark, 2006), 199. See Setel, "Roundtable Discussion."

[38] Lily Montagu, "Address Given at the Girl's Club," November 26, 1911, London Metropolitan Archives, ACC/3529/3/7, 5.

[39] See Lily Montagu, *Prayers for Jewish Working Girls* (London: Wertheimer, Lea & Co., 1895).

that religion need not be a rigid set of laws, but should fill the ordinary daily lives of women.[40]

In *Naomi's Exodus* the heroine is dutiful, although the rigid legalism Naomi Saul associates with her aunt's observance is personally troubling. Her "soul," we are told, hungers "for understanding love."[41] The choice of festival for the opening scene demonstrates Lily Montagu's awareness of the rigid Evangelical code of Sabbath observance. The novel also reveals that although Shabbat is a ritual central to traditional Judaism and its hierarchical system, it may be reworked in a non-hierarchical manner that maintains its special quality.[42] Naomi, typical of the idealized spiritual Jewess of late nineteenth-century Jewish fiction,[43] takes her place at the Shabbat table:

> As Naomi returned to her seat on this Sabbath eve, Jacob commenced intoning the appointed psalms in a nasal sing-song, the women bursting every now and then into murmuring accompaniment. Naomi lolled back in her seat and stared around her. She did not understand the words that were being sung. She was hardly conscious that they had a sacred meaning, but she was as zealous and sincere as her aunt in wishing that every portion of the service should be exactly fulfilled.[44]

Judaism is a communal religion. Whether as part of the smaller family unit, or as a member of the congregation at large, Jews are part of a group. Many rituals assume a family structure, such as the Shabbat and the Passover meal, and Jews are expected to pray together, with most prayers written in the plural. Jacob Mann leads the ceremony, which for Naomi is devoid of sacred meaning. She is

---

[40] Montagu, *Naomi's Exodus*, 114.

[41] Montagu, *Naomi's Exodus*, 114.

[42] Judith Plaskow, *Standing Again at Sinai: Judaism from a Feminist Perspective* (1990; rpt. New York: HarperCollins Publishers, 1991), 236.

[43] See Elizabeth Jay, *The Religion of the Heart: Anglican Evangelicalism and the Nineteenth-Century Novel* (Oxford: Clarendon Press, 1975).

[44] Montagu, *Naomi's Exodus*, xiv.

unable to accommodate herself to the ritualism of the festival as it
fails to affect her spiritually. She longs for religion of the heart and
begins, as per the notion of "self-help" – "heaven helps those who
help themselves" – her spiritual struggle, taking personal responsibility for her actions.[45] Indeed, perhaps Christian Evangelicalism's
strongest critique of traditional Judaism was concerning its alleged
neglect of spirituality. Naomi's life is minutely regulated by her
aunt, and occasionally Jacob, both of whom Pharisaically observe
the letter of the law: "But now it happened frequently that some
flippant act or irreverent word would … spoil the performance of
some sacred observance, and render it hateful in its incongruity."[46]

Naomi Saul's subordination to Jacob Mann is a case in point
and relates to contemporaneous analyses of the marital economy,
and of marriage as a commercial transaction. Amy Levy's "Middle-
Class Jewish Women of To-Day" offers a bleak feminist analysis of
acculturated Anglo-Jewry, its "marriage market," and the "shame"
of spinsterhood. The article concludes that given their intellectual
and social limitations, Anglo-Jewish women must either settle for
mercenary marriage or seek fulfillment in gentile society.[47] Indeed,
Levy's examination of the marital economy was not unrepresenta-
tive. Mona Caird, in "Marriage" (1888), also analyzes respectable
marriage as a form of "woman-purchase."[48] During the 1860s and
1870s, most women regarded an equal marriage partnership as unusual and enterprising, yet by the 1880s and 1890s the concept of
equality had become an integral feminist and Reform concern in
England and Germany. Levy's article castigates the "Oriental" Jewish community for its failure to respond to the feminist advances of
society at large. As Nadia Valman concludes: "For Amy Levy, what
binds Jews together also binds Jewish women down: in its refusal
to countenance female economic and social autonomy, Anglo-

---

[45] Samuel Smiles, *Self Help* (Teddington: Echo Library, 2006), 1.

[46] Montagu, *Naomi's Exodus*, 6.

[47] Amy Levy, "Middle-Class Jewish Women of To-Day (By a Jewess)," *Jewish Chronicle*, September 17, 1886, 7.

[48] Mona Caird, "Marriage," in *The Morality of Marriage and Other Essays
on the Status and Destiny of Woman* (London: George Redway, 1897), 95, 99-
100. See Valman, "'Barbarous and Mediaeval.'"

Jewry continues to be 'a society constructed on … a primitive basis.'"[49] More recently, Rachel Adler has linked the notion of marriage as a commercial transaction to scripture. The verb "to marry" is *lakahat* – "to take." Hence, if a woman is young and living under her father's protection, the husband or his negotiators present a bride price, or *mohar*. According to Adler, it is unclear as to whether the bride must offer her consent, and Rebecca is the sole example of a woman in the Bible whose permission is sought. Deuteronomy describes marriage as a two-stage process through which the man designates a woman to be his own. After an interval of one year, the acquisition is completed when he takes her under his roof and consummates the marriage. Adler notes that these texts portray the marriage of a young virgin as a private commercial transaction, which is reflected in the relational terminology. *Ba'al*, the word for husband, also implies master, owner, possessor of property, and bearer of responsibility. Comparatively, no relational term exists for wife aside from *isha* - woman. Adler concludes that marital ownership transcends mere commercial interests, as adultery, similar to idolatry and murder, pollutes the land. Infidelity represents an act of war against the physical terrain and the social order. According to Adler, the marital relationship, more than any other relationship of possession, is a prime metaphor for Israel's Covenant with its God.[50]

In *Naomi's Exodus*, Lily Montagu reveals the shame of spinsterhood and the perils of organized marriage. The narrator of *Naomi's Exodus* laments: "Like most of her friends, she [Naomi] was deeply imbued with the belief that marriage was a necessity and spinsterhood a degradation. Therefore she had accepted the engagement merely as a necessary episode in the natural course of events; love as a romantic idea never occurred to them."[51] Naomi's prospective marriage to Jacob Mann is figured as a transaction, of which the bride is not consulted. It is irrelevant "Whether Naomi objected or not," as she is condemned to domesticity: "Jewish girls

---

[49] Valman, *The Jewess*, 175.
[50] Adler, *Engendering Judaism*, 170-72.
[51] Montagu, *Naomi's Exodus*, xiii.

always live at home."[52] Mrs. Saul, the self-appointed negotiator, is merely a "gossip":

> "They say in the market that Miriam Green is engaged to a young fellow, been here a fortnight; these girls take anybody. She's only sixteen. And Daisy Samuel's young man has found out she wears false teeth, and won't have her. And Reuben Aaronson has run away – he took some of his mother's money – he's a bad 'un. And the Ezekiels have gone to the East and taken a business near the London hospital."[53]

Montagu, perhaps unintentionally, reinforces the early rabbis association of women with light-mindedness and gossip, though in *Naomi's Exodus* idleness and immorality result from the absence of religious guidance. The derogatory, and sweeping, alignment of women with "gossip" and vacant pursuits recurs throughout *Naomi's Exodus*, although it is not biologically inherent; more a product of women's limited educational and social opportunities: "Come what may, she [Naomi] must not seek lodging among her own co-religionists, who would have no difficulty in discovering her identity, and would make existence intolerable both for her and her aunt by circulating gossip about them."[54]

Lily Montagu was particularly scornful of those unwilling to treat prayer with reverence or *kavanah* (spiritual intention), as her description of her father's leading of prayer testifies:

> He read every word from beginning to end, and many of his hearers behaved as if nothing was going on which was even remotely connected with religion. They joined in the singing without even the slightest reverence; they joked and laughed; and my father went on reading, and, at the end, with unquestioning faith asked God to accept the divine service. I remem-

---

52 Montagu, *Naomi's Exodus*, 17, 73.
53 Montagu, *Naomi's Exodus*, 11-12.
54 Montagu, *Naomi's Exodus*, 50.

ber rushing up to my eldest brother after one of these Seders and expostulating. "I feel ashamed," I said, "at the behavior of many of the people. How dare they think they are praying? If that is religion, I hate it and would rather take the religion of ____" (mentioning a rigid Christian of my acquaintance).[55]

The halakhic exemption of women from formal and public prayer enforces an indifferent or negative attitude, leading to alienation from the liturgy. As women rarely pray at home, prayer becomes an occasional feature of synagogue attendance, which is hardly an incentive to serious prayer.[56] Women's suppression, based on centuries of their association with raw physicality and chaotic sexuality in rabbinic writing,[57] along with the laws of containment, have contributed to women's sense of inferiority and men's "superiority."[58] These halakhot associate women with pollution and disorder justifying their regulation,[59] and also occasionally assume their depravity.[60]

Naomi, by playfully resisting a *"Shabbos"* kiss, accidently touches a candle, to her aunt's disgust. Mrs. Saul is more concerned with the strict observance of halakhah, which Liberal Judaism marginalizes and even rejects:

"Come Naomi," cried Jacob, "I want my Shabbos kiss"! The girl playfully resisted, and in the little tussle that followed accidently touched one of the candles. "Be careful, child"! shrieked Mrs Saul, "the Shabbos candle." In an instant the girl withdrew

---

[55] Montagu, *The Faith of a Jewish Woman*, 9.

[56] Blu Greenberg, *On Women and Judaism: A View from Tradition* (1981; rpt. Philadelphia: The Jewish Publication Society of America, 1983), 8-9.

[57] Tova Hartman, *Feminism Encounters Traditional Judaism; Resistance and Accommodation* (New England: UPNE, 2007), 49, 51.

[58] Leonard Swidler, *Women in Judaism: The Status of Women in Formative Judaism* (Metuchen: Scarecrow, 1976), 138.

[59] Judith Baskin, "The Separation of Women in Rabbinic Judaism," in *Women, Religion, and Social Change*, eds. Yvonne Haddad and Ellison Findly (Albany: State University of New York Press, 1985), 14.

[60] Plaskow, *Standing Again at Sinai*, 184-85.

her arm from the table … It was a serious offence to touch
any lighted candle on the Sabbath, and the Shabbos candle in
particular must be left to burn itself out undisturbed, if the
rest, which it symbolized, was to remain in the home.[61]

Indeed, there has been no greater battleground for the coexistence
of Orthodoxy and feminism than the issues of ritual observance
and the liturgy. The traditional liturgies of all faiths are ubiquitous
in their frequent reference to fathers and kings, and have long been
the target of feminist critics as the blatant portrayers of patriarchy.
Nevertheless, although the Reform and Liberal movements later
championed egalitarian worship by removing the *mechitzah* curtain,
and by marginalizing the masculine imagery of the liturgy, Orthodoxy has generally resisted the egalitarian impulse. Although some
of the tradition's overtly patriarchal features are subject to evolution within halakhic realms, such as through better seating ar-
rangements, women's prayer groups, and gendered access to the
Torah scrolls, Orthodoxy has a built in legal system to oppose reform.[62]

During the observance of Shabbat, Mrs. Saul prays for Naomi
to emulate the matriarchs: Sarah, Rebecca, Rachel, and Leah.[63] The
reference, however, reveals Lily Montagu's proto-feminist critique
of the tradition and its masculine defined texts (in the Talmud God
regularly appears as "father"). The matriarchs of Genesis are strong
women who figure prominently in the family narrative. As "independent" personalities they possess intuitive knowledge of God's
plans for their sons. Both Sarah and Rebecca, for example, seem to
understand God better than their husbands, and accordingly, he
defends Sarah when she casts out Hagar, and orders Abraham to
obey his wife (Genesis 21:12). However, despite their intuition,
wiliness, and resourcefulness, it is not the women who receive the
Covenant or pass on its lineage. The establishment of the patriar-

---

[61] Montagu, *Naomi's Exodus*, xvi.

[62] Hartman, *Feminism Encounters Traditional Judaism*, 62.

[63] Montagu, *Naomi's Exodus*, xv-xvi.

chal family and the patrilineal lineage takes precedence over the matriarchal stories.[64]

Naomi Saul regularly attends synagogue, and recites Hebrew prayers, through which we are to infer that the community, prayer, and *shul* (synagogue) are vitally important to her. She is, however, unable to explain the spiritual void that burdens her existence, and so leaves home, justifying herself through religious faith rather than reason, and with a sense of mission that she will work for the betterment of others, reflecting the Evangelical call to service and individual responsibility toward social care.

Compared to Christianity, there is less emphasis on personal spirituality within traditional Judaism. The Reformers, and the Liberal Jewish movement, in their determination that Judaism assimilate the religious norms of the host culture, concluded that the ethical aspects of the tradition had been obscured by the emphasis on ritual, and that despite the sacred role of the community, the internal struggle for each individual was a supremely religious act.[65] Reform Rabbi Morris Joseph concluded from the pulpit in 1893:

> Now and then Jews of an impressionable age are caught by the glitter of the Church, and think, with a sigh, how beautiful it would be if the rites of the Synagogue were not characterized by so severe a simplicity. They are attracted by the Christian service with its impressive ritual, its stirring and tuneful hymns, or they are captivated by the winning hero of the Gospels. Occasionally, regret manifests itself in action of a pronounced kind, and the homely religion is abjured for the more romantic one. It is well that young people of our race, who exclaim

---

[64] Plaskow, *Standing Again at Sinai*, 3-4. For an overview of women in rabbinic literature see Brayer Menachem, *The Jewish Woman in Rabbinic Literature: A Psychohistorical Perspective* (New Jersey: Ktav Publishing House, 1986); Jacob Neusner, *Rabbinic Judaism: Structure and System* (Atlanta: Scholars Press, 1999); Rachel Biale, *Women and Jewish Law: The Essential Texts, Their History & Their Relevance for Today* (New York: Schocken Books, 1995); Adler, *Engendering Judaism*.

[65] Jonathan Romain, *Reform Judaism and Modernity: A Reader* (London: SCM, 2004), 168-69.

"how superior"! when they think of the religion of their Christian companions, should be at pains to examine it in its entirety
before pronouncing judgment. A religion whose surface looks
so beautiful may prove to be far less satisfactory when examination is extended to the core.[66]

Liberal Judaism, like its Reform predecessor, came about as a response to the counter-attractions of Protestant society, and therefore sought to develop a religious culture at ease rather than polarized with the host nation, as Jonathan Romain concludes:

> In the more tolerant climate of the late nineteenth century, it
> seemed that Christian welcome could be as dangerous as
> Christian hostility. Some Jews found Christianity very attractive
> because its emphasis on spirituality and the aesthetic appeared
> to contrast favorably with the obsession over ritual minutiae
> which they felt had characterized much of Jewish life. There
> were also those who, more cynically, saw it as offering a gate-
> way into social acceptance and political opportunity. Reverend
> Joseph was sufficiently concerned to issue a public warning to
> those considering conversion.[67]

In *Naomi's Exodus* too, the heroine's spiritual struggle is reminiscent
of Evangelical conversion. Naomi Saul's regeneration results from
her personal and immediate experience of the divine presence, and
the power of God to intervene in human lives. Naomi seeks personal communion with the divine, as Lily Montagu herself had:
"Think of God's infinite patience with us who aspire to receive His
friendship."[68] This spiritual experience, resonant of Evangelical-

---

[66] Morris Joseph, "Morris Joseph on the Lure of Christianity
(1893)," in Romain, *Reform Judaism*, 65-66.

[67] Romain, *Reform Judaism*, 65.

[68] Lily Montagu, "August 5th," in "Addresses Given on the Club
Holiday at Littlehampton, August, 1916," London Metropolitan Archives,
ACC/3529/3/7, 5.

ism's romantic conception of religion, is highly emotional, intense, and even imaginative. Naomi prays:

> "Oh God, what shall I do? Oh, God, help me"!
> That was the first prayer Naomi Saul had ever made.
> Almost immediately her troubled spirit seemed somewhat soothed. The tension on her feelings was relieved as she gave herself up to the Power not herself of which she was becoming conscious. She lay for a whole hour, half waking, half-sleeping, in communion with her God.[69]

For Montagu, all Liberal Jews are witnesses before God and responsible to him, as the prophets were.[70] She argued: "The Bible heroes held communion with the divine.- [sic] but not in a passive way surely, but with hearts and brains aflame with the desire to serve, with the zeal of sacrifice – of self-devotion to a great cause."[71]

Naomi Saul, however, understandably finds the transformation difficult as she has not communed with her God before,[72] and in traditional Judaism there is radical separation between the divine and the individual:[73] "Naomi, whose God still dwelt in a splendid white aloofness, trembled at connecting Him with such sordidness, it seemed almost like blaspheming her Jewish conception, and she half dreaded some punishment might overtake her for profanity." She had previously associated religion with obedience, but begins

---

[69] Montagu, *Naomi's Exodus*, 26.

[70] Lily Montagu, "How Much Do I Count"? sermon, November 1943, London Metropolitan Archives, ACC/3529/3/21, 3; Lily Montagu, "May 8th, 1920," sermon, London Metropolitan Archives, ACC/3529/3/7, 1.

[71] Lily Montagu, "Who Is Self-Made"? sermon, February 2, 1924 (this date is crossed out and rewritten as what appears to be "Aug 1925"), London Metropolitan Archives, ACC/3529/3/7, 2.

[72] Montagu, *Naomi's Exodus*, 54.

[73] See Claude Montefiore, *Liberal Judaism and Convenience: and Do Liberal Jews Teach Christianity?* Papers for Jewish People, 25 (London: Jewish Religious Union, 1924).

to question the validity of the rituals she had observed without question:

> For the first time she became seriously thoughtful; but she would have been afraid to formulate her thoughts even if she had the power to do so. She began almost in spite of herself, to question the significance and importance of some of the observances which were rigidly followed in her home, and which had hitherto possessed a strong hold over her everyday life, adding considerably to its happiness.[74]

Naomi gradually realizes that her estrangement is common to assimilated women. Indeed, Angela Marks, another young Jewish woman in *Naomi's Exodus*, can attribute no spiritual meaning to the Hebrew prayers:

> At length dinner was nearly over, but before the dessert was passed the butler handed Mr Marks and Clement their hats, and Naomi heard the long Hebrew grace recited very much as Jacob used to recite it at home. She stared in bewildered amazement. Till that moment she had not realized that the resemblance between Clement's Judaism and that of Jacob could extend beyond their common source. Yet here was Clement's own father, sitting in these strange "English surroundings," waited upon by "English" servants, speaking the same familiar words with the same funny intonation to which she was accustomed in the Ghetto shop. She looked into Clement's serious face, and asked herself if he could possibly have recited these words. Angy, she could see, did not patronize them. She sat with a half smile on her face and an air of aloofness.[75]

Resonant of the Evangelical tradition, Naomi undergoes a type of conversion, or spiritual regeneration, by experiencing the presence

---

[74] Montagu, *Naomi's Exodus*, 5-6.
[75] Montagu, *Naomi's Exodus*, 141- 42.

of God. The search is her own, independent of doctrinal or legal coercion, in line with Montagu's own experience: "We cannot find God unless we seek him. We may cry with our lips but our hearts will remain untouched."[76] Accordingly, Naomi's devoted prayers abate her spiritual crisis:

> The prayer was spoken in utter exhaustion of spirit; the soul realized its weakness, and could no longer find rest within itself. It threw itself on the God without for help in its sore need. And the help was given. Naomi was much too tired to know how she reasoned, or whether she reasoned at all. It seemed as if she snatched from the inmost depths of her being the love, faith and hope which she had planted there for Clement, and with that cry to God threw them at His feet. And He accepted them.[77]

Her exodus or "awakening" complete,[78] Naomi Saul returns home with renewed inner-spirituality and reverence for Shabbat: "She had been born a Jewess, and no spiritual yearnings, no discontent, no remorse could rob her of this birthright":

> Naomi felt an inexplicable thrill of excitement at the thought that after the lapse of so many weeks, she was again to join in that ceremony of welcome, in that ceremony which she had once thought herself able to despise. ... The familiar Sabbath candles, too, appeared strangely familiar to-night. The glow which they threw on the spotless tablecloth, seemed possessed with a mysterious sanctity which Naomi had never noticed before.[79]

---

[76] Lily Montagu, "Loneliness," sermon, December 2, 1916, London Metropolitan Archives, ACC/3529/3/7, 15.

[77] Montagu, *Naomi's Exodus*, 162.

[78] Montagu, *Naomi's Exodus*, 24.

[79] Montagu, *Naomi's Exodus*, 41, 190-91.

During her time away from the family home, and the "ancient" faith, Naomi had been first taken in by Christian girls, discovering the essence of "true" religion: "Here was no question of terms, no question of respectability; here was simply love; here ... was religion."[80] She also boarded at the Working Girls' Club and Home, gradually becoming aware of the universal "God of love," finding "Him in the ritual customs of her people, in the small duties of her daily life, in her neighbors, in the world around her."[81] Indeed, *Naomi's Exodus* is notable for its universalistic underpinnings, and its apologetic gratitude to contemporaneous Protestantism. Naomi develops several mutually beneficial friendships with Christian women of all social backgrounds, and frequently takes their advice on religious issues.[82] As Miss Miles states: "There is a great Peace somewhere, and it flows into this world and fills the empty wells in many human hearts, and there are quite as many channels as there are hearts, and nobody can tell which it will use."[83] Moreover, Mrs. Finch's universal and charitable interpretation of religion imbues Naomi with her sense of mission and commitment to social service:

> "Don't you see that if we, who profess to commit our ways to God and to listen to His commandments every day and all day, if we were as good as we should be, our lives would offer the most perfect testimony to the purity of our creed. We should be turned into living sermons, such sermons as influence people."[84]

Philanthropy was central to Reform and Liberal Judaisms, as it was to Evangelical Christianity. Rabbi David Woolf Marks argued that

---

[80] Montagu, *Naomi's Exodus*, 41, 61.

[81] Montagu, *Naomi's Exodus*, 165, 196-97.

[82] Alternatively, in Montagu's short-story "A Child Plays," a Jewish woman helps awaken the spirit of universal love in a Christian woman; see *What Can A Mother Do? And Other Stories* (London: George Routledge & Sons, 1926).

[83] Montagu, *Naomi's Exodus*, 117.

[84] Montagu, *Naomi's Exodus*, 4-5.

charity should not be viewed as a meritorious act, but as a moral obligation. More so given that wealth is merely a temporary loan from God, with the moral duty to distribute it wisely to others rather than hoarding it for oneself.[85] Finally, we are informed of the "purity of her soul" and that Naomi had taken up active social service, becoming a nurse: "one of the cleverest nurses this hospital has ever trained."[86]

As we have seen, several Evangelical perspectives and criticisms of traditional Judaism are central to Lily Montagu's novel and the Liberal ideology and proto-feminism that underpins it. The Reformers believed that it was the rabbi and the Talmud who had transmitted the tradition, while in the liberal climate of toleration in post-emancipation England the same institutions were unnecessary and even objectionable.[87] The *Jewish Chronicle*, Anglo-Jewry's communal mouthpiece, assumed that Christian society imagined the tradition to be incapable of development, and beyond reason.[88] Accordingly, the Reformers and their Liberal Jewish counterparts, were determined to alter the negative perception of Judaism propagated in Christian Evangelical circles. As David Feldman notes: "The parallels between religious reform and the evangelical critique of Judaism are impressive."[89] Bibliocentrism, anti-rabbinism, and anti-ceremonialism are central to *Naomi's Exodus*, and indeed Liberal Jewish ideology. Again Feldman:

> The arguments generated by the reform tendency represented an attempt to revise Judaism in the face of criticism from inside and outside of Jewry which counterpoised degenerate "rabbinism" to a religion of the "spirit." Internal reform was a response to criticism from the non-Jewish world. The dominant answer to the charges of "rabbinism" was to fall back on the Bible and to cleanse the synagogue of those elements

---

[85] Romain, *Reform Judaism*, 59.

[86] Montagu, *Naomi's Exodus*, 198, 207.

[87] M. Angel, *The Law of Sinai and its Appointed Times* (London: 1858), 178.

[88] Feldman, *Englishmen and Jews*, 61.

[89] Feldman, *Englishmen and Jews*, 63.

which contradicted not only the norms of Victorian decorousness but which also offered the impression that Jews attended synagogue for any purpose other than prayer and spiritual elevation.[90]

"Rabbinism," the popular term for Judaic practice, for the Evangelicals, was conflated with "Popery," so an attack on Judaism was also an attack on Catholicism.[91] The Liberal Jewish estrangement from the tradition, and critique of rabbinism, helped to align the movement with Protestant culture, which remained far more hostile to Catholicism, a perversion of Christianity, than it did toward Judaism. The Evangelicals did not regard Judaism as a totally negative force, as it was after all the precursor of Christianity. Accordingly, the Jews were "princes in degradation." Their survival and decline confirmed Christian "truth,"[92] as we read in *Naomi's Exodus*:

> Naomi had behind her the racial pride of her ancestors. The persistent, dogged tenacity with which they [Jews] had clung to their religious inheritance, even deifying its casings in their passionate zeal; the fiery jealousy with which they had cherished their isolation among all the peoples of the earth; these seemed suddenly to make their influence felt on the girl. She had been born a Jewess, and no spiritual yearnings, no discontent, no remorse could rob her of this birthright. Even though she had no understanding of the ancient religion, in spite of all her recent self-questionings and misgivings, a passionate devotion of Judaism was indelibly stamped in her blood.[93]

These lines are not for the benefit of Jewish readers, but reinforce Evangelical views that Jewish survival can be attributed to their religion. Within this context, Liberal thinkers such as Montagu, aware of their multiple Christian and Jewish audiences, were able to

---

[90] Feldman, *Englishmen and Jews*, 65.
[91] Feldman, *Englishmen and Jews*, 55.
[92] Feldman, *Englishmen and Jews*, 56.
[93] Montagu, *Naomi's Exodus*, 40-41.

defend the tradition by glorifying, for example, prophetic Judaism and its democratizing, humanitarian, and populist values, and denigrating the rabbinic legal minutiae, the Talmud, and Orthodox ritual as "ancient" or in need of spiritual revitalization.

Naomi's Exodus, by outlining Liberal Judaism's theology of divine immanence, intension to spiritually vitalize ritual, and bibliocentrism (or reverence for the Hebrew Bible), demonstrates the movement's determination to assimilate aspects of Protestant Evangelicalism. Moreover, the proto-feminist aspirations of the story, depicted through Naomi Saul, are quintessentially Evangelical. In fact, as we have seen, David Bebbington and Olive Banks both conclude that Evangelicalism did more than the feminist movement to expand women's sphere:[94]

> By the second half of the nineteenth century this ideal of female superiority appears to have gained wide acceptance not only amongst moral reformers, both male and female, but amongst women writers catering for the emotional needs of middle-class women not necessarily either feminists or moral reformers. The novels of the period portrayed women not only as fundamentally different from men, but as basically superior creatures. Less forcefully, but along very similar lines, they present such feminine traits as sensitivity, consideration and the expression of emotions more desirable than the more aggressive masculine qualities.[95]

Indeed, Christian Evangelicalism impacted on the lives of Anglo-Jewish women. Montagu's novel is a classic example of First-Wave feminism. The heroine is regenerative, yet remains within the "natural," acceptable boundaries of the cult of true womanhood, or doctrine of female superiority. Naomi, as moral guardian, is committed to philanthropy, educational and cultural improvement, and spirituality. She returns home, dutifully, to the family she abandoned in her personal quest for spiritual fulfillment, and heeding

---

[94] Bebbington, *Evangelicalism*, 129; Banks, *Faces of Feminism*, 13-27.
[95] Banks, *Faces of Feminism*, 91.

the (Evangelical) call to social service, she is determined to work for others, so becomes a nurse. Certainly, Montagu's concerted drive to provide Jewish women with formal education and training, and the inclusionist policies of the Liberal Jewish movement, such as the abolishment of sex segregation in the synagogue and the *minyan*, the removal of the morning blessing in which men thank God for not having been created a woman ("Blessed are You, Lord our God, King of the universe, who has not created me a woman"), and the development of prayers particular to women, demonstrate not only Montagu's commitment to reversing the spiritual alienation of her female congregants and Club members, but also her intention to counter Evangelical criticisms of the tradition and the community.

5   LILY MONTAGU, *SHEKHINAH*, AND LIBERAL JEWISH THEOLOGY

Jewish feminist scholars have often located precedence for contemporary theorem in the Jewish movements of the past.[1] Anglo-Jewish women writers, however, particularly those such as Lily Montagu, have, until now, been overlooked as fore-bearers of the Second and Third-Waves of Jewish feminism, and the theological and spiritual theories that underpin these phases of activism. This chapter therefore demonstrates the theological continuities, however tentative or conceptual, between Montagu's theological discourse and the theologies of the *Shekhinah* appropriated by, particularly the Second, but also the Third-Wave of Jewish feminism. Additionally, this chapter provides a much needed corrective to the extant historiography that has declined to analyze Montagu's writing and activism in terms of theology at all. Indeed, her application of Liberal theology ensured the immediacy of the divine rather than the radical separation between the individual and the holy in the tradition,[2] and her appropriation of the *Shekhinah* (the word is grammatically feminine) might be regarded as an early attempt at theological gender "completion."[3]

---

[1] See Naomi Shepherd, *A Price Below Rubies: Jewish Women as Rebels and Radicals* (London: Weidenfeld and Nicolson, 1993).

[2] See T. Drorah Setel, "Roundtable Discussion: Feminist Reflections on Separation and Unity in Jewish Theology," *Journal of Feminist Studies in Religion* 2 (1986): 113-118.

[3] Melissa Raphael, *The Female Face of God in Auschwitz: A Jewish Feminist Theology of the Holocaust* (London: Routledge, 2003), 11. See Phyllis Trible, "Depatriarchalizing in Biblical Interpretation," *Journal of the American*

Lily Montagu did not apply the Hebrew term, *Shekhinah*, in her writing or sermons as she was aiming for accessibility.[4] In fact, she rarely uses Hebrew words, particularly as the girls of her West Central Club could not speak Hebrew. Indeed, the extensive use of Hebrew in the liturgy was a source of alienation for many women in the Orthodox community, and to a lesser extent in the Reform community. As we are told of Judith Quixano in *Reuben Sachs*, Amy Levy's late nineteenth-century portrayal of the Reform Synagogue and its services: "These prayers, read so diligently, in a language of which her knowledge was exceedingly imperfect";[5] and of Naomi Saul in Montagu's *Naomi's Exodus*: "She did not understand the [Hebrew] words that were being sung. She was hardly conscious that they had any sacred meaning."[6] In *Thoughts on Judaism*, Montagu summarizes each of the Jewish festivals, though Pesach is referred to as Passover, Shavuot as Pentecost, *Sukkot* as the festival of Tabernacles, Rosh Hashanah as "The New Year," and Yom Kippur as the Day of Atonement.[7] It was essential to the Liberal Jewish project that services were in the vernacular and that the movement was accessible to assimilated Jews, and specifically, women. Many acculturated Jewish men and women did not speak Hebrew and identified themselves as English citizens first, and if they had any interest in religion, members of the Jewish faith second. Montagu concluded: "Hebrew may be alright for some people, but it is no use for those who do not understand it."[8]

During the late nineteenth-century women were encouraged to write a form of practical theology by applying biblical truths to

---

Academy of Religion 41 (March 1973): 32-35; Phyllis Trible, *God and the Rhetoric of Sexuality* (Philadelphia: Fortress Press, 1978).

[4] *Shekhinah* is not mentioned in the Talmud, except by its root word, "to dwell."

[5] Amy Levy, *Reuben Sachs* (London: Macmillan and Co., 1888), 92.

[6] Lily Montagu, *Naomi's Exodus* (London: T. Fisher Unwin, 1901), xiv.

[7] See Lily Montagu, *Thoughts on Judaism* (London: R. Brimley Johnson, 1904).

[8] Lily Montagu, "The Spiritual Contribution of Women as Women," in Lily Montagu, *Lily Montagu: Sermons, Addresses, Letters, and Papers*, ed. Ellen Umansky (New York: Edwin Mellen Press, 1985), 173.

their own experience through fiction, devotional exercises, and tracts. Although Christian women writers adapted biblical scholarship in the period for a general audience (as did George Eliot), they did not, generally, produce theology themselves as this would have been deemed an inappropriate assumption of spiritual influence. John Ruskin, for example, argued in 1865 that "theology" is a "dangerous science" for women.[9] Accordingly, women's work on biography remained within approved boundaries. The focus on individual lives, and specifically women, eschewed any wider discussion of what was deemed important in theology, that is, salvation doctrine.[10] Nonetheless, by then the religious sisterhoods and the deaconesses were providing women in the Anglican Church with a vocation besides the roles of wife and mother. Even by the mid nineteenth-century, demands by women for greater participation in the Church were supported by those aware that the surplus of unmarried women necessitated the expansion of women's religious role.[11] As Michael Hill notes:

> It is no accident that the revival of the religious life in the nineteenth-century Church of England should have been initiated by women's communities. Victorian women, faced with a choice between a highly valued role of wife and mother and an indeterminate role as spinster, sought to make provision for a

[9] John Ruskin, "Of Queen's Gardens," in *The Works of John Ruskin*, 39 vols. *Vol 18: Sesames and Lilies, The Ethics of the Dust, The Crown of Wild Olive*, eds. E. Cook and Alexander Wedderburn (London: George Allen, 1905), 127.

[10] Rebecca Styler, "A Scripture of Their Own: Nineteenth-Century Bible Biography and Feminist Bible Criticism," *Christianity and Literature* 57, no. 1 (Autumn 2007): 67-68.

[11] See Ellen Umansky, *Lily Montagu and the Advancement of Liberal Judaism: from Vision to Vocation*, Studies in Women and Religion, vol. 12 (New York: Edwin Mellen Press, 1983).

greater range of laywomen's roles within a church that had previously allocated almost no roles to women.[12]

By 1878 there were forty-three sisterhoods; by 1912 this had grown to at least 1,300. By the *fin-de-siècle*, women were overrepresented in the conversionist societies, missionary work, philanthropy, Bible classes, and Sunday schools. A proportion were paid, full-time scripture readers, "mission ladies," parish visitors, and in the Evangelical movement, preachers. Indeed, it was not unusual, or unprecedented, that Lily Montagu assumed the leadership of a religious organization.[13] As Ellen Umansky points out:

> It seems, by 1890, when Lily Montagu first began to hold children's services at the New West End, a variety of nontraditional activities had already been assumed by women within both the Church of England and the dissenting congregations.
>
> In light of Anglo-Jewry's desire to appear British, it is not surprising that Lily Montagu eventually gained acceptance as a religious leader.[14]

Undoubtedly, Lily Montagu's theological writing internalizes contemporaneous Evangelical discourses concerning the spiritually regenerative role of women. This is not surprising, as prior to the Holocaust acculturated Jewish women frequently turned to Christianity as a religion of spiritual and humanistic solace, by contrast to the perceived legalism of the tradition.[15] This criticism had been answered by affirmation of Judaism as a religion of the "spirit."

---

[12] Michael Hill, *The Religious Order: A Study of Virtuoso Religion and its Legitimation in the Nineteenth Century Church of England* (London: Heinemann Educational Books, 1973), 300.

[13] Umansky, *Lily Montagu*, 37-39.

[14] Umansky, *Lily Montagu*, 39.

[15] See Rachel Feldhay Brenner, *Writing as Resistance: Four Women Confronting the Holocaust: Edith Stein, Simone Weil, Anne Frank, Etty Hillesum* (University Park: Pennsylvania State University Press, 1997).

Indeed, Reform Jews looked to the Bible in order to cleanse the synagogue of those elements which contradicted Victorian norms and which implied that Jews attend synagogue for reasons other than prayer and spiritual elevation.[16] Just as the Evangelicals rejected the authority of Church legislature for which they could find no basis in the Bible, so the founders of the West London Synagogue rejected the second days of the festivals for the same reason.[17] The bibliocentric, anti-ceremonialist, anti-rabbinic perspective is central to Montagu's proto-feminist discourse. She argued: "Unfortunately, the legal minutiae added by the Rabbis, have here and there somewhat distorted the vision of believers, who have been so misled as to call themselves Jews merely because they kept 'Koscher' homes."[18]

Lily Montagu lionized Jewish women, seeing them as the vanguard of humanity for the creation of peace. It was women's place, she assumed, to substitute politics with the ethics of religion. Also, women are more imaginative, sensitive, and redemptive, she concluded, than their male contemporaries. This redemptive potential, Montagu suggested, is indicative of those created in the image of God.[19] She argued that the moral and spiritual authority of women is a natural law, as the "girl in the background" tends toward righteousness, peace, temperance, purity, love, and truth.[20] In a sermon delivered on 15 May 1921, Montagu correlated "practical well doing" with belief in God:[21] "As a Jewess [Montagu underlines], I

---

[16] David Feldman, *Englishmen and Jews: Social Relations and Political Culture, 1840-1914* (New Haven: Yale University Press, 1994), 62-65.

[17] Michael Hilton, *The Christian Effect on Jewish Life* (London: SCM, 1994), 130.

[18] Montagu, *Thoughts on Judaism*, 114.

[19] Ellen Umansky in Montagu, *Lily Montagu: Sermons*, 159.

[20] Lily Montagu, "The Girl in the Background," in *Studies of Boy Life in Our Cities*, ed. E. J. Urwick (1904; rpt. New York: Garland Publishing, Inc., 1980), 233; Lily Montagu, "Sept. 20. 1919," sermon, London Metropolitan Archives, ACC/3529/3/7, 9. See Lily Montagu, "The Responsibility of Leisure," paper read, London Metropolitan Archives, ACC/3529/3/17, 8.

[21] Lily Montagu, *The Relation of Faith to Conduct in Jewish Life*, Papers for Jewish People, 2 (London: Jewish Religious Union, 1907), 5. See Lily

must believe in the ultimate of good and it is this faith which gives
me the courage to fight evil which at first sight may appear uncon-
querable."[22] She contended that girls must be introduced to culture,
art, and country life if their development and natural gifts are to be
maximized in the service of God.[23] Jewish women, she noted, have
throughout history been at the forefront of humanity as God's representatives in the creation of peace.[24] She stated (internalizing the
cult of true womanhood):

> Indeed, we believe that the power of women over men is
> based on a law of nature against which rebellion is impossible.
> It is one of the cherished principles underlying the national life
> of countries which boast of Western civilization that the influ-
> ence of the "girl in the background" tends towards purity,
> temperance, righteousness, and peace. ... The fact that woman
> has inspired most of the evil as well as most of the good
> known to human experience has happily not shaken our belief
> in her blessed potentialities.[25]

According to Montagu, women possess a blessed potential that can
only be cultivated by equipping them with sufficient moral, intellectual, and physical strength. She argued that this particularly applied
to working-class girls whose industrial life is regarded as mere pre-
liminary to either the marital economy or financial insecurity. Montagu concluded that motherhood, and wifehood, although the ideal,
need not be the only options available to single women. Instead, it
is necessary, she claimed, that women receive educational training

---

Montagu, "The Just Shall Live by His Faith," *Liberal Jewish Monthly* 17, no.
4 (April 1946): 29-30.

[22] Lily Montagu, "Judaism and Social Service," sermon, May 15
1921, London Metropolitan Archives, ACC/3529/3/7, 4.

[23] Montagu, "The Girl in the Background," 249, 254. See Lily Montagu, "The Place of Judaism in the Club Movement," *Liberal Jewish Monthly*
1, no. 3 (June 1929): 27-29.

[24] Lily Montagu, "Women's Contribution to the Spiritual Life of
Humanity," in Montagu, *Lily Montagu: Sermons*, 159.

[25] Montagu, "The Girl in the Background," 233-34.

in order that they might apply themselves to the service of God and develop individuality, as they "hold the keys of a future destiny – the woman's most sacred trust";[26] this "destiny" being "divine and therefore unknowable."[27]

There is little revolutionary about Lily Montagu's writing, per se. Unsurprisingly, she assumed the gender particularistic mission of women, endowed with transcendental qualities, to morally redeem "mankind." As she noted:

> It was the time of great changes in the lives of girls in the so-called leisured homes. Their education was too good to allow of their being any longer content with the small home duties which in another generation satisfied unmarried girls. They felt the need to justify their existence by some form of useful effort. My parents led strong, purposeful lives, and were not opposed to our having interests outside the home. They applauded our desire to assist others less fortunately placed than ourselves.[28]

Although First-Wave feminists succeeded in overcoming the confinements of domesticity, they had done so without actually rejecting the doctrine of a special feminine nature naturally expressed in domestic and in motherly roles. The cult of domesticity had simply been transformed into the ideal of female moral and spiritual superiority. Accordingly, in biblical terms, Eve the eternal temptress had become Eve the innocent victim or the guardian of moral sanctuary. As part of the feminization of religion evident in all denominations, and the doctrine of female superiority, it became women's mission to redeem society from its sin. This had earlier involved philanthropy or religious mission, but had come to include social

---

[26] Montagu, "The Girl in the Background," 234-35, 237-38, 241, 243-44, 246-47.

[27] Lily Montagu, "Joy of Service," sermon, June 22, 1921, London Metropolitan Archives, ACC/3529/3/7, 14.

[28] Lily Montagu, *The Faith of a Jewish Woman* (London: George Allen & Unwin, 1943), 13.

reform.[29] Montagu's appraisal of the opportunities available to working-class women demonstrates her awareness of New Woman fiction and journalism at the *fin-de-siècle*, though perhaps unsurprisingly, it does not suggest an *avant-garde* feminist discourse. Similarly, Montagu's role for women in Liberal Judaism, while revolutionary by comparison to Anglo-Reformism and Orthodoxy, was not particularly groundbreaking in the light of women's role in the Protestant Church. She notes:

> From the beginning it was determined that in our Synagogue men and women must be absolutely equal in their congregational privileges. Boys and girls were confirmed together, and men and women sat together as they chose in any part of the Synagogue. There was no women's gallery, such as we find in Orthodox Synagogues. Women had, as a matter of course, their seats on the Council, and took their share as voters in the shaping of Synagogue policy and in the responsibility of maintaining and developing its religious influence.[30]

However, the contexts, and sources employed in her theological writing and statements, derived from the rabbinic and mystical traditions, are unique to feminist discourse in the period.

Lily Montagu appears to have located in the mystical and rabbinic traditions Jewish theological authorities for the *fin-de-siècle* doctrine of female spiritual and moral hegemony. She argued that as men and women possess inherently different attributes, women are more emotional, more creative, and more practical than men:[31] "Because women's creative faculty is great, she must serve in the vanguard of humanity in the creation of peace. ... woman with her quicker sensitiveness and imaginative power can appeal to the desire to redeem, which is latent in the heart of every one created in

---

[29] Olive Banks, *Faces of Feminism: A Study of Feminism as a Social Movement* (Oxford: Basil Blackwell, 1988), 85-86, 90-91, 95.

[30] Montagu, *The Faith of a Jewish Woman*, 38.

[31] Umansky in Montagu, *Lily Montagu: Sermons*, 155, 157.

the image of God Who Himself can redeem the universe."[32] Indeed, Montagu's proto-feminist discourse reveals an interpretation of themes that are associated with the Kabbalistic *sefirah*, *Binah* ("the higher *Shekhinah*"): intelligence, processed wisdom, or deductive reasoning associated with women and the feminine.[33] As we know, she did not use the Hebrew term, *binah*, as she was aiming for accessibility.

Each *sefirah* describes a phenomenon that has a counterpart in the inner life of God. The *Zohar* summarizes *Binah* as the Supreme Mother. Additionally, despite the anti-Talmudism and anti-ceremonialism indicative to Montagu's writing, her belief that women are more intuitive, articulate, instinctive, practical, and impulsive is also elaborated by rabbinic Judaism,[34] reflecting the interpretive liberty of her Liberal perspective. The Talmud's commentary on Genesis 2:22 concludes that women possess intuitive ability that when nurtured exceeds that of men. Women are "built" by God (2:22), rather than "formed" of the dust (2:7), thus: "*Binah yeterah natun l'nashim*" – "an extra measure of *binah* was given to women."[35] Montagu similarly elucidated of women: "Her influence has been recognized since the day when Adam attempted to justify himself in the Garden of Eden. Indeed, we believe that the power of women over men is based on a law of nature against which rebellion is impossible."[36] Montagu, particularly in her writings on the synagogue service, often assumed the leader of the congrega-

---

[32] Montagu, "Women's Contribution," 159.

[33] See Leah Novick, *On the Wings of Shekhinah: Rediscovering Judaism's Divine Feminine* (Wheaton: Quest Books, 2008). Novick's book maps the history of *Shekhinah* from a Jewish Renewal perspective. The Jewish Renewal tradition employs Hasidic and mystical perspectives, along with meditation, music, and ideas from Buddhism and Sufism. Critics have labelled the movement a "new age" Judaism.

[34] See Judith Romney *Wegner, Chattel or Person? The Status of Women in the Mishnah* (New York: Oxford University Press, 1988), 153-54.

[35] Judith Hauptman, "Images of Women in the Talmud," in *Religion and Sexism*, ed. Rosemary Ruether (New York: Simon and Schuster, 1974), 197-208.

[36] Montagu, "The Girl in the Background," 233.

tion to be a woman, ignoring the ubiquitous "he" of the sacred texts:

> I discovered that the leader must actually pray with the Congregation as one of the group. She must not be anywhere outside them. Indeed, she only addresses them when she is actually preaching; otherwise, she must invite her congregation to seek God with her, realizing the dignity and the difficulty of the search, never speaking for them, for prayer to be effective must be wrung from the inmost depths of the human soul.[37]

Rabinically, the intellectual capacity, *binah*, is an ability to distinguish between diverse situations that on the surface appear similar. The definition of *binah* is located in the blessing said every morning: "You have given the rooster *binah* to distinguish between night and day": when the rooster crows it appears to be night, although it is, actually, the beginning of the day. The rooster's ability to differentiate between night and day is *binah*. Given the importance of bibliocentrism to the Liberal Jewish movement, it is not surprising that *binah* also appears throughout the Torah. Indeed, the matriarchs used *binah* to create the Jewish people.[38]

Since the exodus from Egypt, *binah* has been a prominent Midrashic theme, more so given that women have a role to play in the Messianic future.[39] Accordingly, Sarah's *binah* permits her to forewarn that Ishmael will eventually turn to murder, adultery, and idolatry. God intervenes on her behalf (Genesis 21:12), forcing Abraham to heed his wife's urging. Likewise, Rebecca's *binah* understands that Esau will gradually undermine Jacob, and she advises him to disguise himself in order to gain Isaac's blessing. The patriarch subsequently acknowledges her foresight (27:33). Similarly, both Rachel and Leah were aware of Laban's intention to infect the

---

[37] Montagu, *The Faith of a Jewish Woman*, 18.

[38] See Savina Teubal, *Sarah the Priestess: The First Matriarch of Genesis* (Athens: Swallow Press, 1984).

[39] Midrash ("exegesis"): Jewish method of commentary or biblical interpretation.

nascent Jewish nation with paganism, and urged Jacob to sever all ties with him (31:14). Consequently, the family departed.[40] And more generally, Jewish women refused to contribute their jewelry to the creation of the Golden Calf (Exodus 32:1-6), and were rewarded by God with the monthly holiday of Rosh Hodesh. Later, when the men are concerned that the distractions of everyday life and work will interfere with their relationship with God after the entry to Israel, it is the women who remain convinced of their spiritual bond with the divine presence. Finally, when Korach, his son, and several hundred others rebel against Moses' leadership, it is the women who take action. The wife of On refuses to allow her husband to join the rebellion, and serves him wine till he passes out. She then sits outside the front door with her hair exposed (forbidden in traditional Judaism). She thus renders her home, or more particularly her husband, unapproachable. Accordingly, Korach and his followers lose their lives (Numbers 16:32).

Lily Montagu's accommodation of Claude Montefiore's Liberal theology, combined with her feminist reading of *binah*, encourages women to engage in the spiritual and cultural life of the community through the study of Judaism, to actively participation in the synagogue: "Let us [women] seek more knowledge, let us study God's word as revealed in the Bible,"[41] and to seek personal, and immediate, experience of the divine presence. She advised her girls to "pause … in perfect quiet and feel the blessedness of God's spirit in our midst."[42] Accordingly, she was critical of women's exclusion from traditional education and the authoritative interpretation of the sacred texts, the *minyan*, and the liturgy:

---

[40] See Phyllis Bird, "Images of Women in the Old Testament," in *Religion and Sexism*, 41-88.

[41] Lily Montagu, "Loneliness," sermon, December 2, 1916, London Metropolitan Archives, ACC/3529/3/7, 15.

[42] Lily Montagu, "Return Unto Me," sermon, September 7, 1918, London Metropolitan Archives, ACC/3529/3/7, 7. See also Lily Montagu, "The Power of Quiet," *Liberal Jewish Monthly* 5, no. 4 (July 1934): 28-30; Lily Montagu, *Suggestions for Sabbath Eve Celebrations*, 2nd ed. (London: Wightman & Co., 1944); Lily Montagu, "The Conception of Prayer," in *Aspects of Progressive Jewish Thought, with an introduction by Israel Mattuck* (London: Victor Gollancz, 1954), 94-98.

In the past, the girl's place in the Jewish community has been inferior to that of boys. Of course, she was cherished and protected from harm as far as possible, but there was no place for her in the Synagogue, and the Synagogue was the factor of supreme importance in molding the life of the Jew. The boy was taught his Hebrew prayer, and it mattered very much that he had a complete Jewish education. It was hardly to be expected that the girl would need much Hebrew. Her life would be led, so the parent anticipated, mainly in the home. Her mother would teach her domestic observances, and beyond that, why, she did not help to make up a congregation. Ten men over the age of 13 were needed for a congregation. The girl was of no use. This conception was entirely wrong, and the fruits of the wrong have been evil, bitter fruits. To-day girls are beginning to realize that they need the help of religion quite as much as do their brothers.[43]

For Montagu, "true" religion entailed the active pursuit of God ("We complain of the inadequacy of religion – instead of practicing it more and more,"[44] she argued) and the development of subjective liturgies relevant to the personal experience of her girls.[45] Her all-female Sabbath groups, based on the joy of Sabbath prescribed by Isaiah (58:13), cultivated this (Evangelical) search for God: "Once more turn the light of the Sabbath rest as a search-light on your soul,"[46] even given, "it is … hard not to be afraid to love Him in private."[47] For Montagu: "The Sabbath lights were blessed by

[43] Lily Montagu, "August 12th, 1916," in "Addresses Given on the Club Holiday," London Metropolitan Archives, ACC/3529/3/7, 11.

[44] Lily Montagu, "Religious Perplexities," sermon, February 3, 1923, London Metropolitan Archives, ACC/3529/3/7, 4.

[45] See *Prayers, Psalms, and Hymns for Jewish Children*, ed. Lily Montagu and Theodora Davis (London: Eyre & Spottiswoode, 1901).

[46] Lily Montagu, "Backwards and Forwards," sermon, March 29, 1924, London Metropolitan Archives, ACC/3529/3/7, 7.

[47] Montagu, "August 12th, 1916," 18. The early rabbis sanctioned independent prayer, more so given the halakhic prohibitions on women's

the mother, whose love for her home rendered her face quite spiritual as she pronounced the simple blessing for the Sabbath."[48] Although these initiatives, the creation of gender inclusionary rituals for women,[49] and the development of subjective feminist liturgies, would later come to be associated with the Second-Wave of Jewish feminism,[50] Montagu's apparent reading of the rabbinic and the mystical *Binah*, and her inclusionary monotheism, also relates to her interpretation of the *Shekhinah*, though again, her desire for accessibility leads her to ignore use of the Hebrew term. Indeed, for Montagu: "Human love in its finest aspects reflects the divine in its inclusiveness."[51]

Jewish feminism, by asking the question, "who is God" since the 1970s, has concluded, though not exclusively, to name the God of their experience *Shekhinah*.[52] The *Shekhinah*, as a manifestation of God, or God-She, is defined by her presentness and, according to the rabbis, *Shekhinah* is not present in laziness, light heartedness, idle conversation, or laughter, but manifests itself in joy, creativity, and prophecy (Pesachim 117a). Traditionally, the *Shekhinah* denotes Judaism's faith in God's immanence, and as the attribute of presence it does not imply God is identical to the world. The rabbis

---

public religious activities. Certainly, in the *aggadah*, the prayers of Esther and Hannah are both given favorable commentaries (Linda Kuzmack, "Aggadic Approaches to Biblical Women," in *The Jewish Woman: New Perspectives*, ed. Elizabeth Koltun (New York: Schocken Books, 1976), 251.

[48] Lily Montagu, My Club and I: the Story of the West Central Jewish Club (London: Herbert Joseph, 1941), 43-44.

[49] See Rebecca Alpert, "Our Lives Are the Text: Exploring Jewish Women's Rituals," *Bridges* 2 (Spring 1991): 66-80; Adelman Penina, *Miriam's Well, Rituals for Jewish Women Around the Year* (Fresh Meadows: Biblio Press, 1986); *A Ceremonies Sampler: New Rites, Celebrations and Observances of Jewish Women*, ed. Elizabeth Resnick Levine (San Diego: Women's institute for Continuing Jewish Education, 1991).

[50] See Marcia Falk, "Notes on Composing New Blessings: Toward a Feminist Jewish Reconstruction of Prayer," *Journal of Feminist Studies in Religion* 3 (Spring 1987): 41.

[51] Montagu, "Kinship with God," in Montagu, *Lily Montagu: Sermons*, 115.

[52] See *New Jewish Feminism: Probing the Past, Forging the Future*, ed. Elyse Goldstein (Woodstock: Jewish Lights Publishing, 2009).

frequently used *"Shekhinah"* as a synonym for God. The word is derived from *shakan*, meaning to dwell with or to pitch one's tent. For the rabbis, *Shekhinah*, now the Second Temple was gone, had accompanied the Israelites in the wilderness, and suggested the accessibility of God.[53] It was even muted that the *Shekhinah*, who dwelt with people on earth, still lived on the Temple Mount. Alternatively, some rabbis believed that the Temple's destruction had freed the *Shekhinah*, allowing it to inhabit the rest of the world. Similar to the Holy Spirit or divine "glory," the *Shekhinah* was God's presence on earth. In fact, the rabbis assumed that the *Shekhinah* had been with them even in Egypt and Babylonia. The image and idea of *Shekhinah* allowed exilic Jews to experience God's presence wherever they were. Indeed, *Shekhinah* went from synagogue to synagogue throughout the diaspora, standing at the door to hear the *Shema* (Jewish proclamation of faith). Moreover, when Jews study Torah together, the *Shekhinah* sits with them, and can only return with the strict observance of the *mitzvot*.[54]

God's transcendence ensures that the divine will and purpose are unconditioned by human interference, while God's immanence ensures that humanity can become God's *shuttaf* (partner) in bringing God's purposes to fulfillment in the immanent dominion. The *Shekhinah*, as a separate feminine hypostasis, however, was developed by the Kabbalists during the twelfth and thirteenth-centuries. In the *Zohar*, or *Book of Splendor*,[55] the *Shekhinah* is God's interface with the universe, and while the rabbis viewed *Shekhinah* as the presence of God, Kabbalah describes her as a *female* element within God – the *sefirah* (emanation) through which the divine presence interacts with the world.[56] Indeed, *Shekhinah*, for the early Kabbalists, was the tenth *sefirah*, also known as *Malkuth* ("Kingdom"). Lily

---

[53] The First Temple was demolished in 586 BCE by the Babylonians, while the Second Temple was destroyed by the Romans in 70 CE. Rabbinic Judaism only came about after the destruction of the Second Temple.

[54] Karen Armstrong, *A History of God* (London: Vintage Books, 1999), 92-94, 319.

[55] The *Zohar* appeared toward the end of the thirteenth-century and is generally attributed to Rabbi Moses de Leon.

[56] Raphael, *The Female Face*, 152-153.

Montagu's proto-theology, similar to the Kabbalistic theologies, seeks "completion" (the unification of masculine and feminine in the Godhead) alike Second and Third-Wave discourse on the *Shekhinah*, as Melissa Raphael notes: "Whatever their historical predicament, where women are fully and normatively female subjects, and God is known in God's fullness as a divine personality revealed in both female and masculine modes, these are together prerequisite to and prefigurative of *shalom* – the peace or completion of a world and a God that is to come."[57] And also Judith Plaskow:

> Two of the virtues of the image of Shekhinah from a feminist perspective are that it is an image of divine immanence and an image of God in non-hierarchical relation. It thus deliberately offsets the picture of God as dominating Other and at the same time fits in well with the general emphasis on mutual relation in feminist spirituality. The Shekhinah, as opposed to the totally unknowable *Kadosh Barukh Hu* (holy one, blessed be he), is precisely that aspect of God with which we can be in relation, and it is experienced in joint study, community gatherings, and other moments of common and intimate human connection.[58]

In traditional Judaism, despite the centrality of monotheism, there has never been a continuous theological tradition. In fact, Judaism has not attached the importance to theology that Christianity has. The Bible itself concentrates on what God does, and what God expects of humanity, and does not describe who or what God is. Genesis, for example, discusses creation, but not the creator. Accordingly, Abraham, the first Jew, did not find God, instead, God found him and subsequently issued a series of commands informing Abraham how he and his descendents must live. Therefore, it is not surprising that traditional Judaism was described by the nineteenth-century Reformers as a religion of "deed rather than

---

[57] Raphael, *The Female Face*, 11.
[58] Judith Plaskow, *Standing Again at Sinai: Judaism from a Feminist Perspective* (1990; rpt. New York: HarperCollins Publishers, 1991), 139-140.

creed."[59] Even rabbinic Judaism, through its study of the Bible and halakhah, did not attempt to set out its theology in systematic form. God is assumed, and his existence need not be proved or explored. However, the rabbis did adhere to several theological beliefs, namely: the unity of God, the uniqueness of God, and the rejection of polytheism and idolatry. For the rabbis, God is transcendent and unknowable, yet active in the world. He has shared in Israel's exile and suffering, and his justice is both majestic and ruthless. On the other hand, he is loving, forgiving, and all-good. He demands that men and women lead righteous lives, yet permits evil to exist in the world. The Torah is a symbol of the Covenant between God and his chosen people, Israel, his witnesses (according to some traditions) responsible for the redemption of all mankind. Rabbinic theology, founded on the unity of God, and the three pillars of creation, redemption, and revelation, is synonymous with Orthodox Judaism.[60]

Perhaps the earliest significant development in the history of Jewish theology was in the writing of Moses Maimonides, the first Jew to set down a fundamental dogmatic theology.[61] He arguably gave Jewish rationalism its classical formulation. His Aristotelianism and Neoplatonist ideas strengthened his belief in the power of human reason. As such, Maimonides combined reason, prophecy, revelation, and the religious tradition, and implicitly devalued Talmudic study, the crown of Jewish education, as the exercise of faith without reason. Despite the controversy over his importation of non-Jewish philosophical categories into Judaism, his Thirteen Principles have remained popular among Orthodox Jews:[62]

[59] Jonathan Romain, *Reform Judaism and Modernity: A Reader* (London: SCM, 2004), 144.

[60] See Michael Berger, *Rabbinic Authority* (New York: Oxford University Press, 1998).

[61] Melissa Raphael, "Standing at a Demythologized Sinai? Reading Jewish Feminist Theology Through the Critical Lens of Radical Orthodoxy," in *Interpreting the Postmodern: Responses to "Radical Orthodoxy,"* eds. Rosemary Radford Ruether and Marion Grau (New York: T & T Clark, 2006), 204.

[62] Nicholas de Lange, *Judaism* (Oxford: Oxford University Press, 1987), 107, 113.

Great is the living God and to be praised:
existing and unlimited by time.
Unique is his uniqueness he is One,
concealed in his infinite unity.
He has no body, no substance or form,
no image can define his holiness.
Preceding all created things, the First,
with no beginnings to his primacy.
Eternal Lord is he, and all the world
declared his greatness and his majesty.
To men he chose to glorify his name
he gave abundant gifts of prophecy.
No prophet has there been in Israel
like Moses, who beheld him face to face.
Through him, the prophet "faithful in his house,"
God gave his people the one true Torah.
Nor will he ever abrogate his law
or substitute another in its place.
He sees into the secrets of our hearts
and knows the end of all things in advance.
For all good deeds he grants a due reward,
but punishes the sinner for his sin.
Finally our Anointed will he send
to save those who await the glorious end.
The dead our loving God to life will raise:
For ever be his name adored with praise![63]

Nonetheless, Maimonides also acknowledged the limits of reason and demonstrated willingness to depart from Aristotelian doctrines. He argued, for example, against the doctrine of the eternity of the world, instead preferring the biblical notion of the creation.[64]

By the twentieth-century, however, the traditional communities that maintained the spirit of rabbinic Judaism, and the prioriti-

---

[63] Moses Maimonides, "Thirteen Principles," quoted by de Lange, *Judaism*, 106. Each principle consists of two lines.

[64] De Lange, *Judaism*, 114.

zation of halakhah, continued to express reservations about Jews doing theology at all. The Hebrew University, Jerusalem, for example, has barred Jewish theology from the classroom. Alas, despite Maimonides best intentions, Judaism did not become a creedal faith. The philosophers were little interested in theology, and the halakhists had no time for purely doctrinal considerations.[65] Nevertheless, since the *Haskalah* German Reform theologians have theorized numerous meta-halakhic theologies.

The Reform Judaism of the early nineteenth-century, convinced that the rabbinic tradition had undermined the pursuit of theology by its propensity towards regulations and prohibitions, sought to re-engage Jews with the divine presence. In certain respects this involved the employment of typically Jewish terms: God was still a king, a father and an all powerful creator. He was also personally knowable and intimate. However, Reform Judaism departed from the tradition with its subjective will that individuals construct their own theologies.[66] As Morris Joseph stated in 1903: "The Jewish Creed has always been in a fluid condition, and Judaism leaves us free to construct our own theology, so long as we do not trench upon certain easily recognized principles which could not be discarded without destroying the religion itself."[67] Similarly, *fin-de-siècle* Reform rabbis, such as Leo Baeck (1905), have written extensively on the personal relationship between the individual and the deity:

> Whoever knows himself to be bound to the one and eternal God knows no loneliness, for his life is never solitary. No matter how intimately we may come into contact with our fellow man we still remain alone in our innermost soul, for every person is unique upon earth and loneliness is part of individuality. But in God our life finds its peace.[68]

---

[65] Raphael, "Standing at a Demythologized Sinai," 204.
[66] Romain, *Reform Judaism*, 145.
[67] Quoted by Romain, *Reform Judaism*, 145.
[68] Quoted by Romain, *Reform Judaism*, 147.

The Reform theologies, by contrast to the tradition, stressed the immediacy of the divine presence. These ideas were developed by Franz Rosenzweig in the early twentieth-century. Rosenzweig was a disciple of Hermann Cohen's writing on the nature of God and his relationship to man. He left Judaism as a young man, became an agnostic, and then returned to Orthodoxy. As one of the first existentialists, Rosenzweig developed a unique, and universal, conception of Judaism. He argued that religion was essentially an encounter with the divine, and concluded that each individual is alone until God redeems them from anonymity. Accordingly, God does not reduce individuality, but encourages self-consciousness.

Martin Buber developed a similar theology, visualizing Judaism as a spiritual process and as a striving for elemental unity. Similar to Franz Rosenzweig, he talked of religion as an encounter with the divine, though symbolized and enacted in our meetings with other human beings. Thus, life is an endless dialogue with God. Whereas Rosenzweig used the Torah, and Buber, the Torah and Hasidism, Abraham Joshua Heschel, another Jewish existentialist theologian writing in the twentieth-century, returned to the rabbis and the Talmud. Heschel, from an Orthodox background, argued that the *mitzvot* could enable Jews to overcome the dehumanizing aspects of modernity, as these were actions that fulfilled God's will as opposed to our own, and demonstrated his presence. As such, although Heschel was not Reform orientated, his faith in God resulted from an immediate apprehension that had little to do with rationality or law for the sake of law alone.[69] This intra-Judaic struggle between halakhah and ethics, typified by the Reform, Kantian, and existentialist approaches has dominated modern Jewish thought. The Reformers, as we have seen, viewed Orthodoxy as archaic, ritualistic, and exclusivist, and instead prioritized motivational spirituality as opposed to the legality and super-naturalist doctrines of the tradition. Moreover, the Reformers spiritualized Judaism effectively making it palatable to both assimilated Jews and their Christian neighbors.[70]

---

[69] Armstrong, *A History of God*, 434-36, 453-54.

[70] Raphael, "Standing at a Demythologized Sinai," 204-05.

Aside from traditional Judaism, the Reform, and Enlightenment theologies, several other meta-denominational Jewish theological schools developed prior to modernity. Kabbalah, or Jewish
mysticism, has three distinct theosophical elements: knowledge of
God, love of God, and communion with God. In short, the God
of Kabbalah is divinely immanent and personally knowable. This
tradition developed in mediaeval Spain and elaborated on the nature of God. Kabbalah, as such, appealed to those Jews who
wished to achieve a deeper understanding of theological questions.
Similarly, the Hasidim of Poland developed from the Lurianic
Kabbalah, though replaced the intellectual philosophy central to
the Kabbalah with an enthusiasm for prayer, the aim of which is to
detach from the corporeal existence into personal union with the
divine nothingness, or God. Although Kabbalah has been too eso-
teric to be integrated into the mainstream of Jewish life, Jewish
mysticism can still be found in the liturgy, and the tradition has
been widely appropriated in Haredi Holocaust-theology, in post-
Holocaust non-Orthodox theology, and in First, Second, and
Third-Wave Jewish feminist contexts.

In sum, although a body of theology existed prior to the Holocaust, it was often apologetic in nature. From the mediaeval period to the early modern era, dogma had been at least in part an
historical contingency. These theologies were a response to the
Christian theological polemic against Judaism, and of the determination to convert the Jews. The creedal posture of the Reformers
was based on the ongoing dispute with Orthodoxy, and was also
bound up with the Jewish drive for civil liberties in the age of
emancipation.[71] As we have seen, it was following the failure of
Reform Judaism in England that Anglo-Liberal Judaism was born.

Claude Montefiore developed his Liberal theology on the basis of monotheism, the spiritual and moral teachings of the prophets, and the tradition of Judaism throughout the ages. Liberal Judaism, and its anti-rabbinical ideologies, was a "back to the Bible"
movement. Montefiore determined that for Liberal Jews, the Torah
could no longer play the same role as it had done for Orthodoxy,
as allegedly, the great prophets had not known the Torah as it is

---

[71] Raphael, "Standing at a Demythologized Sinai," 204.

known today.[72] His de-ritualized, de-nationalized version of Judaism, as Geoffrey Alderman states, had formed "a system of ethics based on a vague monotheistic doctrine."[73] Liberal Judaism is figured upon the necessity of personal communion with, or immediate experience of, the divine presence.[74] The immediacy of the divine presence was not always an explicit element of rabbinic Judaism, although it was incorporated by the majority of meta-halakhic theologies. Montefiore, however, was aware of the importance of the community, as opposed to the individual, in biblical religion. He presented Liberal Judaism as biblically grounded, yet also as a progressive religion at ease with modern science and able to absorb external influences. He rejected the inessential ceremonialism of Orthodoxy, claiming that it hindered spiritual growth. He also rejected the concept of a personal Messiah, the restoration of the Temple, and the return to Zion. His theology, nonetheless, had its roots, not in religious obligation, but in historical necessity.[75] Maurice Bowler argues:

> Because he [Montefiore] rejected the Zionist solution (of isolation *from* the Western world) and also the voluntary ghetto solution (of isolation *within* the Western world) he felt that Judaism had to be reconstituted if it was to meet the challenge of assimilation which, if uncontrolled, could lead to Anglo-Jewry's disappearance. By definition, the nature of the problem of assimilation and its solution must relate to the cultural force to which the Jewish community was seen to be integrating itself. In Montefiore's day this was a powerful Christianity.[76]

---

[72] A. Hanson, "Claude Montefiore, a Modern Philo," *Modern Churchman* 20, no. 3 (Spring 1977): 110.

[73] Geoffrey Alderman, *Modern British Jewry*, new ed. (Oxford: Clarendon Press, 1998), 203-04.

[74] Yahweh began as a highly personalized deity with passionate human likes and dislikes; it was only later that God became a symbol of transcendence.

[75] Raphael, "Standing at a Demythologized Sinai," 204.

[76] Maurice Bowler, "C. G. Montefiore and His Quest," *Judaism* 30, no. 4 (Fall 1981): 453.

Like Franz Rosenzweig, Montefiore intended Judaism to absorb the best of the surrounding host culture.[77] Thus, perhaps unsurprisingly, Montefiore was criticized for his employment, and praise of, the New Testament, and his analysis of Jesus as a Jewish prophet.[78] Achad Ha'am said that Montefiore had turned his back on Judaism, while Solomon Schechter labeled Montefiore's teachings a type of "Liberal Christianity." Likewise, some Christians thought he had "come over to their side."[79] Problematically, while earlier reclamations of Jesus for Jewish contexts stressed his Jewish attributes, and commitment to first-century Judaism, Montefiore established a prophetic base reminiscent of Paul's description of the law as temporary. This subordination of the law is diametrically opposed to Moses Maimonides belief that the prophecy of Moses, the prototype of the prophets,[80] and the law given to him on Sinai, is true and unchanged.[81] Instead, Montefiore stated: "We recognize no binding outside authority between us and God, whether in a man or in a book, whether in a church or in a code, whether in a tradition or in a ritual."[82] Montefiore committed himself to a prophecy-orientated position, by contrast to Orthodoxy's law-based stance, and in the process indefinitely polarized Liberal Judaism and Orthodoxy.[83]

---

[77] Bowler, "C. G. Montefiore," 454.

[78] See Claude Montefiore, *Some Elements in the Religious Teaching of Jesus* (London: Macmillan, 1910); Claude Montefiore, *Liberal Judaism and Convenience: and Do Liberal Jews Teach Christianity?* Papers for Jewish People, 25 (London: Jewish Religious Union, 1924); Claude Montefiore, *Rabbinic Literature and Gospel Teaching* (London: Macmillan, 1930).

[79] Maurice Bowler, *Claude Montefiore and Christianity* (Atlanta: Scholars Press, 1988), 84.

[80] Armstrong, *A History of God*, 54.

[81] Bowler, "C. G. Montefiore," 457.

[82] Quoted by Bowler, "C. G. Montefiore," 458.

[83] Bowler, "C. G. Montefiore," 458. See Claude Montefiore, *The Religious Teachings of Jesus* (London: Macmillan, 1910); Claude Montefiore, *Liberal Judaism and Convenience: and Do Liberal Jews Teach Christianity?* Papers for Jewish People, 25 (London: Jewish Religious Union, 1924).

As we have seen, the mediaeval Jewish philosophers, including Moses Maimonides, refused to ascribe any gender to God and separated humanity from the unknowable, non-personal, and unnamable divine presence. The early Kabbalists, by contrast, were intent on restoring the divine-human relationship by postulating a divinely immanent God knowable through the ten aspects.[84] The later Kabbalists imaged the *Shekhinah* as the bride of God, or Shabbat bride (Shabbat *Hamalka*) symbolized in the songs and writing of the sixteenth-century Rabbi Isaac Luria (the Shabbat itself is visualized as a bride, or queen, or a lady with many lighted candles). As the final sphere of divine emanation, she is the closest point of the divine presence in the world, and a divine hypostasis in her own right.[85] Luria regrouped the ten *sefirot* into five "Countenances" (*parzufim*), the last of which being *Malkuth* or the *Shekhinah* (Zeir's Woman). In the process of *Tikkun* (repair), Luria used the idea of conception, birth, and the development of human personality as an allusion to a similar evolution in God. The five "Countenances," described by Luria using sexual symbolism, represent the mating of the male and female aspects of God, and the restoration of order.[86]

Contemporary Jews, particularly those with liberal sympathies, have been well disposed to the notion of a feminine aspect to God; reunion with whom brings psycho-spiritual completion. Jewish feminists, on the other hand, have incorporated the *Shekhinah* into their liturgy and theology with specific reference to her exile, and have used the *Shekhinah* to denote, not a separate Goddess or feminine divine, but the maternal intimacy of the divine presence as

---

[84] The notion of divine immanence is central to Liberal theology. See Lily Montagu, *Home Worship and Its Influence on Social Work*, paper read at the Conference of Jewish Women (Southampton: Cot & Sharland, May 1902), 14; Lily Montagu, "Paper to be Read on October 13th 1918," sermon, London Metropolitan Archives, ACC/3529/3/7, 4; Lily Montagu, "Some Thoughts on Home Worship," *Liberal Jewish Monthly* 8, no. 4 (June 1937): 22-23; Lily Montagu, *Religious Education on the Home*, Papers for Jewish People, 26 (London: Jewish Religious Union, 1925).

[85] Some Christians believe the *Shekhinah* is present in the New Testament.

[86] Armstrong, *A History of God*, 317.

an aspect of the one God who can be reclaimed from patriarchy, and who should no longer be erotically or metaphysically subordinated to masculine roles or male interests.[87] This is not at all to say that Lily Montagu envisioned the restoration of the Goddess, but that she too explored the maternal/feminine dimension of the divine presence.[88] Her reading of the *Shekhinah*, as we will see, is bound up in her interpretation of the prophet Isaiah's references to the deity's feminine aspect, in mystical discourse on God's immanence, and in the centrality of the divine-human relationship.

In traditional Judaism, the *Shekhinah*, the indwelling presence of God, is the single developed female image of the deity and represents: "women's divine image, obscured as it has been by the sin of patriarchy, it is engaged in a restorative struggle – the very process of *tikkun*."[89] The radically monotheistic Talmud and Midrash refer to the *Shekhinah*, generally, without reference to the femaleness of the divine presence (except Kiddushin 31b), while as we know, Kabbalah employs the feminine element in conjunction with the masculine, "Holy One, Blessed be He," as Rita Gross argues:

> The most profound, intriguing, and inviting of all Jewish theologies – the *Kabbalah* – teaches us that *galut* – exile – is the fundamental reality and pain of present existence. It teaches us that one of the causes of *galut* is the alienation of the masculine from the feminine in God, the alienation of God and the *Shekhinah*. Now the masculine and feminine have been torn asunder and the feminine dismembered and banished, both from the discourse about divinity and from the human community, such a *tikkun* is obligatory, is a *mitzvah*. When the masculine and feminine aspect of God have been reunited and the female

---

[87] Raphael, *The Female Face*, 153.

[88] See Melissa Raphael, "Goddess Religion, Postmodern Jewish Feminism, and the Complexity of Alternative Religious Identities," *Nova Religio* 1 (1998): 198-214; Starhawk, *The Spiral Dance: A ReBirth of the Ancient Religion of the Great Goddess* (San Francisco: Harper & Row, 1979); Raphael Patai, *The Hebrew Goddess* (New York: Ktav Publishing House, 1967).

[89] Melissa Raphael, *The Female Face*, 149.

half of humanity has been returned from exile, we will begin to have our *tikkun*. The world will be repaired.[90]

The marriage between God and Israel, the *Shekhinah*-bride, is transferred to the inner life of God as a holy union within the Godhead. The *Shekhinah*-bride is accordingly symbolized through feminine terms such as queen, princess, daughter, mother, moon, matron, wisdom, faith, and the community of Israel. Despite the widespread popularity of *Shekhinah* imagery, however, the concept has not been incorporated into the traditional liturgy as an accepted balance to the masculinity of God. Judith Plaskow notes that in mainstream Jewish thinking God's non-sexuality is integral to the moral order, though in Jewish mysticism the *Zohar* and Lurianic Kabbalah use extensive sexual imagery, particularly in relation to the ninth *Yesod* (foundation) *sefirah* through which all higher *sefirot* course into the feminine *Shekhinah*. This process, as we know, is portrayed in phallic terminology and interpreted as the male procreative force active in the universe. The marriage to the *Shekhinah*, the celestial bride, is central to the *sefirot*. Therefore, the separation of the masculine and feminine aspects within God is a disaster key to the drama of creation.[91] Hence, the reunion between the masculine and the feminine is the very meaning of redemption itself. According to Plaskow, it is not surprising, given the importance of sexuality to Kabbalistic interpretations of divinity, that the mystical tradition is a source of positive attitudes towards marital sexuality. The feminine aspect of the divine presence, Plaskow notes, is evident in prophetic Judaism. Isaiah, for example, refers to God as a

[90] Rita Gross, "Steps Toward Feminine Imagery of Deity in Jewish Theology," *Judaism* 30 no. 2 (Spring 1981): 234. Gross is now a practitioner of Buddhism, although she has written extensively on, and practiced, Judaism.

[91] See Tamar Ross, "Can We Still Pray to Our Father in Heaven"? in *A Good Eye: Dialogue and Polemic in Jewish Culture*, a Jubilee book in honor of Tova Ilan (Hakibbutz: Hameuchad Publishing House, Ltd, 1999), 264-278.

mother (42:14, 66:13),[92] and God also appears as a wet-nurse, a midwife, and as a provider of water and food in the Hebrew Bible. Plaskow, on this and other counts, concludes that the Jewish feminist approach to God-language must incorporate women's God-wrestling into the fullness of the Torah which, she assumes, might be achieved by locating images that can evoke and communicate the experience of the divine presence to a diverse, egalitarian, and empowered community of Israel.[93]

Lily Montagu also sought to make the divine presence relevant to the women of her congregation by highlighting the *feminine*, as well as the masculine, elements of God. Montagu believed that her girls already possessed "divine attributes" that could be enhanced through reading and awareness of the gender equalizing aspects of prophetic Judaism.[94] She was introduced and tutored in the prophets by the Reverend Simeon Singer,[95] and compared her own humanitarianism and belief in divine mission to their example.[96] Indeed, only those who renounce pleasure will see the *Shekhinah* in the next world.[97] Montagu's writing is dominated by references to Isaiah and she frequently began her sermons with a quotation by the prophet, despite the fact that Isaiah is not a unified text and contains images of punitive divine violence.[98] As the prophets mo-

---

[92] The book of Isaiah may have been the work of three major prophets. Hence, it is often split into three sections for analysis: first (1-39), second (40-55), and third (56-66).

[93] Plaskow, *Standing Again at Sinai*, 122, 124, 138-139, 188.

[94] Montagu, "Women's Contribution," 167.

[95] Montagu, *The Faith of a Jewish Woman*, 11.

[96] Lily Montagu, "Man's Ambition and God's Law," sermon, January 18 1919, London Metropolitan Archives, ACC/3529/3/7, 8? (many of the pages in this document are not numbered). See also Lily Montagu, *Religious and Social Service*, Papers for Jewish People, 18 (London: Jewish Religious Union, 1918); Lily Montagu, "Social Teaching of Judaism for To-Day," in *In Spirit and In Truth: Aspects of Judaism and Christianity*, ed. George Yates (London: Hodder & Stoughton, 1934), 105-119.

[97] Armstrong, *A History of God*, 286.

[98] Lily Montagu, "Immortality in Literature," sermon, February 16, 1924, London Metropolitan Archives, ACC/3529/3/7, 1. In this instance she quotes Isaiah 59:21. Montagu's ethically selective approach to the tradition was, and is, frequently employed by adherents of Reform and

ralized and spiritualized revelation, Montagu believed that the reformative nature of their rhetoric made them the true exponents of a progressive religion similar to her own Liberal Judaism.[99] Montagu thus used the prophetic tradition to substantiate the gender inclusionary aspects of her Liberal theology of completion: "Throughout the Old Testament God the Ruler is also God the Father. 'As a father pitieth his children, so does the Lord pity them who fear Him.' God's extreme tenderness is further expressed: 'As one who his Mother comforteth so will I comfort thee.'"[100] These labels and descriptions, such as God the "mother," and the gender-neutral aspects of the creation, including, for example, hills, wells, rocks, and fountains,[101] are an important reminder that God is not literally male, even while these terms have been overshadowed by masculine terminology.[102] Like the prophets, Montagu attributed her passions and emotions to God. She located in the prophet Isaiah, and his populist, democratic views and sensitivity toward the plight of the poor,[103] spiritual, moral, and religious authority. She frequently cited Isaiah 55 as her favorite biblical passage:

> I have regarded [Isaiah 55] as my favorite [passage] throughout my life. This chapter seems to me to carry within itself the essence of pure religion. It contains a call to man to seek God, and assurance that if that search is undertaken with sincerity and faith, all other of life's activities will fit in accordingly to a correct measure of values. The chapter gives glorious assur-

---

Liberal Judaisms. The "pick and choose" approach allows interpreters to discard elements of the tradition unpalatable to modern audiences, while highlighting those aspects which are egalitarian, democratic, and universalistic.

[99] Eric Conrad, *Lily H. Montagu: Prophet of a Living Judaism* (New York: National Federation of Temple Sisterhoods, 1953), 36-37, 44.

[100] Lily Montagu, "Kinship with God," in Montagu, *Lily Montagu: Sermons*, 116.

[101] Rachel Adler, *Engendering Judaism: An Inclusive Theology and Ethics* (1998; rpt. Boston: Beacon Press, 2005), 95.

[102] Plaskow, *Standing Again at Sinai*, 124.

[103] Armstrong, *A History of God*, 52.

ance that God will cause goodness to triumph, and that, ruling
as He does by law, we can count on His law to lead to the establishment of righteousness. Moreover, we find in these
verses the wonderful comfort for all seekers after truth, who,
in spite of their love and faith, must ever remain to some degree perplexed and bewildered. "God's thoughts are not our
thoughts, and His ways are not our ways." We have no power
to explain God. If we could, we should be God ourselves. Our
minds can only conceive a part of His activity. The perfect
whole is beyond us. So we must give rest to our souls. We
must make active effort to reach nearer to God: we can be sure
He is waiting for us and helping us: we can be sure that He is
Love and Goodness, Justice, Truth and Beauty, all the good
things for which our human hearts and minds can contain.[104]

Montagu was particularly attracted to the verse: "God's thoughts
are not our thoughts, His ways are not our ways" (Isaiah 55:8).[105]
Accordingly, Isaiah confirmed for her (she bibliocentrically differentiated between the prophet who reveals God's law, and the sage
who interprets it) the basis of ethical monotheism, the anti-
materialist (55:3),[106] anti-ceremonialist (see also Micah 6:7-8, and
Amos 4:4-5, 5:21-24), and the universalistic aspects of her writing.[107] She stated: "If, as is far more probable, we are able by a
strongly organized religious movement to arrest our own spiritual

[104] Montagu, *The Faith of a Jewish Woman*, 41.

[105] Conrad, *Lily H. Montagu*, 51.

[106] Montagu stated regarding the forfeiting of her inheritance: "we
shall be happy without money" ("Letter to Louis," March 8, 1911, London Metropolitan Archives, ACC/3529/3/6/C, 4). Moses Maimonides
sought to protect the Mosaic Law from changes based on prophetic inspiration. For the rabbis, the Oral Law is divinely ordained and does not
require further alteration.

[107] Lily Montagu, *The World Union for Progressive Judaism: The Story of its
First 25 Years – 1926 until 1951* (New York: World Union for Progressive
Judaism, 1951), 7. See Stephen Sharot, *Modern Judaism: a Sociology* (Newton
Abbot: David and Charles, 1976). In the Hebrew Bible many non-
Israelites experience God's acceptance, including Jethro (Exodus 3:1),
Rahab (Joshua 2:8-11, 6:22-25), and Ruth.

degeneration and to revive our faith, that mission of the Lord's Servant unto the nations, which was the highest aspiration of the Second Isaiah, may even yet be turned from vision to reality."[108] In sum, Isaiah 55 symbolized for Montagu the essence of "true" religion, defining her mission:[109] "We must no longer grimly reiterate the fact that Judaism has ceased to appeal to us, and lack the energy to inquire into the cause of its degeneration. We must boldly follow Isaiah, Jeremiah and Ezekiel, and allow a place to progress in religious thought."[110]

Above all, Lily Montagu most related to Isaiah's insistence on "justice, truth, purity, and beauty,"[111] and his alluding to the feminine aspect of the divine presence, which we know as the *Shekhinah*.[112] The prophets frequently describe God in feminine terms. Isaiah, for example: "*now* will I cry like a travailing woman" (42:14); as a provider of water (55): "Ho, every one that thirsteth, come ye to the waters";[113] and the maternal aspect: "As one whom his mother comforteth, so will I comfort you" (66:13), and more specifically, Isaiah (6:1) also refers to symbols such as thrones and robes which the rabbis associate with the *Shekhinah* (the divine presence in the world): "I saw the Lord sitting upon a throne high and lifted up, and his train filled the Temple." These frequent references to the maternal and feminine elements of the divine presence had a profound effect on Montagu's theological discourse. In her sermons she reminded her congregants, using symbology that has since been appropriated by Second-Wave Jewish feminists, "that from darkness we go to light – from death to life,"[114] alluding

---

[108] Lily Montagu, "Spiritual Possibilities of Judaism To-Day," *Jewish Quarterly Review* 11 (1899): 230-231.

[109] Conrad, *Lily H. Montagu*, 47.

[110] Montagu, "Spiritual Possibilities," 225.

[111] Lily Montagu, "Who Is Self-Made"? sermon, February 2, 1924 (this date is crossed out and rewritten as what appears to be Aug 1925), London Metropolitan Archives, ACC/3529/3/7, 4.

[112] Polytheism flourished in Israel until after the Babylonian exile.

[113] Lily Montagu, "Club Letter No. 3," in Montagu, *Lily Montagu: Sermons*, 51.

[114] Lily Montagu, "If Winter Comes," sermon, March 10, 1923, London Metropolitan Archives, ACC/3529/3/7, 10.

to Isaiah 30:26: "The light of the moon shall become like the light of the sun." She frequently quoted: "'He every one that thirsteth, come ye to the waters.' This call, taken from Isaiah 55, is a call to prayer."[115] These references to the light and the moon demonstrate Montagu's appropriation of symbols and imagery that would later become integral to the Second-Wave appropriation of the *Shekhinah*.

The Babylonian Talmud expands on the moon imagery, as does Isaiah 5:20: "Woe unto them that call evil good, and good evil; that put darkness for light, and light for darkness." Rabbi Simeon ben Lakish argues that the he-goat or sin offering on the New Moon is an atonement for the Lord having made the moon (*Shekhinah*) smaller (Hullin 60a), as there could not have been two great lights. Sanhedrin 42a also refers to the following blessing that even women may pronounce: "Blessed be the One Who renews the moons." The rabbinic exchange continues: "The moon [*Shekhinah*] He ordered that she should renew herself as a crown of beauty for those whom He sustains from the womb, and who will someday, like her, be renewed and magnify their maker in the name of the glory of His kingdom."[116] Indeed, the debate suggests that the moon and the sun were equal at the creation. God reduced the moon's brightness, however, at the time of the *Shekhinah*-God's mournful exile.[117] Thus, the *Shekhinah* will return to her former glory in the days of justice and love, and will again be equal to the sun after Messianic redemption. Arlene Agus interprets this rabbinic debate as a veiled comment on the possibility of transformation in the relationship between men and women in Judaism. She assumes that the moon symbolizes women and the sun men. The tradition reminds the women of Israel that they were originally equal to men and that historically they did not give their jewelry for the creation of the Golden Calf at Sinai, and were rewarded with

---

[115] Montagu, "Club Letter No. 3," 51.

[116] Quoted by Arthur Waskow, "Feminist Judaism: Restoration of the Moon," in *On Being A Jewish Feminist: A Reader*, ed. Susannah Heschel (1983; rpt. New York: Schocken Books, 1995), 261.

[117] See Emmanuel Levinas, "Judaism and the Feminine Element," trans. by Edith Wyschogrod, *Judaism* 18 (1969): 30-38.

Rosh Hodesh, an exemption from work on the renewal of the moon at the beginning of the Jewish month. According to Arthur Waskow, the moon symbolizes female spirituality, and for Isaiah, and the Talmudic rabbis, the moon's diminished status, coupled with its potential to return in splendor, is analogous to the weeping *Shekhinah* who will also return, symbolizing *Tikkun*: the repair of the world.[118] Perhaps for Lily Montagu, the ascent of the moon signaled the redemptive return of women to their true status as divine creatures; as daughters of Israel. Although at the very least, her reference to the symbology of the moon demonstrates her concern for theological "completion."

Lily Montagu read and re-read Isaiah, and perhaps, as he had, experienced *mysterium tremendum*. The prophet was introduced to the new Yahweh. No longer would the deity be merely the "God of the armies" (*saboath*), nor would the divine presence remain a mere tribal deity biased in favor of the Israelites or confined to the Promised Land. The Hebrew God would fill the entire world.[119] Like Isaiah, Montagu, frequently described as a prophet herself, heard God's question: "Whom shall I send'? And replied, "Here am I; send me" (Isaiah 6:8). As we have seen, she imported to her reading of Isaiah, and its feminine and maternal perspectives, ideas that have come to be symbolized as the *Shekhinah* by Second and Third-Wave Jewish feminists. Like the prophet, she inspired a new vision of the divine presence for a progressive era, seeking to overcome the gender exclusionism of the tradition and its masculine defined theology. Thus, it is perhaps incorrect to situate the rise of Jewish feminist theology, and Jewish feminism's appropriation of the *Shekhinah*, in 1970s *America*. Montagu too, as we have seen, had already attempted to establish the *feminine* aspect of the divine presence in early twentieth-century *England*. Although Second-Wave Jewish feminists were unaware of Montagu's theological writing, and were not influenced by it, the connection, however tentative,[120]

---

[118] Waskow, "Feminist Judaism," 261-262, 266.

[119] Armstrong, *A History of God*, 53.

[120] I have borrowed Ann Heilmann's methodology in making this comment. Her study, alternatively, explores the conceptual links between

demonstrates an Anglo-Jewish foundation to the ongoing Jewish feminist theological project.

The *Shekhinah*, either as a feminine reunion between male and female within the divine self, or as a Goddess in her own right, was appropriated by Second-Wave Jewish feminists seeking to restore feminine characteristics, metaphors, and imagery to the divine presence. Rita Gross (who has now taken up Buddhism), Judith Plaskow, and Melissa Raphael have written extensively on the feminine aspect of the Godhead, as have Carol Christ,[121] Lynn Gottlieb,[122] and Marcia Falk.[123] For Arthur Waskow also, the restoration of the feminine has been vital to the redemption of Judaism and to the recovery of women's spiritual experience. Arthur Green likewise notes that feminine imagery has never been altogether absent from Judaism, although women's commentary on male produced literature is not sufficient to redress the gender imbalance.[124] Lily Montagu's liberation theology visualizes a universalistic God, both masculine and feminine, present in history, inspiring visions of liberty from one generation to the next. In the biblical period, the prophets, through their message of social and moral justice, and their remit to spiritualize Judaism, considered themselves the purveyors of God's will. Montagu entrusted this mission, however, to the Jewish women of her day. In effect, she associated all women with the feminine aspect of the divine presence, as had thirteenth-century Kabbalistic interpretations of *kavod* (glory), the codeword for *Shekhinah*.[125] "If God, as we believe, is the God of life, then we

---

New Woman fiction and Second-Wave feminism, see *New Woman Fiction: Women Writing First-Wave Feminism* (Basingstoke: Macmillan, 2000).

[121] See Carol Christ, "Women's Liberation and the Liberation of God: An Essay in Story Theology," in *The Jewish Woman*, 11-17.

[122] See Lynn Gottlieb, *She Who Dwells Within: A Feminist Vision of a New Judaism* (New York: HarperSanFrancisco, 1995).

[123] See Marcia Falk, *The Book of Blessings: New Jewish Prayers for Daily Life, the Sabbath, and the New Moon Festival* (San Francisco: HarperSanFrancisco, 1996); Marcia Falk, "Toward a Feminist-Jewish Reconstruction of Monotheism," *Tikkun* 4, no. 4 (July/August 1989): 53-56.

[124] Susannah Heschel, introduction to *On Being a Jewish Feminist*, 221.

[125] Arthur Green, "Bride, Spouse, Daughter: Images of the Feminine in Classical Jewish Sources," in *On Being A Jewish Feminist*, 256-258.

must seek to harmonize our lives with His."[126] The author of Kabbalah's *Gates of Lights*, Joseph Gikatillia also: "In the time of Abraham our father, of blessed memory, the *Shekhinah* was called Sarah. In the time of Isaac our father, she was called Rebecca. In the time of Jacob our father, she was called Rachel."[127]

---

[126] Lily Montagu, "For Reform Synagogue, Berlin," in *Four Centuries of Jewish Women's Spirituality: A Sourcebook*, eds. Ellen Umansky and Diane Ashton (Boston: Beacon Press, 1992), 157-158.

[127] Quoted by Green, "Bride, Spouse, Daughter," 258.

CONCLUSION: LILY MONTAGU AND THE JEWISH FEMINIST THEOLOGICAL PROJECT

The primary importance of this study has been to provide a long overdue corrective to the historiographical picture of Lily Montagu as a mere disciple of Claude Montefiore, and the false depiction of her as a dowdy, idealess social worker. These negative assumptions have been rejected and replaced with an account of Montagu's innovative theological discourse – *Shekhinah* – and re-evaluation of the role her writing, particularly her novel *Naomi's Exodus*, played in the formative years of Liberal Judaism. Finally, it is necessary to delineate Montagu's place, or legacy, in the Jewish feminist theological project that followed her death in 1963.

Indeed, Lily Montagu was certainly not a Goddess feminist; she recognized the masculine and *feminine* aspects of the divine presence. Writing in the early 1970s, the period often regarded as Second-Wave Jewish feminism, Adrienne Rich (who was actually raised Christian despite her Jewish ancestry) argues that feminine images of the divine demonstrate an awareness of women's intrinsic importance, their existence at the centre of the sacred, and their spiritual validation.[1] Comparably, Judith Plaskow would later argue that it is contradictory to assume that the Hebrew God transcends sexuality, that anthropomorphism is not to be taken literally, and at the same time to insist that new metaphors sully monotheism.[2] It is widely agreed, even by Plaskow, that the reinstatement of the Goddess will not necessarily lead to an enhancement of women's status

---

[1] Adrienne Rich, *Of Women Born: Motherhood as Experience and Institution* (New York: Norton, 1976), 93-94.

[2] Judith Plaskow, *Standing Again at Sinai: Judaism from a Feminist Perspective* (1990; rpt. New York: HarperCollins Publishers, 1991), 150.

or of their sense of self-worth.[3] The writer Cynthia Ozick expresses a "Maimonidean" discomfort toward the application of anthropomorphic discourses,[4] and warns against "applying positive attributes to God."[5] Indeed, Ozick rejects the assertion that the marginalization of women has anything to do with the tradition's theistic language.

Notably, the First-Wave was characterized by women's activism toward gaining political emancipation, and equal opportunities in education, the vote, the "Marriage Question," and the right to pursue formerly gender exclusive careers. Accordingly, Reform and Liberal Judaisms generally sought a degree of separation from the tradition, and the rejection, or qualification, of halakhah. The ethos of the Second-Wave, however, symbolized by an identifiable equal-rights movement, was characterized by the drive for equal access in all Jewish denominations, and the call for more opportunities in the workforce, as well as the ending of legal and unofficial sex discrimination. Indeed, the primary locus of the movement came from within the Conservative movement in the United States, largely through the feminist group Ezrat Nashim, or "help for women"; the name being a reference to the women's section in the synagogue. The group included such notables as Judith Plaskow, Paula Hyman, Elizabeth Koltun, Martha Ackelsberg, and Judith Hauptman. Their "Call for Change" to the Rabbinical Assembly of the Conservative movement demanded gender equalization in all areas of religion, including an end to women's disabilities in family halakhot, and questions regarding the necessity of the *mechitzah*, and women's exclusion from the *minyan*. Likewise, Reform activists complained that women were not being called up to read the Torah, and Orthodox feminists critiqued the inability of women to

[3] Tamar Ross, *Expanding the Palace of Torah: Orthodoxy and Feminism* (Waltham: Brandeis University Press, 2004), 131.

[4] Tova Hartman, *Feminism Encounters Traditional Judaism: Resistance and Accommodation* (Lebanon: Brandeis University Press, 2007), 71. See Cynthia Ozick, "Notes Toward Finding the Right Question," in On *Being A Jewish Feminist: A Reader*, ed. Susannah Heschel (1983; rpt. New York: Schocken Books, 1995), 120-51.

[5] Moses Maimonides, *The Guide of the Perplexed of Maimonides (1135-1204)*, trans. M. Friedlander (New York: Hebrew Publishing, 1953), 222.

initiate divorce, and their exclusion from authoritative interpretation of the sacred texts.

The feminist theologies of the Second-Wave were inescapably
post-Holocaust Jewish theologies. Ultra-Orthodoxy aside, these
theologies, in general, have demonstrated an understandable loss of
confidence in the divine. Certainly, some have attributed the mass
genocide to God's tendency to hide his face, and as a perplexing
mystery at the heart of the divine presence. Indeed, Eliezer Berkovits (Orthodox) assumed that God had inexplicably hidden his
face.[6] The Holocaust set the classical understanding of God the
gargantuan challenge of justifying how a perfectly free, all-good,
just God, active in history, caring, and with a special interest in his
people, could permit deliberate evil on such a grand scale. Faith
and reason have perhaps been surrendered, given that after
Auschwitz faith can no longer be considered rational. Accordingly,
while the classical God of rabbinic Judaism is an omnipresent God
of law, the post-Holocaust God is unpredictable, not omnipresent,
and subject to protest for being complicit in evil. Hence, most reflections on the Holocaust, such as those by Eliezer Berkovits,
Martin Buber, David Blumenthal, and Elie Wiesel, have envisaged a
God who is no guarantor of moral progress. For Irving Greenberg,
the Holocaust temporarily suspended the obligation to the Covenant.[7] Accordingly, Richard Rubenstein, for example, iterated the
"death of God" theology in his book, *After Auschwitz*,[8] though re-

---

[6] See Eliezer Berkovits, *Faith After the Holocaust* (New York: Ktav,
1973); Eliezer Berkovits, *With God in Hell: Judaism in the Ghettos and Deathcamps* (New York: Sanhedrin, 1979).

[7] Melissa Raphael, "Standing at a Demythologized Sinai? Reading
Jewish Feminist Theology Through the Critical Lens of Radical Ortho-
doxy," in *Interpreting the Postmodern: Responses to "Radical Orthodoxy,"* eds.
Rosemary Radford Ruether and Marion Grau (New York: T & T Clark,
2006), 206-07; See *Contemporary Jewish Responses to the Holocaust*, ed. Steven
Jacobs (Lanham: University Press of America, 1993).

[8] Nicholas de Lange, *Judaism* (Oxford: Oxford University Press,
1987), 122-23; see Richard Rubenstein, *After Auschwitz: Radical Theology and
Contemporary Judaism* (Indianapolis: Bobbs-Merill, 1966).

mained attracted to Jewish mysticism.[9] By contrast, Emil Fackenheim concludes that there is no theology that can explain the Holocaust.[10] Comparably, Ignaz Maybaum analyzed the Holocaust as an epoch making event through which human progress might be achieved.[11] However, despite efforts to regain a sense of divine presence and response, the overall mood in the post-Holocaust period has been bleak; what George Steiner has labeled the "recession of God."[12]

The constructive Jewish feminist theological project is a work in progress that might never be completed. The first serious issue confronted by the Second-Wave movement, perhaps unsurprisingly, related to the tradition's masculine imagery of God; an issue Lily Montagu had attempted to solve with her *Shekhinah* theology of gender completion. Indeed, Rita Gross argues that the omnipresent "he" could be replaced with female pronouns and images. She concludes that the exclusively masculine imagery of God tells us nothing about the deity, but merely explains the androcentricity of the tradition.[13] Gross rejects the use of neuter language to describe God, and suggests that "she" would be preferable.[14] Problematically, however, the use of "she" is equally as limiting as "he."[15] By contrast, Marcia Falk, utilizing feminist and Reconstruc-

---

[9] Karen Armstrong, *A History of God* (London: Vintage Books, 1999), 447.

[10] See Emil Fackenheim, *God's Presence in History: Jewish Affirmations and Philosophical Reflections* (New York: Harper & Row, 1972); Emil Fackenheim, *The Jewish Return Into History: Reflections in the Age of Auschwitz and a New Jerusalem* (New York: Schocken Books, 1978).

[11] De Lange, *Judaism*, 123-24. See Ignaz Maybaum, *The Face of God After Auschwitz* (Amsterdam: Polak and Van Gennep, 1965).

[12] Raphael, "Standing at a Demythologized Sinai," 207.

[13] See Rita Gross, "Androcentrism and Androgyny in the Methodology of the History of Religions," in *Beyond Androcentrism: New Essays on Women and Religion*, ed. Rita Gross (Missoula: Scholars Press, 1977), 7-21.

[14] Rita Gross, "Female God Language in a Jewish Context," in *Womanspirit Rising: A Feminist Reader in Religion*, eds. Carol Christ and Judith Plaskow (San Francisco: Harper & Row, 1979), 173.

[15] Armstrong, *A History of God*, 464. See Rita Gross, "Steps Toward Feminine Imagery of Deity in Jewish Theology," *Judaism* 30, no. 2 (Spring 1981): 183-93.

tionist perspectives, has developed a liturgical-theology symbolic of universal spirituality.[16] She concludes that the divine "is about a loss of otherness, a merging, a … release into the Wholeness."[17] This perspective assumes natural, or non-personal, interpretations of the divine presence as, for example, rock, tree, or lion,[18] and avoids the issue of gender.[19] Falk's blessings have been criticized for attempting to replace the rabbinically ordained formula: "*Barukh atah Adonai Eloheynu melekh ha-olam*" – "Blessed are you, Adonai/Lord our God, king of the universe." Instead, by addressing the community, Falk avoided having to refer to God as either masculine or feminine.[20] Rabbi Lynn Gottlieb, another liturgist-theologian, focuses on the *Shekhinah*, though has used a variety of metaphors to describe God. Indeed, she explores the use of Hebrew names with feminine meanings, such as "mother of wombs" (*Rahmana*) or "giver of life" (*Rakmaniah*). For example, her "Meditation on the Feminine Nature of Shekinah [she spells differently]":

Shekinah is She Who Dwells Within,
The force that binds and patterns creation.
She is Birdwoman, Dragonlady, Queen of the Heavens,
Opener of the way.
She is Mother of the Spiritworld, Morning and Evening Star.
Dawn and Dusk.

---

[16] Reconstructionism was inspired by Mordecai Kaplan and employs naturalistic theologies. The movement prefers to describe Judaism as a civilization as opposed to a religion. See Neil Gilman, *Sacred Fragments: Recovering Theology for the Modern Jew* (Philadelphia: Jewish Publication Society, 1990).

[17] Quoted by Rachel Adler, *Engendering Judaism: An Inclusive Theology and Ethics* (1998; rpt. Boston: Beacon Press, 2005), 90.

[18] See Tikva Frymer-Kensky, "On Feminine God-Talk," *Reconstructionist* 69 (Spring 1994): 49.

[19] Adler, *Engendering Judaism*, 90. Marcia Falk, "Toward a Feminist Jewish Reconstruction of Monotheism," *Tikkun* 4 (July/August 1989): 53-56.

[20] See Marcia Falk, *The Book of Blessings: New Jewish Prayers for Daily Life, the Sabbath, and the New Moon Festival* (San Francisco: HarperSanFrancisco, 1996).

She is Mistress of the Seas, Tree of Life,
Silvery Moon, Fiery Sun.
All these are Her names.
Shekinah is Changing Woman, Nature herself,
Her own Law and Mystery.
She is cosmos, dark hole, fiery moment of beginning.
She is dust cloud, nebulae, the swirl of galaxies.
She is gravity, magnetic field,
the paradox of waves and particles.
Shekinah is Grandmother, Grandfather,
    Unborn child.
Shekinah is life loving itself into being.
Shekinah is the eros of life, limitless desire,
Cosmic orgasm, wave upon wave of arousal,
hungry, and tireless, explosive and seductive,
the kiss of life and death, never dying.
Shekinah is home and hearth, root and rug,
the altar on which we light our candles.
We live here, in Her body.
She feeds multitudes from her flesh,
Water, sap, blood, milk, fluids of life, elixir of
    the wounded.
Shekinah is the catalyst of our passion,
Our inner spiritfire, our knowledge of self-worth,
Our call to authenticity.
She warms our hearts, ignites our vision.
She is the great turning round,
breathing and pulsating, pushing life toward
    illumination.
Woman and grave, End and Beginning.
All these are her names.[21]

Gottlieb also imports Kabbalistic, Canaanite and Native American traditions. According to Susannah Heschel, the problem of method is central to women engaging in Jewish feminist theology. Neither

---

[21] Lynn Gottlieb, *She Who Dwells Within: A Feminist Vision of a New Judaism* (New York: HarperSanFrancisco, 1995), 27-28.

theology, nor the most sacred texts, according to Heschel, can claim to be the explicit word of God. Rather, theological interpretations present the understandings of that word and will by a specific generation, transmitted, or mediated to later generations. Heschel suggests that women have will have to become part of the interpretation, heritage, and commentary of the tradition and perhaps a missing dimension of Jewish spirituality will be restored.[22]

Similar to Rita Gross, Judith Plaskow concludes that the Otherness of women is expressed through God-language. According to Plaskow, the traditional God, who supposedly transcends sexuality, is known through partial and selectivist masculine pronouns. By contrast, the female images of the Bible and the mystical tradition structure an underground stream that underlies the inadequacy of Jewish imagery, yet fails to transform its predominantly male perspective.[23] Plaskow concludes that recognition of the feminine aspect of the divine presence that can be incorporated into the Godhead is required. Hence, new understandings of God, Torah,[24] and Israel, along with new, gender inclusivist definitions of Jewishness are necessary.[25] Alternatively, Rachel Adler (initially Orthodox and then Reform) suggests that it might not be possible for Judaism to link with its past without affirming a personal God,[26] leading to questions of gender. Even Plaskow's self-identified Jewish feminist theology, *Standing Again at Sinai*, reads more as an ethical sociology of community than as a theology,[27]

---

[22] Susannah Heschel, introduction to *On Being A Jewish Feminist*, 217-18.

[23] See Saul Berman, "The Status of Women in Halakhic Judaism," *Tradition* 14 (Winter 1973): 5-28; David Feldman, "Women's Role and Jewish Law," *Conservative Judaism* 26 (Summer 1972): 29-39.

[24] See Eliezer Berkovits, *Jewish Women in Time and Torah* (Hoboken: Ktav, 1990).

[25] Judith Plaskow, "The Right Question is Theological," in *On Being a Jewish feminist*, 227-29, 231-32. See also Judith Plaskow, "The Coming of Lilith: Toward a Feminist Theology," in *Womanspirit Rising*, 198-209; *Feminist Perspectives on Jewish Studies*, eds. Lynn Davidman and Shelly Tenenbaum (New Haven: Yale University Press, 1994).

[26] Adler, *Engendering Judaism*, 90.

[27] See Plaskow, *Standing Again at Sinai*.

and perhaps generates more questions than it answers. For Plaskow, reform of halakhah is irrelevant, as the problem is inherent to
Judaism: if God is male and humanity is created in his image, maleness is considered the norm and women are perpetual "Other."[28]
However, twenty years after *Standing Again at Sinai*, the daughters
of the Second-Wave appear little interested in theology.[29] Perhaps
the recent anthology *New Jewish Feminism*, edited by Rabbi Elyse
Goldstein, is more encouraging.[30] A section is devoted to "Women
and Theology." This is not surprising as many of the authors are
themselves rabbis. Nonetheless, the conclusions drawn are perhaps
little different to the discussions of Jewish feminist theology ut-
tered during the 1980s and 1990s. As Donna Berman argues: "The
exclusion of women from traditional theological discourse within
Judaism reflected a denial of women's full humanity. The question
for Jewish feminist thinkers ... is, can we dislodge the manifesta-
tions of this denial and still have something that is recognizably
Jewish"?[31]

While the Second-Wave was germane to the creation of a
gendered theology, the actual project was highly amorphous. Feminist theologians continue to disagree over proper subject matter,
methods, categories, and sources.[32] Alienated by the tradition,
many Jewish feminists have focused on the historical Jewish woman, more or less, who can, from the resources of her personal experience, and socio-religious circle, produce alternative models of
God, and free readings of biblical and *aggadic* texts. This impetus,
combined with the postmodernist refusal of normativity, has rendered a normative Jewish feminist theology impossible to most

---

[28] Plaskow, "The Right Question," 226-28. See Paula Hyman, "The
Other Half: Women in the Jewish Tradition," *Response* 18 (Summer 1973):
67-75.

[29] See *Yentl's Revenge: The Next Wave of Jewish Feminism*, ed. Danya
Ruttenberg (New York: Seal Press, 2001).

[30] *New Jewish Feminism: Probing the Past, Forging the Future*, ed. Elyse
Goldstein (Woodstock: Jewish Lights Publishing, 2009).

[31] Donna Berman, "Major Trends in Jewish Feminist Theology: The
Work of Rachel Adler, Judith Plaskow, and Rebecca Alpert," in *New Jewish
Feminism*, 13.

[32] Adler, *Engendering Judaism*, xviii.

Jewish women.[33] More recently, Tamar Ross (Orthodox) has argued that the theology and imagery of any religion must be viewed in terms of its primary function: to capture the nature of the divine and to enhance the spiritual capacity of human beings for experiencing it. Questions of gender aside, the concepts of a transcendental divine presence do affect the way Jewish women relate to spirituality.[34] Perhaps the problem is that Jewish feminist theology, generally, is geared toward women achieving positions of leadership in the community, and to becoming full participants in Jewish study, ritual, and halakhah,[35] despite the fact that these are not matters of belief about God per se.

As we have seen, attempts to overcome the masculine imagery of God have ranged from Lily Montagu's early attempts at gender completion, to the importation of theological ideas unfamiliar to traditional Judaism. Ultimately, to refer to God as either "he" or "she" inevitably alienates, while neuter language can be equally problematic. It is perhaps unsurprising surprising that Melissa Raphael has concluded that Jewish feminism has emptied Judaism of theology. Certainly, Jewish feminist theology can only justify Judaism to women on the basis of its prophetic concern for social justice, of its being a spiritual connector between the foremothers of the current generation of Jewish women and their daughters, and as an imaginal and ritual focus for communal identity.[36] Thus, the creation of women's groups and spiritual collectives composed of women without theological training has proffered little with regard to the creation of a Jewish feminist theology or attempt to articulate the transformative immanence of the divine presence: the tran-

---

[33] Raphael, "Standing at a Demythologized Sinai," 201.

[34] Ross, *Expanding the Palace of Torah*, 135-36.

[35] Plaskow, "Calling All Theologians," in *New Jewish Feminism*, 8.

[36] Raphael, "Standing at a Demythologized Sinai," 200-01, 207 n27, 209-10, 214. See Daphne Hampson, *Theology and Feminism* (Cambridge: Blackwell, 1990); Arthur Green, "Keeping Feminist Creativity Jewish," *Sh'ma* 16, no. 305 (January 10, 1986): 33-35; T. Drorah Setel, "Feminist Reflections on Separation and Unity in Jewish Theology," *Journal of Feminist Studies in Religion* 2 (Spring 1986): 113-18.

scendent or *mysterium tremendum*,[37] that is, any para-doctrinal Jewish and feminist discourse on God as the basis of values and practices. Indeed, God has become sexually, politically, and historically elusive to women (Raphael's *The Female Face* seeks to combat this absence for women).[38] In sum, the Second and Third-Waves of Jewish feminism have been a product of the modern, and postmodern, shift toward egalitarianism and the focus upon the immediacy of women's experience.[39] This personally subjective impetus is partly a legacy of nineteenth and early twentieth-century Reform and Liberal Judaisms.

Lily Montagu's many sermons, theological essays, addresses, and monographs, demonstrate her belief in an immanent divine presence, and in a God with both paternal and maternal characteristics. Jewish feminist theology, since the 1970s, has perhaps continued Montagu's project, particularly, as we have seen, through the Jewish feminist movement's adoption of the immanent divine presence of their experience, the *Shekhinah*. This has generally stopped short of imaging the divine presence as a Goddess in her own right. Jewish feminist theology, and Liberal Judaism in particular, fully in Montagu's spirit, encourages the individual to experience the immanence of God on her own terms – to maintain a relationship, however tenuous as it might sometimes appear, to Judaism. As Alexandra Wright argues: "Feminist theology, like all theology, begins not with God, but with the self."[40] Indeed, Liberal Judaism's primary aim was to counter the secularization of the community through appeal to the reason and choice of the modern individual, and it still is.

---

[37] See Martha Ackelsberg, "Spirituality, Community and Politics: B'not Esh and the Feminist Reconstruction of Judaism," *Journal of Feminist Studies in Religion* 2 (Fall 1986): 109-20.

[38] Raphael, "Standing at a Demythologized Sinai," 197, 199, 200 f8. See Melissa Raphael, *The Female Face of God in Auschwitz: A Jewish Feminist Theology of the Holocaust* (London: Routledge, 2003).

[39] Raphael, "Standing at a Demythologized Sinai," 198.

[40] Alexandra Wright, "Alexandra Wright on the Feminist Revolution (1994)," in Jonathan Romain, *Reform Judaism and Modernity: A Reader* (London: SCM, 2004), 255.

GLOSSARY

aggadah: (lit. "narration") the (non-legal) sayings, legends, interpretations, and folklore of rabbinic literature.

Agunah: (lit. "bound," "tied," or "anchored") a deserted wife whose husband cannot be located to grant her a get.

Aliyah: (lit. "ascending") being called up to read the Torah aloud to the congregation, or can refer to immigration to Israel.

almanah: widow.

Amida: the central prayer of all four services: *shacharit* (morning), *mincha* (afternoon), *maariv* (evening), and *mussaf* (additional).

Amoraim: rabbis of the Talmudic period cited in the Gemara.

Ashkenazim (plural): (Hebrew corruption of "Allemagne") Jews of central and Eastern European origin.

ba'al: husband.

Bar Mitzvah: (lit. "Son of the Commandment") a boy who has obtained legal and religious maturity on his thirteenth birthday.

Bat Mitzvah: (lit. "Daughter of the Commandment") a girl who has obtained legal and religious maturity on her twelfth or thirteenth birthday.

berakhah: blessing.

Beth Din: (lit. "house of judgment") rabbinical court.

Binah: (lit. "understanding") *Sefirah* in Kabbalah associated to women and the feminine. In rabbinic Judaism *binah* refers to intuitive ability exceeding that in men.

Challah: ritual separation of a portion of dough.

chametz: leavened food.

chevrot: Ashkenazi fraternity.

Chukkat ha-goy: rabbinic prohibition on the use of gentile practices.

da-ta-kala: weak-minded.

derash: (lit. "exposition") inquire or seek.

Eshet Chayil: woman of worth or valor.

galut: exile.

gashmiut: physicality.

Gemara (Aramaic): (lit. "study") commentary on the Mishnah.

get: bill of divorce.

goy: (plural: *goyim*) non-Jew.

Haggadah: (lit. "telling") book from which the *seder* service is conducted on Pesach.

halakhah: (lit. "the way") Jewish law, including the oral tradition and the Torah; halakhic: connected to Jewish law; halakhot (plural).

Hanukkah: the Festival of Lights celebrating the Maccabean victory of 167 BCE.

Haskalah: (lit. "cultivation of the intellect") the Jewish Enlightenment.

Havdalah: ceremony to mark the end of a holiday.

hazzan: cantor.

herem: expulsion from the community.

hesed: kindness.

isha: woman.

Kabbalah: (lit. "received tradition") the Jewish mystical tradition.

Kaddish: prayer recited in the daily services and by mourners.

Kadosh: holiness.

Kadosh Barukh Hu: holy one, blessed be he.

Kashrut: (lit. "fit" or "proper") Jewish dietary law.

kavanah: spiritual intention, particularly during prayer.

kavod: honor, respect.

Kavod ha-tzibbur: the honor of the community.

Kedushah: holiness: the absolute otherness of God and the radical separation of the individual from the divine presence. *Kedushah* also refers to the third section of all *Amida* recitations.

Ketubah: (lit. "document") Jewish marriage contract.

kinyan: an act that formalizes a legal transaction.

Kol isha: law prohibiting men from hearing women sing.

kosher: food fit for consumption according to *Kashrut*.

Ladino: Mingling of Spanish and Hebrew sometimes spoken by the Sephardim.

lakahat: (lit. "to take") to marry.

lulav: palm branch.

Malkuth: Kingdom.

Mashiach: Messiah.

Maskilim: followers or adherents of the Jewish Enlightenment.

matzah: unleavened bread.

mechitzah: (lit. "divider") partition in some synagogues which separates the sexes.

menuha: haven.

midrash: (lit. "inquiry" or "investigation") Jewish biblical exegesis. Midrash (capitalized) refers to the body of rabbinic literature.

mikveh: ritual bath used by a married woman after menstruation.

minyan: (lit. "number") quorum of ten required for a prayer service. In most Orthodox communities only males count toward the *minyan*.

Mishnah: (lit. "repetition" or "study and review") second-century CE rabbinic legal codes collated by the Tannaim. The codes are the basis of the legal commentaries in the Talmud.

mitzvah: commandment; *mitzvot* (plural).

mohar: bride price.

Nashim: women or wives.

Nerot: the ritual lighting of candles.

Niddah: a menstruating woman required to undertake ritual immersion.

Onah: rabbinic sexual obligation a man owes his wife.

Ostjudische (German): immigrants.

Parzufim: "Countenances."

Pesach: Passover (commemorating the exodus from Egypt).

Purim: (lit. "lots") Festival commemorating Jewish deliverance from Haman's genocidal plans as told in the *Megillah*.

Rahmana: "mother of wombs."

Raknaiah: "giver of life."

responsa: legal opinions written by the rabbis.

Rosh Hashanah: (lit. "Head of the Year") beginning of the Jewish new year.

Rosh Hodesh: (lit. "Head of the Month") the New Moon, or first day of the Hebrew month.

ruhniut: spirituality.

Saboath: God of the armies.

Sanhedrin: supreme judicial body in ancient Jerusalem.

seder: order or arrangement.

Sefirah: ('Numeration') one of the ten stages of emanation of the Godhead in Jewish mysticism; *Sefirot* (plural).

Sephardim (plural): refers to Jews of Spanish or Portuguese origin.

Shabbat: (lit. "rest" or "cessation") the Jewish Sabbath, Friday evening to Saturday night; *Shabbos* (Yiddish).

Shabbat *Hamalka*: Shabbat bride.

shakan: to dwell or to pitch one's tent.

Shavuot: (lit. "weeks") the Festival of Weeks.

Shekhinah: Jewish mysticism describes her as the feminine aspect of the divine presence, although the biblical and rabbinic traditions refer to *Shekhinah* as the divine presence in the world.

Shema: (lit. "hear") refers to Deuteronomy 6:4 and is part of a prayer said twice daily: "Hear O Israel the Lord our God the Lord is One."

Shoah: (lit. "chaos," "tragedy," or "destruction") term increasingly used to refer to the Holocaust (Greek: "the destruction of life by fire"), the murder of six million Jews by the Nazis.

shofar: ram's horn trumpet.

shtetl (Yiddish): Eastern European village.

shul (Yiddish): synagogue.

shuttaf: partner.

Siddur: (lit. "order") prayer book.

Siddur Nashim: prayer book for women.

sukkah: booth.

Sukkot: the Feast of Booths.

tallit: (lit. "cloak") prayer shawl.

Talmud: (lit. "instruction" or "learning" or "study") sixty-three volumes containing the Mishnah and the Gemara. The Babylonian version was completed in approximately 500 BCE and the Jerusalem version in the preceding century.

Tanakh: The Hebrew Bible (thirty-nine books) including the Torah, *Nevi'im* (prophets), and *Ketuvim* (writings).

Tannaim: rabbis contributing to the Mishnah. These were the first generation of legists who edited the Oral Law, or Mishnah.

tefillah: prayer.

tefillin: phylacteries – small black cases containing biblical passages which are fixed to the head and arms by straps during weekday morning prayers (as commanded by Deuteronomy 6:4-7).

Tehinot (Yiddish): special prayers for women.

Tikkun: rehabilitation, repair, restoration, even redemption.

Tikkun Olam: (lit. "repair of the world") the imperative to contribute to the betterment of humankind.

Torah: (lit. "Teaching") the Five Books of Moses, the Written Law.

Tumah: ritual impurity.

Tzniut: modesty.

Yahweh: the name of God in Israel.

yeshivah: (lit. "sitting") traditional academy devoted to the study of the sacred texts.

Yesod: foundation.

Yiddish: the historical language of the Ashkenazim made up of primarily German and Hebrew, but also Aramaic, Old French, Old Italian, and Slavic languages.

Yom Kippur: Day of Atonement.

Zohar: (*Book of Splendor*) Kabbalah's main text.

BIBLIOGRAPHY

Archival Collections

London Metropolitan Archives, 40 Northampton Road, London. ACC/3529.

Published Works

Abrahams, Israel. *Jewish Life in the Middle* Ages. New York: Atheneum, 1973.

_____, and Claude Montefiore. *Aspects of Judaism: Being Sixteen Sermons*. London: Macmillan & Co., 1895.

_____, and S. Levy. *Macaulay on Jewish Disabilities*. Edinburgh: Jewish Historical Society of England, 1909.

A Ceremonies Sampler: New Rites, Celebrations and Observances of Jewish Women. Edited by Elizabeth Resnick Levine. San Diego: Women's institute for Continuing Jewish Education, 1991.

Ackelsberg, Martha. "Spirituality, Community and Politics: B'not Esh and the Feminist Reconstruction of Judaism." *Journal of Feminist Studies in Religion* 2 (Fall 1986): 109-20.

Adler, Rachel. *Engendering Judaism: An Inclusive Theology and Ethics*. 1998; rpt. Boston: Beacon Press, 2005.

_____. "The Jew Who Wasn't There." *Davka* (Summer 1971): 7-11.

Aguilar, Grace. *Collected Works*, 8 vols. London: R. Groomridge, 1861.

_____. *Grace Aguilar: Selected Writings*, edited by Michael Galchinsky. Peterborough: Broadview Press, 2003.

Alderman, Geoffrey. *Modern British Jewry*, new ed. Oxford: Clarendon Press, 1998.

_____. *The Federation of Synagogues, 1887-1987*. London: Federation of Synagogues, 1987.

_____. *The Jewish Community in British Politics*. Oxford: Oxford University Press, 1983.

Alpert, Rebecca. "Our Lives Are the Text: Exploring Jewish Women's Rituals." *Bridges*, 2 (Spring 1991): 66-80.

Angel, M. *The Law of Sinai and its Appointed Times*. London: 1858.

Ardis, Ann. *New Women, New Novels: Feminism and Early Modernism*. London: Rutgers UP, 1990.

A Reader of Early Liberal Judaism: The Writings of Israel Abrahams, Claude Montefiore, Lily Montagu and Israel Mattuck. Edited by Edward Kessler. London: Valentine Mitchell, 2004.

Armstrong, Karen. *A History of God: From Abraham to the Present: the 4000-Year Quest for God*. London: Vintage, 1999.

Bach, Alice. *Women in the Hebrew Bible: A Reader*. London: Routledge, 1999.

Baeck, Leo. *Judaism and Christianity*. Philadelphia: JPSA, 1960.

Banks, Olive. *Becoming a Feminist: The Social Origins of "First Wave" Feminism*. Brighton: Wheatsheaf Books, 1986.

_____. *Faces of Feminism: A Study of Feminism as a Social Movement*. Oxford: Basil Blackwell, 1988.

Baron, Salo. *A Social and Religious History of the Jews*, 18 vols., 2nd ed. New York: Columbia UP, 1952-1983.

Bayme, Steven. "Claude Montefiore, Lily Montagu and the Origins of the Jewish Religious Union." *Transactions of the Jewish Historical Society of England* 27 (1982): 61-71.

Beauvoir, Simone de. *The Second Sex*, translated by Howard Parshley. 1949; rpt. New York: Knopf, 1972.

Bebbington, David. *Evangelicalism in Modern Britain: A History from the 1730s to the 1980s*. London: Unwin Hyman, 2002.

Beer, Gillian. *Darwin's Plots: Evolutionary Narrative in Darwin, George Eliot and Nineteenth-Century Fiction*. London: Routledge & Kegan, 1983.

Bentwich, Norman. *Solomon Schechter: A Biography*. Philadelphia: Jewish Publication Society of America, 1940.

Berger, Michael. *Rabbinic Authority*. New York: Oxford University Press, 1998.

Berkovits, Eliezer. *Faith After the Holocaust*. New York: Ktav, 1973.

_____. *Jewish Women in Time and Torah*. Hoboken: Ktav, 1990.

_____. *With God in Hell: Judaism in the Ghettos and Deathcamps*. New York: Sanhedrin, 1979.

Berman, Saul. "The Status of Women in Halakhic Judaism." *Tradition* 14 (Winter 1973): 5-28

Bermant, Chaim. *The Cousinhood: The Anglo-Jewish Gentry*. London: Eyre & Spottiswoode, 1971.

Best, Geoffrey. *Mid-Victorian Britain, 1851-1875*. New York: Schocken Books, 1972.

Beyer, Bryan. *Encountering the Book of Isaiah*. Grand Rapids: Baker Academic, 2007.

Biale, Rachel. *Women and Jewish Law: The Essential Texts, Their History & Their Relevance for Today*. 1984; rpt. New York: Schocken Books, 1995.

Bitton-Jackson, Livia. *Madonna or Courtesan? The Jewish Woman in Christian Literature*. New York: Seabury, 1982.

Black, Eric. *The Social Politics of Anglo-Jewry, 1880-1920*. Oxford: Basil Blackwell, 1988.

Bland, Lucy. *Banishing the Beast: English Feminism and Sexual Morality 1885-1914*. London: Penguin Books, 1995.

Blumenthal, Aaron. "The Status of Women in Jewish Law." *Conservative Judaism* 31, no. 3 (Spring 1977): 24-40.

Blumenthal, David. *Facing the Abusing God: A Theology of Protest*. London: John Knox Press, 1993.

Bouten, Jacob. *Mary Wollstonecraft and the Beginnings of Female Emancipation in France and England*. Philadelphia: Porcupine Press, 1975.

Bowler, Maurice. "C. G. Montefiore and His Quest." *Judaism* 30, no. 4 (Fall 1981): 453-59.

———. *Claude Montefiore and Christianity*. Atlanta: Scholars Press, 1988.

Brantlinger, Patrick. "Nations and Novels: Disraeli, George Eliot, and Orientalism." *Victorian Studies* 35 (1992): 255-75.

Broner, Esther. *A Weave of Women*. New York: Holt, Rinehart, and Winston, 1978.

Brown, Heloise. *"The Truest Form of Pacifism": Pacifist Feminism in Britain, 1880-1902*. Manchester: Manchester University Press, 2003.

Bruggemann, Walter. *The Theology of the Book of Jeremiah*. Cambridge: Cambridge University Press, 2007.

Buber, Martin. *Hasidism and Modern Man*. New York: Horizon Press, 1958.

Bunt, Sidney. *Jewish Youth Work in Britain: Past, Present and Future*. London: Bedford Square Press, 1975.

Butler, Judith. *Gender Trouble: Feminism and the Subversion of Identity*. New York: Routledge, 1990.

Caird, Mona. *The Morality of Marriage and Other Essays on the Status and Destiny of Woman*. London: George Redway, 1897.

———. *The Daughters of Danaus*. 1894; rpt. New York: The Feminist Press, 1989.

Calisch, Edward. *The Jew in English Literature: As Author and Subject*. Port Washington: Kennikat Press, Inc., 1969.

Cantor, Aviva. *Bibliography on the Jewish Woman: A Comparative and Annotated Listing of Works Published 1900-1979*. New York: Biblio Press, 1979.

Cesarani, David. *The Jewish Chronicle and Anglo-Jewry, 1841-1991*. Cambridge: Cambridge University Press, 1994.

Chadwick, Owen. *The Secularization of the European Mind in the Nineteenth Century*. Cambridge: Cambridge University Press, 1975.

Cheyette, Bryan. *Constructions of the "Jew" in English Literature and Society: Racial Representations: 1875-1945*. Cambridge: Cambridge University Press, 1993.

———. "From Apology to Revolt: Benjamin Farjeon, Amy Levy and the Post-Emancipation Anglo-Jewish Novel, 1880-1990." *Transactions of the Jewish Historical Society of England* 24 (1982-86): 253-65.

———. "The Other Self: Anglo-Jewish Fiction and the Representation of Jews in England, 1875-1905." In *The Making of Modern Anglo-Jewry*, edited by David Cesarani, 97-111. Oxford: Basil Blackwell Ltd, 1990.

Childs, Brevard. *Isaiah: A Commentary*. Louisville: John Knox, 2001.

Christ, Carol. *Diving Deep and Surfacing: Women Writers on Spiritual Quest*. Boston: Beacon Press, 1980.

———, Ellen Umansky, and Anne Carr. "Roundtable Discussion: What Are the Sources of My Theology"? *Journal of Feminist Studies in Religion* 1, no. 1 (Spring 1985): 119-31.

Christianity and Rabbinic Judaism: A Parallel History of Their Origins and Early Development. Edited by Hershel Shanks. London: SPCK, 1993.

Clements, R. "The Community of God in the Hebrew Bible." In *The Blackwell Companion to the Hebrew Bible*, edited by Leo Perdue, 276-92. Malden: Blackwell Publishing Ltd, 2005.

Cohen, Gerson. "On the Ordination of Women." *Conservative Judaism* 32 (Summer 1979): 56-62.

Cohen, Lucy. *Some Recollections of C. G. Montefiore.* London: Faber & Faber, 1940.

Cohen, Samuel. *Jewish Theology: A Historical and Systematic Interpretation of Judaism and its Foundations.* New York: Van Gorcum, 1971.

Colby, Veneta. *The Singular Anomaly: Women Novelists of the Nineteenth Century.* New York: New York University Press, 1970.

Conrad, Eric. *Lily H. Montagu: Prophet of a Living Judaism.* New York: National Federation of Temple Sisterhoods, 1953.

Contemporary Jewish Responses to the Holocaust. Edited by Steven Jacobs. Lanham: University Press of America, 1993.

Cooper, Lamar. *Ezekiel.* Nashville: Broadman & Holman, 1994.

Cowen, Anne, and Roger Cowen. *Victorian Jews Through British Eyes.* Oxford: Oxford University Press, 1986.

Daughters of Abraham: Feminist Thought in Judaism, Christianity, and Islam. Edited by Yvonne Yazbeck Haddad and John Esposito. Gainesville: University Press of Florida, 2002.

Darwin, Charles. *The Origin of Species,* edited by Gillian Beer. 1859; rpt. Oxford: Oxford University Press, 1996.

Daughters of the King: Women and the Synagogue. Edited by Susan Grossman and Rivka Haut. Philadelphia: The Jewish Publication Society of America, 1992.

Davies, William. *Paul and Rabbinic Judaism: Some Elements in Pauline Theology.* London: SPCK, 1948.

Disraeli, Benjamin. *Tancred, or The New Crusade.* London: Longmans Green, 1880.

Dobson, Richard. *The Jews of Medieval York and the Massacre of March 1190.* York: Anthony's Hall Publications, 1974.

Dumbrell, William. "The Purpose of the Book of Isaiah." *Tyndale Bulletin* 36 (1985): 111-28.

Elbogen, Ismar. *Jewish Liturgy: A Comprehensive History,* translated by Raymond Schendlin. Philadelphia: Jewish Publication Society, 1993.

Emanuel, Charles. *A Century and a Half of Jewish History Extracted from the Minute Books of the London Committee of Deputies of the British Jews.* 1910; rpt. Charleston: BiblioBazaar, 2009.

Encyclopedia of American Jewish History, 2 vols. Edited by Stephen Norwood and Eunice Pollack. Oxford: Abc-Clio, 2008.

Endelman, Todd. "Communal Solidarity Among the Jewish Elite of Victorian London." *Victorian Studies* 28, no. 3 (Spring 1985): 491-526.

_____. *Comparing Jewish Societies*. Ann Arbor: University of Michigan Press, 1997.

_____. "English Jewish History." *Modern Judaism* 11 (1991): 91-109.

_____. *Radical Assimilation in English Jewish History: 1656-1945*. Bloomington: Indiana University Press, 1990.

_____. "The Frankaus of London: A Study of Radical Assimilation, 1837-1967." *Jewish History* 8, no. 1-2 (1994): 117-54.

_____. *The Jews of Britain, 1656 to 2000*. Berkeley: University of California Press, 2002.

_____. *The Jews of Georgian England: Tradition and Change in a Liberal Society*. Philadelphia: Jewish Publication Society of England, 1979.

Englander, David. "Anglicized Not Anglican: Jews and Judaism in Victorian Britain." In *Religion in Victorian Britain*, vol. 3, edited by Gerald Parsons, 235-73. Manchester: Manchester University Press, 1988.

Fackenheim, Emil. *God's Presence in History: Jewish Affirmations and Philosophical Reflections*. New York: Harper & Row, 1972.

_____. *The Jewish Return Into History: Reflections in the Age of Auschwitz and a New Jerusalem*. New York: Schocken Books, 1978.

Falk, Marcia. "Notes on Composing New Blessings: Toward a Feminist-Jewish Reconstruction of Prayer." *Journal of Feminist Studies in Religion* 3 (Spring 1987): 39-53.

_____. *The Book of Blessings: New Jewish Prayers for Daily Life, the Sabbath, and the New Moon Festival*. San Francisco: HarperSanFrancisco, 1996.

_____. "Toward a Feminist-Jewish Reconstruction of Monotheism." *Tikkun* 4, no. 4 (July/August 1989): 53-56.

_____. "What About God"? *Moment* 10 (March 1985): 32-36.

Feldhay Brenner, Rachel. *Writing as Resistance: Four Women Confronting the Holocaust: Edith Stein, Simone Weil, Anne Frank, Etty Hillesum*. Pennsylvania: Pennsylvania State University Press, 1997.

Feldman, David. *Englishmen and Jews: Social Relations and Political Culture, 1840-1914*. New Haven: Yale University Press, 1994.

_____. "Immigrants and Workers, Englishmen and Jews: Jewish Immigration to the East End of London, 1880-1906." Ph.D. diss., Cambridge University, 1985.

_____. "Women's Role and Jewish Law." *Conservative Judaism* 26 (Summer 1972): 29-39.

Felsenstein. Frank. *Anti-Semitic Stereotypes: A Paradigm of Otherness in English Popular Culture, 1660-1830.* Baltimore: John Hopkins UP, 1995.

Feminist Companion to Literature by Women. Edited by Virginia Blain, Isobel Grundy, and Patricia Clements. New Haven: Yale University Press, 1990.

Feminist Interpretation of the Bible. Edited by Letty Russell. Philadelphia: Westminster Press, 1985.

Feminist Perspectives on Jewish Studies. Edited by Lynn Davidman and Shelly Tenenbaum. New Haven: Yale University Press, 1994.

Finestein, Israel. *Anglo-Jewry in Changing Times: Studies in Diversity, 1840-1914.* London: Valentine Mitchell, 1999.

Fishman, William. *East End Jewish Radicals, 1875-1914.* London: Duckworth, 1975.

_____. *The Streets of East London.* London: Duckworth, 1979.

Four Centuries of Jewish Women's Spirituality: A Sourcebook. Edited by Ellen Umansky and Diane Ashton. Boston: Beacon Press, 1992.

Frankau, Julia [pseud. Danby, Frank]. *Dr. Phillips; A Maida Vale Idyll.* London: Vizetelly, 1887.

Frankel, Ellen. *The Five Books of Miriam: A Woman's Commentary on the Torah.* New York: G. P. Putnam, 1996.

Fretheim, Terence. *Jeremiah.* Macon: Smith & Helwys, 2002.

Frymer-Kensky, Tikva. *In the Wake of the Goddesses: Women, Culture and the Biblical Transformation of Pagan Myth.* New York: Free Press, 1992.

_____. "On Feminine God-Talk." *Reconstructionist* 69 (Spring 1994): 48-55.

_____. "The Bible, Goddesses, and Sex." *Midstream* 34 (October 1988): 20-23.

_____. "Toward a Liberal Theology of Halakha." *Tikkun* 10 (July/August 1995): 42-48.

Gainer, Bernard. *The Alien Invasion: The Origins of the Aliens Act of 1905.* New York: Crane, Russak & Co., 1972.

Galchinsky, Michael. "Otherness and Identity in the Victorian Novel." In *Victorian Literary Cultures: A Critical Companion,* edited by William Bake and Kenneth Womack, 458-507. Westport: Greenwood, 2002.

_____. "The New Anglo-Jewish Literary Criticism." *Prooftexts* 15, no. 3 (September 1995): 272-82.

_____. *The Origin of the Modern Jewish Woman Writer: Romance and Reform in Victorian England.* Detroit: Wayne State University Press, 1996.

Galton, Francis. *Hereditary Genius: An Inquiry into its Laws and Consequences.* London: Macmillan and Co., 1869.

Gartner, Lloyd. *The Jewish Immigrant in England, 1870-1914.* London: Simon Publications, 1973.

Gaster, Moses. *History of the Ancient Synagogue of the Spanish and Portuguese Jews.* London: 1901.

Gates, Judith, and Gail Reimer. *Reading Ruth: Contemporary Women Reclaim a Sacred Story.* New York: Ballantine Books: 1996.

Geiger, Abraham. *Judaism and Its History,* translated by Charles Newburgh. New York: Bloch, 1911.

Gender and Judaism: The Transformation of Tradition. Edited by Tamar Rudavsky. New York: New York University Press, 1995.

Gender Issues in Jewish Law: Essays and Responsa. Edited by Walter Jacob and Moshe Zemer. New York: Bergham Books, 2001.

Gertner, Meir. *Midrashim in the New Testament.* Manchester: Manchester University Press, 1962.

Gibson, Gwen, and Barbara Wyden. *The Jewish Wife.* New York: Peter H. Wyden, 1969.

Gilam, Abraham. *The Emancipation of the Jews in England: 1830-1860.* New York: Garland, 1982.

Gilbert, Alan. *Religion and Society in Industrial England: Church and Chapel in Social Change 1740-1914.* London: Longman, 1976.

Gilbert, Martin. *Exile and Return.* London: Weidenfeld and Nicolson, 1978.

Gilbert, Sandra, and Susan Gubar. *The Madwoman in the Attic: The Woman Writer and the Nineteenth-Century Literary Imagination,* 2nd ed. New Haven: Yale University Press, 2000.

Gill, Sean. *Women and the Church of England: From the Eighteenth Century to the Present.* London: SPCK, 1994.

Gilman, Neil. *Sacred Fragments: Recovering Theology for the Modern Jew.* Philadelphia: Jewish Publication Society, 1990.

Gilman, Sander. *Jewish Self-Hatred: Anti-Semitism and the Hidden Language of the Jews.* Baltimore: John Hopkins University Press, 1986.

_____. *The Jew's Body.* London: Routledge, 1991.

Gleadle, Kathryn. *The Early Feminists: Radical Unitarians and the Emergence of the Women's Rights Movement, 1831-51*. Basingstoke: Macmillan, 1995.

Goldenberg, Naomi. *Changing of the Gods: Feminism and the End of Traditional Religions*. Boston: Beacon Press, 1979.

Goldstein, Morris. *Jesus in the Jewish Tradition*. New York: Macmillan, 1950.

Gordon Kuzmack, Linda. Review of *Lily Montagu and the Advancement of Liberal Judaism: from Vision to Vocation*, by Ellen Umansky. *Journal for the Scientific Study of Religion* 24, no. 3 (1985): 337.

_____. *Woman's Cause: The Jewish Woman's Movement in England and the United States, 1881-1933*. Columbus: Ohio State University Press, 1990.

Gottlieb, Lynn. *She Who Dwells Within: A Feminist Vision of a New Judaism*. New York: HarperSanFrancisco, 1995.

_____. "The Secret Jew: An Oral Tradition of Women." *Conservative Judaism* 30, no. 3 (Spring 1976): 59-62.

Gould, Stephen Jay. *The Mismeasure of Man*. New York: W.W. Norton, 1981.

Grade, Chaim. *The Agunah*. Boston: Twayne, 1974.

Graetz, Heinrich. *History of the Jews*, 6 vols. 1895; rpt. Philadelphia: JPSA, 1956.

Green, Arthur. "Keeping Feminist Creativity Jewish." *Sh'ma* 16, no. 305 (January 10, 1986): 33-35.

Greenberg, Blu. *On Women and Judaism: A View from Tradition*. 1981; rpt. Philadelphia: The Jewish Publication Society of America, 1983.

_____. "Women's Liberation and Jewish Law." *Lilith* 1, no. 1 (Fall 1976): 16-19, 42-43.

Gross, Chaim. *The Book of Isaiah*. Philadelphia: Jewish Publication Society, 1972.

Gross, Rita. "Androcentrism and Androgyny in the Methodology of the History of Religions." In *Beyond Androcentrism: New Essays on Women and Religion*, edited by Rita Gross, 7-21. Missoula: Scholars Press, 1977.

_____. "Hindu Female Deities as a Resource in the Contemporary Rediscovery of the Goddess." *Journal of the American Academy of Religion* 46, no. 3 (September 1978): 269-91.

_____. "Steps Toward Feminine Imagery of Deity in Jewish The-
ology." *Judaism* 30, no. 2 (Spring 1981): 183-93.

Gutwein, Daniel. *The Divided Elite: Economics, Politics and Anglo-Jewry,
1882-1917.* Leiden: Brill Academic Publishers, 1992.

Guy, Frances. *Women of Worth: Jewish Women in Britain.* Manchester:
Manchester Jewish Museum, 1992.

Hackett, Jo Ann. "Can a Sexist Model Liberate Us? Ancient Near
Eastern 'Fertility' Goddesses." *Journal of Feminist Studies in Religion* 5 (Spring 1989): 65-76.

Hagner, Donald. *The Jewish Reclamation of Jesus: An Analysis & Critique of the Modern Jewish Study of Jesus.* Grand Rapids: Academie
Books, 1984.

Hamelsdorf, Ora, and Sandra Adelsberg. *Women and Jewish Law:
Bibliography.* New York: Biblio Press, 1980.

Hampson, Daphne. *Feminism and Theology.* Oxford: Basil Blackwell,
1990.

Hanson, A. "Claude Montefiore, a Modern Philo." *The Modern
Churchman* 20, no. 3 (Spring 1977): 109-14.

Harris, Emily. *Benedictus,* 2 vols. London: George Bell, 1887.

_____. *Estelle,* 2 vols. London: George Bell, 1878.

Harrison, Brian. *Separate Spheres: The Opposition to Women's Suffrage in
Britain.* London: Croom Helm, 1978.

Hartman, Tova. *Feminism Encounters Traditional Judaism; Resistance and
Accommodation.* New England: UPNE, 2007.

Hauptmann, Judith. *Rereading the Rabbis: A Woman's Voice.* Oxford:
Westview Press, 1998.

Hawkins, Mike. *Social Darwinism in European and American Thought,
1860-1915.* Cambridge: Cambridge University Press, 1997.

Hear Our Voice: Women in the British Rabbinate. Edited by Sybil Sheridan. Columbia: University of South Carolina Press, 1998.

Heasman, Kathleen. *Evangelicals in Action: An appraisal of Their Social
Work.* London: G. Bles, 1962.

Heeney, Brian. *The Women's Movement in the Church of England, 1850-
1930.* Oxford: Clarendon Press, 1988.

Heilmann, Ann. *New Woman Fiction: Women Writing First-Wave Feminism.* Basingstoke: Macmillan, 2000.

Heller, James. *Isaac Mayer Wise, His Life, Work, and Thought.* New
York: Union of American Hebrew Congregations, 1966.

Henry, Sondra, and Emily Taitz. *Written Out of History.* New York:
Bloch Publishing Co., 1978.

Herford, R. Travers. *Christianity in Talmud and Midrash*. 1908; rpt. Clifton: Reference Book Publishers, 1966.

Heschel, Susannah. *Abraham Geiger and the Jewish Jesus*. Chicago: University of Chicago Press, 1998.

_____. "Current Issues in Jewish Feminist Theology." *Jewish-Christian Relations: A Documentary Survey* 19, no. 2 (1986): 27-31.

Hetherington, Naomi. "New Woman, 'New Boots': Amy Levy as Child Journalist." *Cambridge Studies in Nineteenth Century Literature and Culture* 47 (2005): 254-68.

Hickok, Kathleen. *Representations of Women: Nineteenth-Century British Women's Poetry*. Westport: Greenwood Press, 1984.

Hill, Michael. *The Religious Order: A Study of Virtuoso Religion and its Legitimation in the Nineteenth Century Church of England*. London: Heinemann Educational Books, 1973.

Hilton, Boyd. *The Age of Atonement: The Influence of Evangelicalism on Social and Economic Thought, 1785-1865*. Oxford: Clarendon Press, 1988.

Hilton, Michael. *The Christian Effect on Jewish Life*. London: SCM Press Ltd, 1994.

_____, and Marshall Gordian. *The Gospels and Rabbinic Judaism*. London: SCM Press, 1988.

Hoffman, Lawrence. *The Canonization of the Synagogue Service*. Notre Dame: University of Notre Dame Press, 1979.

Hoffman, Matthew. *From Rebel to Rabbi: Reclaiming Jesus and the Making of Modern Jewish Culture*. Stanford: Stanford University Press, 2007.

Hollis, Patricia. *Women in Public 1850-1900*. London: Allen and Unwin, 1979.

Holmes, Colin. *Anti-Semitism in British Society, 1876-1939*. London: Edward Arnold, 1979.

Holy Bible containing the Old and New Testaments, King James Version. Cambridge: Cambridge University Press.

Homa, Bernard. *Orthodoxy in Anglo-Jewry, 1880-1940*. London: Jewish Historical Society of Great Britain, 1969.

Hunt Beckman, Linda. *Amy Levy: Her Life and Letters*. Athens: Ohio University Press, 2000.

Hyamson, Albert. *The Sephardim of England*. London: Methuen, 1951.

Hyman, Naomi. *Biblical Women in the Midrash: A Sourcebook*. Northvale: Jason Aronson, 1998.

Hyman, Paula. *Gender and Assimilation in Modern Jewish History: The Roles and Representations of Women.* Seattle: University of Washington Press, 1995.

_____. "The Other Half: Women in the Jewish Tradition." *Conservative Judaism* 26, no. 4 (Summer 1972): 14-21.

Jacobs, Joseph. *The Jews of Angevin England.* Farnborough: Gregg International Publishers, 1969.

Jay, Elizabeth. *The Religion of the Heart: Anglican Evangelicalism and the Nineteenth-Century Novel.* Oxford: Clarendon Press, 1975.

Jelen, Sheila. "Reading and Writing Women: Minority Discourse in Feminist Jewish Literary Studies." *Prooftexts* 25, no. 1/2 (Winter/Spring 2005): 195-209.

Jenkins, Ruth. *Reclaiming Myths of Power: Women Writers and the Victorian Spiritual Crisis.* Lewisburg: Bucknell University Press, 1995.

"Jewish Religious Union Circular." *Jewish Chronicle,* June 6, 1902, 11.

Jewish Tradition and the Challenge of Darwinism. Edited by Geoffrey Cantor and Marc Swetlitz. Chicago: University of Chicago Press, 2006.

Jewish Women: a Comprehensive Historical Encyclopedia. Edited by Paula Hyman. Jerusalem: Shalvi Pub., 2006.

Jewish Women in Historical Perspective. Edited by Judith Baskin. Detroit: Wayne State University Press, 1991.

Jews and Gender: The Challenge to Hierarchy. Edited by Jonathan Frankel. Oxford: Oxford University Press, 2000.

Joseph, Nathan. *Essentials of Judaism,* Papers for Jewish People, 1. London: Jewish Religious Union, 1906.

Jusova, Iveta. *The New Woman and the Empire.* Columbus: Ohio State University Press, 2005.

Kahana, Kalman. *Daughters of Israel: Laws of Family Purity.* New York: Feldheim, 1970.

Kaplan, Marion. *The Jewish Feminist Movement in Germany: The Campaigns of the Jüdischer Frauenbund, 1904-1938.* Westport: Greenwood Press, 1979.

Kaplan, Mordecai. *Judaism as a Civilization: Toward a Reconstruction of American Jewish Life.* New York: Schocken, 1967.

Katz, David. *Philo-Semitism and the Readmission of the Jews to England, 1603-1655.* Oxford: Oxford University Press, 1982.

Keck, Leander. *Who Is Jesus? History in Perfect Tense.* Columbia: University of South Carolina Press, 2000.

Keith, Graham. *Hated Without a Cause? A Survey of Anti-Semitism.* Carlisle: Paternoster Press, 1997.

Kessler, Edward. *An English Jew: The Life and Writings of Claude Montefiore.* London: Vallentine Mitchell, 1989.

Kien, Jenny. *Reinstating the Divine Woman in Judaism.* Florida: Universal Publishers/upublish.com, 2000.

Klein, Charlotte. *Anti-Judaism in Christian Theology.* Philadelphia: Fortress, 1975.

Knox, Robert. *The Races of Men: A Fragment.* Philadelphia: Lea and Blanchford, 1850.

Kraditor, Aileen. *The Ideas of Woman Suffrage Movement 1890-1920.* New York: Columbia University Press, 1965.

Krell, Marc. *Intersecting Pathways: Modern Jewish Theologians in Conversation with Christianity.* Oxford: Oxford University Press, 2003.

Lange, Nicholas de. *Judaism.* Oxford: Oxford University Press, 1987.

Langmuir, Gavin. *Toward a Definition of AntiSemitism.* London: University of California Press, 1996.

Langton, Daniel. *Claude Montefiore: His Life and Thought.* London: Vallentine Mitchell, 2002.

Lansbury, Carol. *The Old Brown Dog: Women, Workers, and Vivisection in Edwardian England.* Wisconsin: The University of Wisconsin Press, 1985.

Laytner, Anson. *Arguing with God: A Jewish Tradition.* Northvale: J. Aronson, 1990.

Ledger, Sally. *The New Woman: Fiction and Feminism at the Fin de Siècle.* Manchester: Manchester University Press, 1997.

Leighton, Angela. "'Because Men Made the Laws.' The Fallen Woman and the Woman Poet." *Victorian Poetry* 27, no. 2 (Summer 1989): 109-27.

_____. *Victorian Women Poets: Writing Against the Heart.* Charlottesville: University Press of Virginia, 1992.

Lerner, Gerder. *The Majority Finds Its Past: Placing Women in History.* New York: Oxford University Press, 1979.

Lerner, Michael. *Jewish Renewal.* New York: G. P. Putnam Sons, 1994.

Levinas, Emmanuel. "Judaism and the Feminine Element," translated by Edith Wyschogrod. *Judaism* 18 (1969): 30-38.

Levine, Philippa. *Feminist Lives in Victorian England: Private Roles and Public Commitment.* Oxford: Basil Blackwell, 1990.

Levitt, Laura. *Jews and Feminism: The Ambivalent Search for Home*. New York: Routledge, 1997.

Levy, Amy. "Middle-Class Jewish Women of To-Day (By a Jewess)." *Jewish Chronicle*, September 17, 1886, 7.

_____. *Reuben Sachs: A Sketch*. London: Macmillan, 1888.

_____. *The Romance of a Shop*, edited by Susan David Bernstein. 1888; rpt. Ontario: Broadview Press, 2006.

Levy, Nellie. *The West Central Story and Its Founders the Hon. Lily H. Montagu CBE, JP, DD and the Hon. Marian Montagu: 1893-1968*, club pamphlet. London: Leeway Business Services.

Lewis, Jane. *Women and Social Action in Victorian England*. Aldershot: Edward Elgar, 1991.

Lichtenstein, Diane. *Writing Their Nations: The Tradition of Nineteenth-Century American Jewish Women Writers*. Bloomington: Indiana University Press, 1992.

Lipman, V. *A Century of Social Service 1859-1959 – The History of the Jewish Board of Guardians*. London: Routledge and Kegan Paul, 1959.

_____. *A History of the Jews in Britain Since 1858*. Leicester: Leicester University Press, 1990.

_____. *Social History of the Jews in England, 1850-1950*. London: Watts, 1954.

_____. *The Jews of Medieval England*. London: Jewish Historical Society of England, 1967.

_____. *Three Centuries of Anglo-Jewish History*. London: Jewish Historical Society of England, 1961.

Lodahl, Michael. *Shekhinah Spirit: Divine Presence in Jewish and Christian Religions*. New York:, Paulist Press, 1992.

Lorber, Judith. *Gender Inequality: Feminist Theories and Politics*. Los Angeles: Roxbury Publishing, 1998.

Lyndon Stanley, Mary. *Feminism, Marriage and the Law in Victorian England, 1850-95*. Princeton: Princeton University Press, 1993.

Maccoby, Hyam. *Jesus the Pharisee*. London: SCM Press, 2003.

_____. *The Mythmaker: Paul and the Invention of Christianity*. London: Weidenfeld and Nicolson, 1986.

MacDonald, Ramsay. *Margaret Ethel MacDonald: a Memoir*. London: Hodder & Stoughton, 1913.

Maimonides, Moses. *The Guide of the Perplexed of Maimonides (1135-1204)*, translated by M. Friedlander. New York: Hebrew Publishing, 1953.

Malthus, Thomas. *An Essay on the Principle of Population*, edited by Anthony Flew. Harmondsworth: Penguin Books, 1982.

Manuel, Frank. *The Broken Staff: Judaism Through Christian Eyes*. Cambridge: Harvard University Press, 1992.

Marcus, Jacob. *The Jew in the Medieval World*. New York: Atheneum, 1974.

Marcus, Sharon. *Between Women: Friendship, Desire, and Marriage in Victorian England*. New Jersey: Princeton University Press, 2007.

Marks, L. *Working Wives and Working Mothers: A Comparative Study of Irish and East European Jewish Married Women's Work and Motherhood in East London 1870-1914*. London: PNL Press, 1990.

Marriage and Impediments to Marriage in Jewish Law. Edited by Walter Jacob and Moshe Zemer. Tel Aviv: Rodef Shalom Press, 1997.

Mattuck, Israel. *The Essentials of Liberal Judaism*. London: Routledge & Kegan Paul, 1947.

Maybaum, Ignaz. *The Face of God After Auschwitz*. Amsterdam: Polak and Van Gennep, 1965.

McClintock Fulkerson, Mary. *Changing the Subject: Women's Discourses and Feminist Theology*. Minneapolis: Fortress, 1994.

Mein, Andrew. *Ezekiel and the Ethics of Exile*. Oxford: Oxford University Press, 2006.

Meiselman, Moshe. *Jewish Woman in Jewish Law*. New York: Ktav Publishing House, 1978.

Menachem, Brayer. *The Jewish Woman in Rabbinic Literature: A Psychohistorical Perspective*. New Jersey: Ktav Publishing House, 1986.

Metzger, Deena. *What Dinah Thought*. New York: Viking Penguin, 1989.

Meyer, Michael. *Responses to Modernity: A History of the Reform Movement in Judaism*. New York: OUP, 1988.

Midgley, Clare. "Ethnicity, 'Race' and Empire." In *Women's History: Britain, 1850-1945: An Introduction*, edited by June Purvis, 247-75. London: Routledge, 2004.

Modder, Frank. *The Jew in the Literature of England*. Philadelphia: Jewish Publication Society of America, 1960.

Montagu, Lily. *A Little Book of Comfort: For Jewish People in Times of Sorrow*. London: Wightman and Co, 1948.

———. *Broken Stalks*. London: R. Brimley Johnson, 1902.

_____. "Home Worship and Its Influence on Social Work," paper read at the Conference of Jewish Women. Southampton: Cot & Sharland, May 1902.

_____. *In Memory of Lily H. Montagu: Some Extracts from Her Letters and Addresses*, edited by Eric Conrad. Amsterdam: Polak and Van Gennep, 1967.

_____. "In the Beginning." In *The First Fifty Years: A Record of Liberal Judaism in England, 1900-1950*, 3-6. Keighley: John Wadsworth, 1950.

_____. *Letters to Anne and Peter*. London: Mamelok Press, 1944.

_____. "Liberal Judaism in Relation to Women." *Jewish Religious Union Bulletin* (June 1914), 5.

_____. *Lily Montagu: Sermons, Addresses, Letters, and Papers*, edited by Ellen Umansky. New York: Edwin Mellen Press, 1985.

_____. "Mazzini: The Man and the Teacher." *Present Day Papers* 4 (June 1901): 188-209.

_____. *My Club and I: the Story of the West Central Jewish Club*. London: Herbert Joseph, 1941.

_____. *Naomi's Exodus*. London: T. Fisher Unwin, 1901.

_____. "Pioneer Personalities of the J.R.U." *Liberal Jewish Monthly* 1, no. 3 (June 1929): 27-29.

_____. *Prayers for Jewish Working Girls*. London: Wertheimer, Lea & Co., 1895.

_____. *Religious and Social Service*, Papers for Jewish People, 18. London: Jewish Religious Union, 1918.

_____. *Religious Education in the Home*, Papers for Jewish People, 26. London: Jewish Religious Union, 1925.

_____. *Samuel Montagu, First Baron Swaythling: A Character Sketch*. London: Truslove and Hanson Limited.

_____. "Social Teaching of Judaism for To-Day." In *In Spirit and In Truth: Aspects of Judaism and Christianity*, edited by George Yates, 105-19. London: Hodder & Stoughton, 1934.

_____. "Some Thoughts on Home Worship." *Liberal Jewish Monthly* 8, no. 4 (June 1937): 22-23.

_____. "Spiritual Possibilities of Judaism To-Day." *Jewish Quarterly Review* 11 (1899): 216-31.

_____. *Suggestions for Sabbath Eve Celebrations*, 2nd ed. London: Wightman & Co., 1944.

_____. "The Conception of Prayer." In *Aspects of Progressive Jewish Thought, with an Introduction by Israel Mattuck*, 94-98. London: Victor Gollancz, 1954.

_____. "The Condition of the Individual in a Socialist State." *Westminster Review* 146 (October 1896): 439-45.

_____. *The Faith of a Jewish Woman*. London: George Allen & Unwin, 1943.

_____. "The Girl in the Background." In *Studies of Boy Life in Our Cities*, edited by E. Urwick, 233-54. 1904; rpt. New York: Garland Publishing Inc., 1980.

_____. "The History of Liberal Judaism in England." *The Judaeans* 4 (1933): 152-62.

_____. *The Jewish Religious Union and Its Beginnings*, Papers for Jewish People, 27. London: Jewish Religious Union, 1927.

_____. "The Jewish Religious Union in War Time." *Liberal Jewish Monthly* 10, no. 6 (November 1939): 55-56.

_____. "The Just Shall Live by His Faith." *Liberal Jewish Monthly* 17, no. 4 (April 1946): 29-30.

_____. "The Letter Which Started the Jewish Religious Union." *Liberal Jewish Monthly* 27, no. 1 (January 1956): 4.

_____. *The Memory of Lily Montagu: Some Extracts from Her Letters and Addresses*, collected by Eric Conrad. Amsterdam: Polak & Van Gennep, 1967.

_____. "The Place of Judaism in the Club Movement." *Liberal Jewish Monthly* 1, no. 3 (June 1929): 27-29.

_____. "The Power of Quiet." *Liberal Jewish Monthly* 5, no. 4 (July 1934): 28-30.

_____. *The Relation of Faith to Conduct in Jewish Life*, Papers for Jewish People, 2. London: Jewish Religious Union, 1907.

_____. *The World Union for Progressive Judaism: The Story of its First 25 Years – 1926 until 1951*. London: World Union for Progressive Judaism, 1951.

_____. *Thoughts on Judaism*. London: R. Brimley Johnson, 1904.

_____. *What Can A Mother Do? and Other Stories*. London: George Routledge & Sons, 1926.

_____. "Why Pray? An Answer." *Liberal Jewish Monthly* 3, no. 1 (April 1931): 4-5.

Montefiore, Charlotte. *Caleb Asher*. Philadelphia: Jewish Publication Society, 1845.

Montefiore, Claude. *Assimilation: Good and Bad*, Papers for Jewish People, 9. London: Jewish Religious Union, 1914.

_____. *Is There a Middle Way?* Papers for Jewish People, 23. London: Jewish Religious Union, 1920.

_____. *Judaism and Democracy*, Papers for Jewish People, 13. London: Jewish Religious Union, 1917.

_____. *Judaism, Unitarianism, and Theism*, Papers for Jewish People, 4. London: Jewish Religious Union, 1908.

_____. "Liberal Judaism." *Jewish Quarterly Review* 20 (April 1908): 363-90.

_____. *Liberal Judaism and Authority*, Papers for Jewish People, 22. London: Jewish Religious Union, 1919.

_____. *Liberal Judaism and Convenience: and Do Liberal Jews Teach Christianity?* Papers for Jewish People, 25. London: Jewish Religious Union, 1924.

_____. *Liberal Judaism and Hellenism: and Other Essays*. London: Macmillan, 1918.

_____. *Liberal Judaism: An Essay*. London: Macmillan, 1903.

_____. *Outlines of Liberal Judaism*. London: Macmillan & Co., 1912.

_____. *Rabbinic Literature and Gospel Teaching*. London: Macmillan, 1930.

_____. *Some Elements in the Religious Teaching of Jesus*. London: Macmillan, 1910.

_____. "The Desire for Immortality." *Jewish Quarterly Review* 14 (October 1901): 96-110.

_____. *The Jewish Religious Union: Its Principles and Its Future*. Papers for Jewish People, 19. London: Jewish Religious Union, 1918.

_____. *The Justification of Liberal Judaism*, Papers for Jewish People, 21. London: Jewish Religious Union, 1919.

_____. *The Old Testament and After*. London: Macmillan, 1923.

_____. *The Place of Judaism in the Religions of the World*, Papers for Jewish People, 12. London: Jewish Religious Union, 1916.

Morell, Samuel. "An Equal or a Ward: How Independent is a Married Woman According to Rabbinic Law"? *Jewish Social Studies* 44, no. 3-4 (Summer/Fall 1982): 189-210.

Morgan, Sue. *A Passion for Purity: Ellice Hopkins and the Politics of Gender in the Late-Victorian Church*. Bristol: University of Bristol, 1999.

_____. "The Power of Womanhood: Religion and Sexual Politics in the Writings of Ellice Hopkins." In *Women of Faith in Victo-*

rian Culture: Reassessing the Angel in the House, edited by Anne Hogan and Andrew Bradstock, 209-24. Basingstoke: Macmillan Press, 1998.

Moss, Celia, and Marion Moss. *Tales of Jewish History*, 3 vols. London: Miller and Field, 1843.

Myers, Michael. *Judaism Within Modernity: Essays on Jewish History and Religion*. Detroit: Wayne State University Press, 2001.

New Jewish Feminism: Probing the Past, Forging the Future. Edited by Elyse Goldstein. Woodstock: Jewish Lights Publishing, 2009.

Newman, Aubrey. *The Board of Deputies of British Jews, 1760-1985*. London: Vallentine Mitchell, 1987.

_____. *The United Synagogue, 1870-1970*. London: Routledge and Kegan Paul, 1977.

Nolan Fewell, Danna, and David Gunn. "'A Son is Born to Naomi': Literary Allusions and Interpretation in the Book of Ruth." *Journal for the Study of the Old Testament* 40 (1988): 99-108.

Novick, Leah. *On the Wings of Shekhinah: Rediscovering Judaism's Divine Feminine*. Wheaton: Quest Books, 2008.

Odell, Margaret, and John Strong. *The Book of Ezekiel: Theological and Anthropological Perspectives*. Atlanta: Society of Biblical Literature, 2000.

On Being A Jewish Feminist: A Reader. Edited by Susannah Heschel. 1983; rpt. New York: Schocken Books, 1995.

Ostow, Mortimer. "Women and Change in Jewish Law." *Conservative Judaism* 29, no. 1 (Fall 1974): 5-12.

Oxford Dictionary of National Biography, 38: Meyrick – Morande. Edited by H. Matthew and Brian Harrison. Oxford: Oxford University Press, 2004.

Panitz, Esther. *The Alien in Their Midst: Images of Jews in English Literature*. London: Associated University Presses, 1981.

Pankhurst, E. *The Suffragette Movement*. London: Virago, 1977.

Patai, Raphael. *The Hebrew Goddess*. New York: Ktav Publishing House, 1967.

Penina, Adelman. *Miriam's Well, Rituals for Jewish Women Around the Year*. Fresh Meadows: Biblio Press, 1986.

Petuchowski, Jakob. *Prayerbook Reform in Europe: The Liturgy of European Liberal and Reform Judaism*. New York: World Union for Progressive Judaism, 1963.

Philipson, David. *The Jew in English Fiction.* Cincinnati: Robert Clarke and Co., 1889.

_____. *The Reform Movement in Judaism: A Sourcebook of its European Origins.* New York: World Union for Progressive Judaism, 1963.

Philosemitism, Antisemitism and "the Jews": Perspectives from the Middle Ages to the Twentieth Century. Edited by Tony Kushner and Nadia Valman. Aldershot: Ashgate Publishing Limited, 2004.

Picciotto, James. *Sketches of Anglo-Jewish History.* London: Soncino Press, 1956.

Plaskow, Judith. "Feminist Anti-Judaism and the Christian God." *Journal of Feminist Studies in Religion* 7, no. 2 (1991): 99-108.

_____. "Halakha as a Feminist Issue." *The Melton Journal* 22 (Fall 1987): 3-5, 25.

_____. *Standing Again at Sinai: Judaism from a Feminist Perspective.* 1990; rpt. New York: HarperCollins Publishers, 1991.

Plaut, W. Gunter. *The Rise of Reform Judaism.* New York: World Union for Progressive Judaism, 1963.

Polack, Maria. *Fiction Without Romance; or the Locket Watch,* 2 vols. London: Effingham Wilson, 1830.

Pollins, Harold. *Economic History of the Jews in England.* Rutherford: Farleigh Dickinson University Press, 1982.

Poupko, Chana, and Devorah Wohlgelernter. "Women's Liberation – An Orthodox Response." *Tradition* 15, no. 4 (Spring 1976): 45-52.

Prayers, Psalms, and Hymns for Jewish Children. Edited by Lily Montagu and Theodora Davis. London: Eyre & Spottiswoode, 1901.

Prell, Riv-Ellen. "The Dilemma of Women's Equality in the History of Reform Judaism." *Judaism* 30, no. 4 (Fall 1981): 418-26.

_____. "The Vision of Woman in Classical Reform Judaism." *Journal of the American Academy of Religion* 50, no. 4 (1983): 575-89.

_____. *Women Remaking American Judaism.* Detroit: Wayne State University Press, 2007.

Prins, Yopie. *Victorian Sappho.* Princeton: Princeton University Press, 1999.

Prochaska, Frank. *Women and Philanthropy in Nineteenth-Century England.* Oxford: Clarendon Press, 1980.

_____. "Women in English Philanthropy, 1790-1830." *International Journal of Social History* 19 (1974): 426-45.

Pryor Hack, Mary. *Consecrated Women*. London: Hodder & Stoughton, 1880.

Pullen, Christine. "Amy Levy; Her Life, Her Poetry and the Era of the New Woman." Ph.D. diss., Kingston University, 2000.

Putnam Tong, Rosemarie. *Feminist Thought: A More Comprehensive Introduction*. Boulder: Westview, 1998.

Radford Ruether, Rosemary. *Faith and Fratricide: The Theological Roots of AntiSemitism*. New York: Seabury Press, 1974.

———. *Sexism and God-Talk: Toward a Feminist Theology*. Boston: Beacon Press, 1983.

———. *Women and Redemption: A Theological History*. London: SCM Press, 1998.

Ragussis, Michael. *Figures of Conversion: "The Jewish Question" & English National Identity*. Durham: Duke University Press, 1995.

———. "The Birth of a Nation in Victorian Culture: The Spanish Inquisition, the Converted Daughter, and the 'Secret Race.'" *Critical Inquiry* 21 (Spring 1994): 477-508.

Ramey Mollenkott, Virginia. *The Divine Feminine: Biblical Imagery of God as Female*. New York: Cross roads, 1984.

———. *Women, Men and the Bible*. Nashville: Abingdon, 1977.

Raphael, Melissa. "Goddess Religion, Postmodern Jewish Feminism, and the Complexity of Alternative Religious Identities." *Nova Religio* 1, no. 2 (April 1998): 198-215.

———. "Standing at a Demythologized Sinai? Reading Jewish Feminist Theology Through the Critical Lens of Radical Orthodoxy." In *Interpreting the Postmodern: Responses to "Radical Orthodoxy,"* edited by Rosemary Radford Ruether and Marion Grau, 197-214. New York: T & T Clark, 2006.

———. *The Female Face of God in Auschwitz: A Jewish Feminist Theology of the Holocaust*. London: Routledge, 2003.

Rashkow, Ilona. *Upon the Dark Places: Anti-Semitism and Sexism in English Renaissance Biblical Translation*, Bible and Literature Series, 28. Sheffield: Sheffield Academic Press, 1990.

Reform Judaism: a Historical Perspective, Essays from the Yearbook of the Central Conference of American Rabbis. Edited by Joseph Blau. New York: Ktav, 1973.

Reform Judaism: Essays on Reform Judaism in Great Britain. Edited by Dow Marmur. London: Reform Synagogues of Great Britain, 1973.

Religion and Sexism. Edited by Rosemary Ruether. New York: Simon and Schuster, 1974.

Religion in the Lives of English Women, 1760-1930. Edited by G. Malmgreen. London: Croom Helm, 1986.

Renton, Peter. *The Lost Synagogues of London.* London: Tymsder Publishing, 2000.

Rich, Adrienne. *Of Women Born: Motherhood as Experience and Institution.* New York: Norton, 1976.

Richardson, H. *The English Jewry Under Angevin Kings.* London: Jewish Historical Society of England, 1960.

Rigal, Lawrence. *A Brief History of the West Central Liberal Synagogue.* London: West Central Synagogue, 1978.

_____, and Rosita Rosenberg. *Liberal Judaism: The First Hundred Years.* London: Union of Liberal and Progressive Synagogues, 2004.

Rigg, J. *Select Pleas, Starrs and Other Records from the Exchequer of the Jews, 1220-1284.* London: Jewish Historical Society of England, 1902.

Romain, Jonathan. *Reform Judaism and Modernity: A Reader.* London: SCM, 2004.

Rosenberg, Edgar. *From Shylock to Svengali: Jewish Stereotypes in English Fiction.* Stanford: Stanford University Press, 1960.

Rosenzweig, Franz. *The Star of Redemption.* New York: Holt, Reinhart and Winston, 1971.

Ross, Tamar. "Can We Still Pray to Our Father in Heaven"? In *A Good Eye: Dialogue and Polemic in Jewish Culture,* a Jubilee book in honor of Tova Ilan, 264-78. Hakibbutz: Hameuchad Publishing House, Ltd, 1999.

_____. *Expanding the Palace of Torah: Orthodoxy and Feminism.* Waltham: Brandeis University Press, 2004.

Roth, Cecil. *A History of the Jews in England.* Oxford: Clarendon Press, 1964.

_____. *A History of the Marranos.* New York: Schocken, 1974.

_____. *Essays and Portraits in Anglo-Jewish History.* Philadelphia: Jewish Publication Society of America, 1962.

_____. *The Evolution of Anglo-Jewish Literature.* London: Edward Goldston, 1937.

_____. "The Jew in the Literature of England." *Menorah Journal* 28, no. 1 (1940): 122-25.

_____. "Wellsprings of European Literature." *Menorah Journal* 25, no. 3 (1937): 340-49.

Rubenstein, Richard. *After Auschwitz: Radical Theology and Contemporary Judaism.* Indianapolis: Bobbs-Merrill, 1966.

Rudavsky, David. *Modern Jewish Religious Movements: A History of Emancipation and Adjustment.* New York: Behrman House, 1967.

Ruskin, John. "Of Queen's Gardens." In *The Works of John Ruskin,* 39 vols. *Vol 18: Sesames and Lilies, The Ethics of the Dust, The Crown of Wild Olive,* edited by E. Cook and Alexander Wedderburn, 109-44. London: George Allen, 1905.

Russell, George. *A Short History of the Evangelical Movement.* London: A. R. Mowbray and Son, 1915.

Sacks, Jonathan. *One People? Tradition, Modernity, and Jewish Unity.* London: Littman Library of Jewish Civilization, 1993.

Said, Edward. *Orientalism.* New York: Vintage, 1979.

Salbstein, M. *The Emancipation of the Jews in Britain – The Question of the Admission of the Jews to Parliament, 1828-1860.* London: The Littman Library of Jewish Civilization, 1902.

Sandmel, Samuel. *Judaism and Christian Beginnings.* Oxford: Oxford University Press, 1978.

Scheinberg, Cynthia. *Women's Poetry and Religion in Victorian England: Jewish Identity and Christian Culture.* Cambridge: Cambridge University Press, 2002.

Schussler Fiorenza, Elisabeth. *Bread Not Stone: The Challenge of Feminist Biblical Interpretation.* Boston: Beacon, 1984.

_____. *In Memory of Her: A Feminist Theological Reconstruction of Christian Origins.* 1983; rpt. New York: Crossroad, 1994.

_____. *Wisdom Ways: Introducing Feminist Biblical Interpretation.* New York: Orbis Books, 2001.

Seldin, Ruth. "Women in the Synagogue: A Congregants View." *Conservative Judaism* 32, no. 2 (Winter 1979): 80-88.

Setel, T. Drorah. "Roundtable Discussion: Feminist Reflections on Separation and Unity in Jewish Theology." *Journal of Feminist Studies in Religion* 2 (1986): 113-18.

Shapiro, James. *Shakespeare and the Jews.* New York: Columbia University Press, 1996.

Sharot, Stephen. *Modern Judaism: a Sociology.* Newton Abbot: Holmes & Meier Publishers, 1976.

_____. "Native Jewry and the Religious Anglicization of Immigrants in London: 1870-1905." *The Jewish Journal of Sociology* 16 (1974): 39-56.

_____. "Reform and Liberal Judaism in London: 1840-1940." *Jewish Social Studies* 41, no. 3/4 (Summer/Fall 1979): 211-28.

Shepherd, Naomi. *A Price Below Rubies: Jewish Women as Rebels and Radicals.* London: Weidenfeld and Nicolson, 1993.

Showalter, Elaine. *Sexual Anarchy: Gender and Culture at the Fin de Siècle.* London: Virago, 1992.

Sidgwick, Mrs. Alfred [pseud. Dean, Mrs. Andrew]. *Isaac Eller's Money.* London: Unwin, 1889.

Simons, Hyman. *Forty Years a Chief Rabbi: The Life and Times of Solomon Hirschell.* London: Robson Books, 1980.

Singer, Simeon, Israel Abrahams, Lily H. Montagu. *The Literary remains of the Rev. Simeon Singer.* 1908; rpt. BiblioBazaar, LLC, 2009.

Spence, Jean. "Lily Montagu: a Short Biography." *Youth and Policy* 60 (1998): 73-83.

_____. "Working for Jewish Girls: Lily Montagu, Girls' Clubs and Industrial Reform 1890-1914." *Women's History Review* 13, no. 3 (2004): 491-509.

Starhawk. *The Spiral Dance: A ReBirth of the Ancient Religion of the Great Goddess.* San Francisco: Harper & Row, 1979.

Steinsaltz, Adin. *The Essential Talmud.* London: Weidenfeld and Nicolson, 1976.

Stendahl, Krister. *The Bible and the Role of Women.* Philadelphia: Fortress Press, 1966.

Stulman, Louis. *Jeremiah.* Nashville: Abingdon Press, 2005.

Styler, Rebecca. "A Scripture of Their Own: Nineteenth-Century Bible Biography and Feminist Biblical Criticism." *Christianity and Literature* 57, no. 1 (Autumn 2007): 65-85.

Suffer Be Still: Women in the Victorian Age. Edited by Martha Vicinus. Bloomington: Indiana University Press, 1973.

Swidler, Leonard. *Women in Judaism: The Status of Women in Formative Judaism.* Metuchen: Scarecrow, 1976.

Tanakh: A New Translation of The Holy Scriptures According to the Traditional Hebrew Text. Philadelphia: The Jewish Publication Society, 1985.

Taylor, Barbara. *Eve and the New Jerusalem: Socialism and Feminism in the Nineteenth Century.* London: Virago Press, 1983.

Teubal, Savina. *Sarah the Priestess: The First Matriarch of Genesis.* Athens: Swallow Press, 1984.

The Absent Mother: Restoring the Goddess to Judaism and Christianity. Edited by Alex Pirani. London: Madala, 1991.

The Babylonian Talmud, 18 vols. Edited by I. Epstein. London: Soncino, 1978.

The Coming of Lilith: Essays on Feminism, Judaism, and Sexual Ethics, 1972-2003. Edited by Judith Plaskow and Donna Berman. Boston: Beacon Press, 2005.

The Encyclopaedia Judaica. Edited by Cecil Roth. Jerusalem: Keter, 1972.

The Fin de Siècle. Edited by Sally Ledger and Roger Luckhurst. Oxford: Oxford University Press, 2000.

The Jewish Family: Myths and Reality. Edited by Steven Cohen and Paula Hyman. New York: Holmes & Meier, 1986.

The Jew in the Text: Modernity and the Construction of Identity. Edited by Linda Nochlin and Tamar Garb. London: Thames and Hudson, 1995.

The Jewish Condition: Essays on Contemporary Judaism Honoring Alexander Schindler. Edited by Aron Hirt-Manheimer. New York: UAHC Press, 1995.

The Jewish Heritage in British History: Englishness and Jewishness. Edited by Tony Kushner. London: Frank Cass, 1992.

The Jewish Woman: New Perspectives. Edited by Elizabeth Koltun. New York: Schocken Books, 1976.

The Late-Victorian Marriage Question: A Collection of Key New Woman Texts. Edited by Ann Heilmann. London: Routledge Theommes Press, 1998.

The New Woman in Fiction and in Fact: Fin-de-Siècle Feminisms. Edited by Angelique Richardson and Chris Willis. Houndmills: Palgrave, 2001.

The Ordination of Women as Rabbis: Studies and Responsa. Edited by Simon Greenberg. New York: Jewish Theological Seminary, 1988.

The Passionate Torah: Sex and Judaism. Edited by Danya Ruttenberg. New York: NYU Press, 2009.

The Pleasure of Her Text: Feminist Readings of Biblical and Historical Texts. Edited by Alice Bach. Philadelphia: Trinity Press International, 1990.

The Role of Religion in Modern Jewish History. Edited by Jacob Katz. Cambridge: Cambridge Association for Jewish Studies, 1975.

The Torah: A Women's Commentary. Edited by Tamara Cohn Eskenazi and Andrea Weiss. New York: URI Press, 2008.

The Uses of Tradition: Jewish Community in the Modern Era. Edited by Jack Wertheimer. New York: Jewish Theological Seminary, 1992.

The Wisdom of the Zohar: An Anthology of Texts, 3 vols. Edited by Isaiah Tishby and Fischel Lachower, translated by David Goldstein. Oxford: Oxford University Press, 1989.

Trible, Phyllis. "Depatriarchalizing in Biblical Interpretation." *Journal of the American Academy of Religion* 41 (March 1973): 30-48.

_____, et al. *Feminist Approaches to the Bible.* Washington: Biblical Archaeology Society, 1995.

_____. *God and the Rhetoric of Sexuality.* Philadelphia: Fortress Press, 1978.

_____. "Naomi." In *Women in Scripture: A Dictionary of Named and Unnamed Women in the Hebrew Bible, the Apocryphal/Deuterocanonical Books and the New Testament*, edited by Carol Meyers, et al., 130-31. Cambridge: Eerdmans, 2000.

Tuckman, Gaye, and Nina Fortin. *Edging Women Out: Victorian Novelists, Publishers, and Social Change.* New Haven: Yale University Press, 1989.

Turnbull, Annemarie. "Gendering Young People – Work, Leisure and Girls' Clubs: the Work of the National Organization of Girls' Clubs and its Successors 1911-1961." In *Community and Youth Work*, edited by Tony Jeffs and Jean Spence, 95-110. Leicester: Youth Work Press, 2001.

Umansky, Ellen. "Beyond Androcentrism: Feminist Challenges to Judaism." *Journal of Reform Judaism* 37, no. 1 (Winter 1990): 25-35.

_____. "Creating a Jewish Feminist Theology: Possibilities and Problems." In *Weaving the Visions: New Patterns in Feminist Spirituality*, edited by Judith Plaskow and Carol Christ, 187-98. 1984; rpt. New York: HarperSanFrancisco, 1989.

_____. "Lily H. Montagu: Religious Leader, Organizer and Prophet." *Conservative Judaism* 34, no. 6 (July/August 1981): 17-27.

_____. *Lily Montagu and the Advancement of Liberal Judaism: from Vision to Vocation*, Studies in Women and Religion, vol. 12. New York: Edwin Mellen Press, 1983.

_____. "The Origins of Liberal Judaism in England: The Contribution of Lily H. Montagu." *Hebrew Union College Annual* 55 (1984): 309-22.

Vadillo, Ana Parejo. "New Woman Poets and the Culture of the Salon at the Fin de Siècle." *Women: A Cultural Review* 10, no. 1 (1999): 22-33.

_____. *Women Poets and Urban Aestheticism: Passengers of Modernity.* Basingstoke: Palgrave Macmillan, 2005.

Valman, Nadia. "A Fresh-Made Garment of Citizenship: Representing Jewish Identities in Victorian Britain." *Nineteenth Century Studies* 17 (2003): 35-45.

_____. "'Barbarous and Mediaeval': Jewish Marriage in Fin de Siècle English Fiction." In *The Image of the Jew in European Liberal Culture, 1789-1914,* edited by Bryan Cheyette and Nadia Valman, 111-29. London: Vallentine Mitchell, 2004.

_____. "Hearts Full of Love for Israel: Converting the Jews in Victorian England." *Jewish Quarterly* 182 (Summer 2001): 15-20.

_____. "Semitism and Criticism: Victorian Anglo-Jewish Literary History." *Victorian Literature and Culture* 27 (1999): 235-48.

_____. "Speculating Upon Human Feeling: Evangelical Writing and Anglo-Jewish Women's Autobiography." In *The Uses of Autobiography,* edited by Julia Swindells, 98-109. London: Taylor & Francis, 1995.

_____. *The Jewess in Nineteenth-Century British Culture.* Cambridge: Cambridge University Press, 2007.

_____. "Women Writers and the Campaign for Jewish Civil Rights in Early Victorian England." In *Women in British Politics, 1760-1860: The Power of the Petticoat,* edited by Kathryn Gleadle and Sarah Richardson, 93-114. Basingstoke: Macmillan Press Ltd, 2000.

Vicinus, Martha. *A Widening Sphere: Changing Roles of Victorian Women.* Bloomington: Indiana University Press, 1973.

_____. *Independent Women: Work and Community for Single Women, 1850-1920.* London: Virago, 1985.

Victorian Women Poets: An Anthology. Edited by Angela Leighton and Margaret Reynolds. Oxford: Blackwell, 1995.

Waard, Jan de. *A Handbook on Jeremiah.* Winona Lake: Eisenbrauns, 2003.

Walkowitz, Judith. *Prostitution and Victorian Society: Women, Class and the State.* Cambridge: Cambridge University Press, 1980.

Wallach Scott, Joan. *Feminism & History*. Oxford: Oxford University Press, 1996.

_____. *Gender and the Politics of History*. New York: Columbia University Press, 1988.

Walton, Ronald. *Women in Social Work*. London: Routledge & Kegan Paul, 1975.

Waskow, Arthur. *Rainbow Sign: The Shape of Hope*. New York: Schocken Books, 1985.

Wiener, Max. *Abraham Geiger and Liberal Judaism: the Challenge of the Nineteenth Century*. Philadelphia: Jewish publication Society of America, 1962.

Wiesel, Elie, *Legends of Our Time*. New York: Avon, 1968.

Wolf, Lucien. *Manasseh ben Israel's Mission to Oliver Cromwell. Being a Reprint of the Pamphlets Published by Manasseh ben Israel to Promote the Readmission of the Jews to England, 1649-1656*. London: 1901.

Wollstonecraft, Mary. *Vindication of the Rights of Woman*, edited by Carol Poston. 1792; rpt. New York: W. W. Norton, 1975.

Wolowelsky, Joel. *Women, Jewish Law, and Modernity: New Opportunities in a Post-Feminist Age*. New York: Ktav, 1997.

Womanspirit Rising: A Feminist Reader in Religion. Edited by Carol Christ and Judith Plaskow. San Francisco: Harper & Row, 1979.

Women, Religion, and Social Change. Edited by Yvonne Haddad and Ellison Findly. Albany: State University of New York Press, 1985.

Women's Bible Commentary. Edited by Carol Newsom and Sharon Ringe. London: Westminster, 1992.

Yentl's Revenge: The Next Wave of Jewish Feminism. Edited by Danya Ruttenberg. New York: Seal Press, 2001.

Zangwill, Israel. *Children of the Ghetto: A Study of a Peculiar People*. London: Heinemann, 1892.

Zatlin, Linda. *The Nineteenth-Century Anglo-Jewish Novel*. Boston: Twayne Publishers, 1981.

Zierler, Wendy. *And Rachel Stole the Idols: The Emergence of Modern Hebrew Women's Writing*. Detroit: Wayne State University Press, 2004.

INDEX